APPLICATIONS OF DATA MINING

APPLICATIONS OF DATA MINING

Edited by

Dr. T. Sudha

Professor and Head
Department of Computer Science
Sri Padmavathi Mahila Visva Vidyalayam (SPMVV)
Tirupati (Andhra Pradesh)
(India)

&

Dr. M. Usha Rani

Associate Professor
Department of Computer Science
Sri Padmavathi Mahila Visva Vidyalayam (SPMVV)
Tirupati (Andhra Pradesh)
(India)

DISCOVERY PUBLISHING HOUSE PVT. LTD.

NEW DELHI-110 002

First Published - 2008
Reprinted - 2017

ISBN: 978-81-8356-330-7

Applications of Data Mining

Published by:
DISCOVERY PUBLISHING HOUSE PVT. LTD.
4383/4B, Ansari Road, Darya Ganj
New Delhi-110 002 (India)
Phone: +91-11-23279245, 43596064-65
Fax: +91-11-23253475
E-mail: discoverypublishinghouse@gmail.com
sales@discoverypublishinggroup.com
web: www.discoverypublishinggroup.com

Printed at:
Infinity Imaging Systems
Delhi

Synopsis

"Applications of Data Mining," presents an overview of the state-of-the-art approaches in this new and multidisciplinary field of data mining. The primary objective of this book is to explore the myriad issues regarding data mining, specifically focusing on those areas that explore new methodologies or examine case studies. This book constitutes the refereed proceedings of the Conference on Applications of Data Mining, held in Tirupati, Andhra Pradesh, India on 24th-25th April 2006. The conference was focussed on sophisticated techniques and tools that can handle new fields of data mining, e.g. spatial data mining, biomedical data mining, and mining on high-speed and time-variant data streams; an expansion of data mining to new applications is also strived for. Along with the invited talks, 20 revised full papers selected from over 150 submissions. The collected papers are sections on association rules, classification, clustering, novel algorithms, text mining, multimedia mining, sequential data mining and time series mining, web mining, biomedical mining, advanced applications, security and privacy issues, spatial data mining, and streaming data mining.

Contents

1

Pros and Cons of Various Approaches to Associative Classification

Sireesha Rodda*

ABSTRACT

In the recent years, the synthesis between association rule mining and classification has led to the development of several associative classifiers. Associative classifiers use association rules to attach attribute values with observed class labels. This paper summarizes such works on associative classifiers, their fruitful results and discusses enhancements proposed and the challenges faced by it.

INTRODUCTION

Data Classification problem aims at predicting the class label of a newly arrived object given its description in terms of a set of attributes. The process is performed in two phases. In the first phase, the classification model is developed based on a good collection of training examples. Each of these training examples is represented in terms of the values of the set of attributes describing the example along with the class to which it belongs. Once the model is built, it is tested on the training data.

* Department of Computer Science and Engineering, College of Engineering, Gandhi Institute of Technology and Management, Visakhapatnam, e-mail: sireesha@gitam.edu

When the classifier is based on the Association Mining, it makes use of the frequent item sets extracted as an end product of Association Rule Mining. Each frequent item set should have invariably the class label attribute in addition to other attributes.

Associative classification though is efficient, needs to take care of some issues:

- Very large search space of candidate rules during the rule discovery;
- Incorporating mined association rules for classification purpose.

The remainder of the paper is about how different associative classifiers address these issues, and the enhancements proposed to improve their performance.

ASSOCIATIVE CLASSIFICATION

Associative classification is a special case of association rule mining in that the rule's consequent contains only the class attribute.

The training data set T has m distinct attributes A1, A_2, ..., A_m and C is a list of class labels.

Attributes can be categorical or continuous. In case of categorical attributes, all possible values are mapped onto a set of positive integers. Continuous attributes are to be discretised before they are used.

Definition1: Each record/instance in the training set contains a set of attributes A_i (along with their associated values) and a class c_j ($\subset$ C)

Definition 2: An item/literal is described by an attribute name A_i and its value a_i

Definition 3: An item set is a set of distinct items in a training set instance

Definition 4: A rule item, r is of the form <X, Y> i. e., $X \rightarrow Y$ where X is a item set ($\subset$ T)

And Y is a class ($\subset$ C)

Definition 5: Support of any rule r is defined as

Sup(r) ={e | e∈ T, e satisfies r}

Definition 6: Confidence of any rule r is given as

Conf(r) = sup(r)/{e | e ∈ T, e satisfies X}

Definition 7: Frequent item set is any item set with support greater than minsupp threshold

Definition 8: An association classification rule is of the form

$(A_{i1}, a_{i1}) \wedge (A_{i2}, a_{i2}) \wedge \ldots \wedge (A_{im}, a_{im}) \rightarrow cj$

Where the antecedent of the rule is an item set and the consequent is a class

Definition 9: A classifier is of the form

$H: A_1, A_2, \ldots, A_n \rightarrow Y$

Where A_i is an attribute and y is a class

The concept of Association rule mining was first proposed in.[2] The support and confidence were considered as parameters for the A-priori algorithm.[3] Association rules could be discovered using two steps:

1. Find all the items(item sets) that have transaction support above minimum support. These item sets are referred as large item sets;
2. Use the large item sets to generate the desired rules.

Using association rules for classification purpose is called Associative Classification.

The main goal of the classifier is to predict the class label of an unseen data as accurately as possible.

General Framework

Figure 1.1 shows general steps used in associative classification. Most of the classifiers, more or less, follow this framework. First step is computationally expensive, and is similar to discovery of frequent item sets in association rule mining. After all the frequent item sets are identified, for each of them which passes minconf threshold, generate a rule of the form X → c.

Where c is the classes having largest frequency among all the classes associated with the itemset X.

Step 3 does the ranking and pruning of the rules obtained from association rule mining. The number of rules generated from association rule discovery is quite large. Hence rule pruning is required. Moreover, to avoid the problem of over fitting, proper rule pruning method is to be employed.

Ranking of the rules is also important. When a test instance has more than one potentially applicable rules, rule ranking is necessary to prefer one over the others.

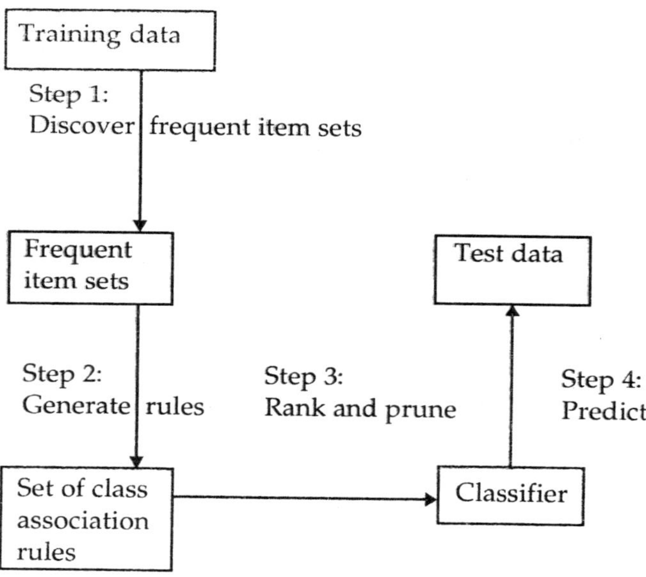

Fig 1.1: **Associative classification steps**

After the classifier is built on the training set, the class labels of the test set are to be predicted. The observed values are then compared with the actual values to calculate the accuracy of the classifier. Over the recent years, it has been observed that associative classifiers have better accuracy than other classification models.

Next section describes different associative classifiers like CBA, CMAR, CPAR and MCAR.

DIFFERENT ASSOCIATIVE CLASSIFIERS

One of the first algorithms to use association rule discovery for classification is CBA.[17] In CBA, the classification Association rules (CARs) are found iteratively in an apriori algorithm-like fashion. At first, frequent 1-rule item sets are generated and are pruned. Using this iteratively, other frequent rule item sets are also found. They are then pruned to get complete set of Classification association rules.

To prune the rules, CBA uses pessimistic error based pruning method in C4.5. The rule ranking is defined as below:

Given two rules r_i and r_j, $r_i > r_j$ (i.e., r_i precedes r_j or r_i has higher precedence over r_j) if one of the following holds good:

1. The confidence of r_i is greater than that of r_j
2. Their confidences are the same but support of r_i is greater than that of r_j
3. Both the confidences and supports of r_i and r_j are the same, but r_i is generated before r_j

After rule ranking, each training instance is covered by the rule having highest precedence among the rules that can cover the case. Every rule correctly classifies at least one training instance. The rules that do not cover any training instance are removed. The training instances that do not fall into any of the observed classes are added to a default class.

CMAR[20] is another associative classifier that performs classification based on multiple association rules. Instead of relying on a single rule, CMAR determines the class label by a set of high confidence, highly related rules and analyses the correlation among them. To avoid bias, weighted xi-square method was implemented. CMAR uses a new data structure, CR-tree to compactly store and retrieve large number of rules for classification. CMAR maintains the distribution of various class labels among data objects matching the pattern. It uses class label distribution to prune.

CPAR[21] is a greedy associative classification algorithm. It adopts FOIL[15] and modifies its strategy for rule generation from training data. It seeks for the best rule condition that brings the most gin among the available ones in the training set. Once the condition is identified, the weights of the positive examples is decreased by a multiplying factor. This process is repeated until all the positive examples in the training set are covered. CPAR used an efficient data structure called PNArray to store the information regarding the information gain. CPAR derives not only the best condition but conditions closely similar to the best condition. It has been claimed that CPAR improves the efficiency when compared with CBA and CMAR.

Corclass[5] is an associative classifier which discover all correlated association rules and then applies the discovered rule sets to classify unseen data. The advantage with this method is that it does not use user-specified support and confidence thresholds (unlike CBA, CMAR etc.) but directly finds association rules by using branch-and-bound algorithm.

By using correlation, pruning is more efficient. It does not generate too many rules like conventional associative classifiers usually do. Moreover, the user specified threshold (maximum number of rules to be generated), will be used. In that case, the threshold could be dynamically raised.

MMAC[9] is a multi-class, multi-label associative classification approach. The algorithm consists of three phases: rule generation, recursive learning and classification. In the first phase, it finds a set of association rules; then ranks the rule set, and from it, removes the redundant rules. In second phase, it recursively tries to find more rules by discarding instances and continues until no more frequent items are found. After every iteration in phase 2, the rule sets generated are merged to produce a multi-label classifier. Third phase performs classification on the results of second phase.

MCAR[12] is another associative classifier which claims that a little over one scan over the entire data set is enough for generation of classification rules. The training set is scanned once to discover all the frequent rule items. MCAR then recursively combines the rule items (using tid-intersection method) generated to produce potential frequent items. Only the items having support and confidence values greater than specified thresholds are considered. These rules are used to build a classifier based on their effectiveness. As the number of passes over the dataset is reduced, the efficiency of the algorithm is improved[17] uses a new framework for associative classification that uses both positive and negative association rules. Negative association rules either associate negations of attributes to class, or negatively associate attribute values to classes. The algorithm generates positive and negative association rules based on the item correlation with the class label. If the absolute value of the correlation is greater than a given correlation threshold, a positive rule is discovered. When the correlation is negative, negative rules are generated. They are added to PCR and NCR respectively if their confidence exceeds minimum confidence threshold.

In the classification phase, a set of rules are generated within a confidence margin. The applicable set of rules are divided among the classes. The average confidence of each class is calculated (by adding the confidence if the rule is positive, or by subtracting the same if the rule is negative). The groups are then ordered according to the average confidence per class. Classification is then made by assigning the new object to the class having highest score.

ISSUES OF ASSOCIATIVE CLASSIFIER

The main problem with associative classifiers is that they generate huge number of classification rules and it is very important to prune them. Most of the pruning techniques are based on redundancy, noise elimination and precedence ranking. One such important technique is database coverage introduced in.[6] Whenever a rule applies correctly to a set of database instances, the rule is marked and all the instances covered by it are remove until are the training instances are covered. Finally, all the unmarked rules are pruned. Though many rules are pruned using database coverage, the remaining number of rules is still large. Further pruning is required[18] provides more enhancements to rule pruning. The technique adopted is shown in figure 1.2.

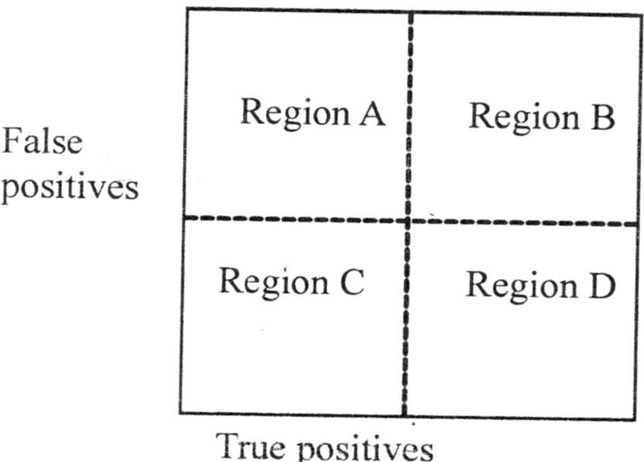

Fig. 1.2

Each rule is plotted with the number of true positives and false positives in the training set. Rules plotted high in the graph incorrectly classify many training instances. Rules plotted towards right of the graph correctly classify many instances. Each of the regions has the following properties:

Region A – Rules that are incorrect more than are correct

Region B – Rules that are frequently used but equally misclassify and classify correctly

Region C – Rules that are infrequently used that equally misclassify and classify correctly

Region D – Good Rules which frequently classify correctly and seldom misclassify

All the rules in Regions A, B, and C could be safely pruned. The resulting number of rules in Region C is still large. Hence, this quadrant pruning is combined with diagonal pruning to get good results. Diagonal pruning uses a diagonal line to identify within .Region C, the rules that misclassify more than they are correct. These rules could be pruned[13] compares several parameters that influence the efficiency of associative classifiers and argues that Certainty Factor is better suited for associative classification than traditional support and confidence thresholds. Certainty factor helps in pruning, in that only association rules with positive certainty factor are useful, since they increase our knowledge and improve classifier accuracy.

One of the common rule ranking techniques was introduced in[16] and used in CBA. It says:

Given two rules p and q, p precedes q (p > q) if:

1. The confidence of p is greater than that of q
2. The confidence values of p and q are the same, but the support of p is greater than that of q
3. The confidence and support values of p and q are the same, but p was generated before q.

Introduces[7] an additional definition to that proposed in CBA: "Confidence, support and cardinality of p and q are the same, but p is associated with a class that occurs more frequently in the training data than q". The paper claims to have achieved greater accuracy by this which is shown in the results provided in the paper. The author argues that accuracy could be increased by associating class distribution frequency with each rule and favours the rules which are associated with the most representative class.

CMAR proposes an additional definition for sorting rules: " If confidence and support values of p and q are the same, but p has fewer attributes on its left hand side than q does".

MMAC also proposes an additional definition for sorting rules: " The confidence and support values of p and q are the same, but p has larger representation than q in the training data".

Apart from rule ranking criteria proposed in CBA[10] proposes a new criterion. It considers the class frequency distribution frequency associated with each rule and favours rules that are associated with the most representative class.

On the other hand,[14] argues that generating classification association rules by conventional association rule mining(ARM) is expensive, that this "overfit and prune" strategy will not be much useful if the datasets are large. The authors have identified three issues in this regard:

(i) ARM is costly because of its exponential complexity of search space;

(ii) It is very likely that the first stage in ARM will generate large number of rules;

(iii) The reliability of the classifier, to some extent, will depend on the choice of support and confidence values.

It also proposes a new method. If there is a rule X → cl, it is unnecessary to consider other rules whose antecedent is a superset of X. But if there is a rule Y → cl2, and Y is a superset of X, which has higher confidence, then we give precedence to Y. To avoid considering all such supersets, the paper proposes a new data structure called P-tree which contains incomplete summation of support counts for relevant sets using P-tree, the algorithm uses an apriori-like procedure to build a T-tree. This T-tree contains all the frequent sets with their associated supports. The nodes/ sets that do not meet the required thresholds will be immediately pruned. The remaining sets could be used to directly generate classification rules.

Proposes[4] a novel algorithm for Cost-sensitive associative-classification. In this technique, rules are generated based on the concept to maximal frequent class item sets, and then selected based on their informative value and on the cost that an error implies. An item set that has no frequent superset is called a maximal item set.

Evaluates[11] four different associative classifiers and comes up with some interesting results. The paper proposes that studies indicate Support threshold's larger impact on the number of rules produced in the classifier, the processing time, and storage needed during the algorithms discovery and generation whereas confidence has a lesser impact on the same concepts. Through experiments, the paper indicates that the performance of MCAR gives slightly better accuracy than that of CBA, CMAR and CPAR.[8]

The crucial differences between Association rule mining and classification were discussed in.[1] It argues that classification is an asymmetric task with respect to attributes whereas Association rule mining is a symmetric task. Classification is an ill-defined, non-deterministic task whereas Association Rule Mining is a defined, deterministic task. The issue of over fitting/under fitting is crucial in Classification problem whereas they are not an issue in Association rule mining. Given a set of facts, the number of classification rules is infinite. Hence inductive bias is necessary in case of Classification and not needed at all for Association Rule Mining.

CONCLUSION AND FUTURE WORK

This paper aims at bringing together different approaches to Associative Classification. The different approaches are discussed and their pros and cons are evaluated. Associative classification was proved to be a much better option than other classification strategies. Future work involves considering multi-label associative classification. Multi-label Associative classification can attribute an item to multiple classes. Cases when these labels are overlapping or interdependent will also be considered.

REFERENCES

1. A. A. Freitas (2004). *Understanding the Crucial Differences Between Classification and Discovery of Association Rules*—A Position Paper. SIGKDD Explorations, 2(1): 65-69, July 2000.
2. Agrawal R., Imielinski, T., and Swami, A. (1993). *Mining Association Rules Between Sets of Items in Large Databases*. In Proc. of the Int. Conf. on Management of Data, SIGMOD, pp. 207-216, Washington, USA, ACM
3. Agrawal, R. and Srikant , R (1994). *Fast Algorithms for Mining Association Rules*. In Proc. Of the Int. Conf. on Very Large Databases, pp. 487-499, SanTiago, Chile.
4. Adriano Veloso, Wagner Meira Jr.(2005). *Rule Generation and Rule Selection Techniques for Cost-sensitive Associative Classification*, SBBD2005, pp. 295-305.
5. Albrecht Zimmermann and Luc De Raedt (2004). CorClass: Correlated Association Rule Mining for Classification, *Proceedings of the 7th International Conference on Discovery Science* (DS-2004), pp. 60-72, Padova, Italy, October 2-5, 2004.
6. Ali, K., Mangaris, S., and Srikant, R. (1997). Partial Classification Using Association Rules. In Proc. *Of 3rd Int. Con. of Knowledge Discovery and Data Mining*, pp. 115-118, 1997.
7. Davy Janssens, Geert Wets, Tom Brijs, Koen Vanhoof.(2003) *Integrating Classification with Association Rule Mining by Proposing Adaptations to CBA Algorithm*.
8. Fadi Thabtah, Peter Cowling, Suhel Hammoud. (2005) Improving Rule Sorting, Predictive Accuracy and Training Time in Associative Classification, *Journal of Expert Systems with Applications*, Elsevier.

9. Fadi Thabtah, Peter Cowling, Yonghong peng (2004). MMAC: A New Multi-label, Multi-class Associative Classification Approach. In proc. of Fourth IEEE International Conference on Data Mining, *Proceedings of the 4th IEEE International Conference on Data Mining* (ICDM 2004), 1-4 November 2004, Brighton, UK. pp. 217-224.

10. Fadi Thabtah, Peter Cowling, and Yonghong Peng (2005). The Impact of Rule Ranking on the Quality of Associative Classifiers, *The Twenty-fifth SGAI International Conference on Innovative Techniques and Applications of Artificial Intelligence (AI-2005)*, Cambridge, UK.

11. Fadi Thabtah, Peter Cowling, Yonghong Peng(2005). A Study of Predictive Accuracy of Four Associative Classifiers, In Journal of *Digital Information Management*, Volume 3, Number 3, September 2005, pp. 202-205.

12. Fadi Thahbtah, Peter Cowling, Yonghomg Peng (2005). MCAR: Multi-class Classification Based on Association Rule, *The 3rd ACS/ IEEE Conference on Computer Systems and Applications*, 2005.

13. Fernando Berzal et. al (2005) *Association Rule Evaluation for Classification Purposes*, TAMIDA 2005, pp. 135-144.

14. Frans Coenen, Paul Leng, and Lu Zhang (2005). *Threshold Tuning for Improved Classification Association Rule Mining*, PAKDD 2005, pp. 216-225.

15. J.R. Quinlan and R. M. Cameron-Jones (1993). FOIL: A Midterm Report. In Proc. *1993 European Conference of Machine Learning*, pp. 3-20, Vienna, Austria, 1993.

16. Liu, B., Hsu, W., Ma. Y (1998). *Integrating Classification and Association Rule Mining*. In Knowledge Discover and Data Mining, pp. 80-86.

17. Maria-Luiza Antonie and Osmar R. Zaiane (2004). An Associative Classifier Based on Positive and Negative Rules. In Proc. *Of the 9th ACM SIGMOD Workshop on Research Issues in Data Mining and Knowledge Discovery*, pp. 64-69, Paris, France.

18. Osmar R. Zaiane and Maria-Luiza Antonie (2005). *On Pruning and Tuning Rules for Associative Classifiers*. KES (3) 2005: 966-973.

19. W. Li, J. Han, J. Pei.(2001) *Accurate and Efficient Classification Based on Multiple Class-Association rules*, IEEE International Conference on Data Mining, 2001

20. W. Li, J. Han, J. Pei. (2001). CMAR: *Accurate and Efficient Classification Based on Multiple-class Association Rules*, IEEE International Conference on Data Mining, 2001

21. Yin, X. and Han, J. (2003). CPAR: Classification Based on Predictive Association Rules. *In Proceedings of the 3rd SIAM International Conference on Data Mining (SDM'03)*. SIAM, Philadelphia, PA.

2

Data Mining
A Shocking Wave for Bioinformatics

A.Bindu*
A.Bhavani**

INTRODUCTION

The new science of Bioinformatics studies the genetic make-up of all living organisms to answer complex biological questions. Its central task concerns with the analysis of data and discovery patterns in data which provides new scientific insight in the problem. It is a fast growing and multi disciplinary field which combines information technology, computer science and biology.

Discovering knowledge in data is the key research topic in the field of Data Mining. The idea is that by automatically sifting through large quantities of data it should possible to extract nuggets of knowledge. Data Mining is useful in Scientific Applications like Bioinformatics to reduce the complexity of data in large bioinformatics databases and for discovering meaningful and useful patterns and relationships in data.

BASICS REGARDING BIOINFORMATICS FOR COMPUTER SCIENTISTS

Basically all organisms' posses the discrete entities called genes, the gene is made of DNA and it is the hereditary material

* **MCA V Semester, Department of Computer Science, SPMVV, Tirupati.**
** **MCA V Semester, Department of Computer Science, SPMVV, Tirupati.**

for all species. This DNA is composed of a Nucleotide sequence called {A, T, G, C} as given below:

#	*1-letter code*	*Nucleotide name*
1	A	Adenine
2	C	Cytosine
3	G	Guanine
4	T	Thymine

From the computer scientist point of view the DNA double helix is a clever robust information storage and transition system like the binary alphabet {0, 1} used in computers. The four letter alphabet of D N A {A, T, C, G} can encode messages of arbitrary complexity. When encoded into long sequence analysis of genomic data, including gene sequence, gene expression and clinical data offers great opportunity for progress in medical science and great opportunity and challenges for sestinas.

BIOLOGICAL DATABASES

Biological information such as 3D protein structure, protein sequence, nucleotide sequence data etc are placed in the databases named Protein Databank, Swiss-prot, TrEMBL, EMBL Nucleotide Sequence D-base etc. The data in these databases is growing rapidly day by day which creates the necessity of Data Mining Techniques to explore them.

DATA MINING TECHNIQUES FOR BIOINFORMATICS AND THEIR IMPLEMENTATION PROCEDURES

The process of data mining in terms of Bioinformatics concerns mainly about pattern matching and discovery. From the biological data bases by using classification, regression, link analysis, segmentation or deviation detection. The process starts with an unknown pattern such as a potential protein structure and ends with a label for the pattern.

The procedure is shown in the figure:

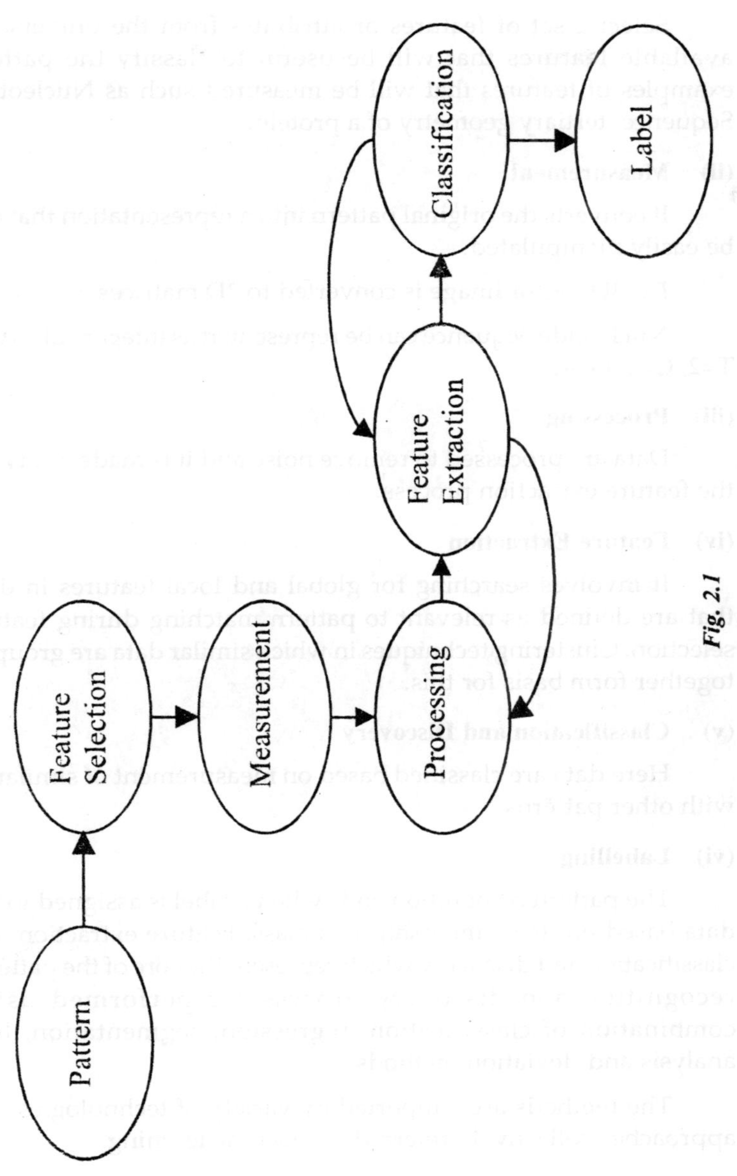
Pattern
Feature Selection
Measurement
Processing
Feature Extraction
Classification
Label

Fig. 2.1

(i) Feature Selection

Select a set of features or attributes from the universe of available features that will be useful to classify the pattern examples of features that will be measured such as Nucleotide Sequence, tertiary geometry of a protein.

(ii) Measurement

It converts the original pattern into a representation that can be easily manipulated.

Ex: 3D vector image is converted to 2D matrices.

Nucleotide Sequence can be represented as integers like A=1, T=2, C=3, G=4.

(iii) Processing

Data are processed to remove noise and it is made ready for the feature extraction process.

(iv) Feature Extraction

It involves searching for global and local features in data that are defined as relevant to pattern matching during feature selection. Clustering techniques in which similar data are grouped together form basis for this.

(v) Classification and Discovery

Here data are classified based on measurement of similarity with other patterns.

(vi) Labelling

The pattern recognition ends when a label is assigned to the data based on its membership in a class. Feature extraction and classification and discovery which represent the core of the pattern-recognition and discovery process are performed using combination of classification, regression, segmentation, link analysis and deviation methods.

The methods are supported by variety of technologies and approaches collectively referred as machine learning.

DATA MINING TECHNOLOGIES FOR PATTERN MATCHING AND DISCOVERY

The pattern matching and pattern discovery components of data mining are often performed by machine learning techniques. Machine learning is not a single technique it encompasses variety of methods such as:

(i) Inductive Logic Programme

It uses set of rules and heuristics to categorise data. It works by incrementally dividing the data into the largest possible spaces until all data has been assigned to a collection.

(ii) Genetic Algorithms

These are based on evolutionary principles where in a particular function or definition that best fits the constraints of an environment survives to the next generation and the other functions are eliminated it continues until best solution is found.

(iii) Neural Nets

These are based on biological neurons. They are said to learn or to be trained, in molecular biology. They learn to associate input patterns with output patterns in a way that allow them to categorise new patterns and extrapolate trends from data. These are used for pattern recognition and classification.

(iv) Statistical Methods

These are some form of feature extraction classification clustering:

(i) *Decision Trees:* These are hierarchically arranged questions and answers that lead to classification.

(ii) *Hidden Marker Model:* It resembles the translation network which produces symbols when translation is made. This model is called order n model where n-number of states affecting the choice of next state. These are used for protein structure prediction, gene prediction.

Following figure shows hidden markova model transition network.

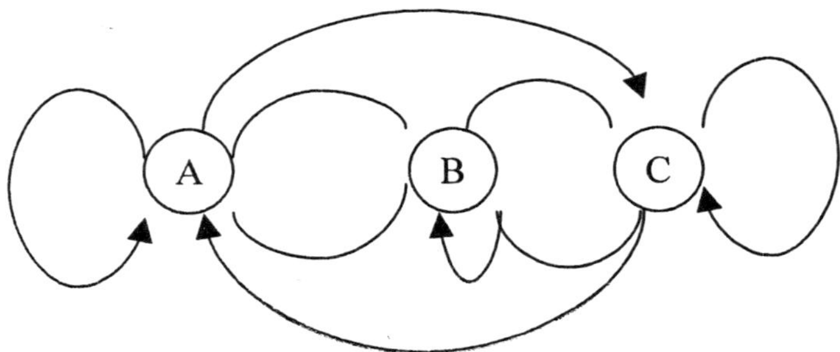

APPLICATIONS

1. Biological activity prediction for chemical compounds.
2. Analysis of gene expression data.
3. Sequence Analysis (DNA, protein).
4. Protein Structure Prediction.

ADVANTAGES

1. We can easily explore large and complex bioinformatics databases.
2. We can easily discover various types of patterns in potentially large data bases.

DISADVANTAGES

1. User should have prior knowledge about biology and computer science.
2. Noise may accrue in data.
3. Size updates are complex to perform for large data sets.

CONCLUSION

Hence this paper controls that data mining is extensively useful in Bioinformatics to explore large and complex information and for the analysis of Gene and protein sequence. The feature of pattern recognition and discovery of the data mining is key process applied to bioinformatics to study the genetic patterns and relationships among the pattern of the species.

REFERENCES

1. *Data Mining Techniques* by Arun.K.Pujari.
2. *Bioinformatics Computing* by Bryan Bergone.
3. *Bioinformatics Sequence and Gene Analysis* by David Mount.
4. *Evolutionary Computing in Bioinformatics* by BFOGEL/DAVID W.CORNE.

3

Privacy Preserving Data Mining Using Multi Group and Multi Authority Randomised Response Technique

P. Vasudeva Reddy*
B.H. Nagarajasri*
G. Anjan Babu*
Dr. M. Padmavathamma*

ABSTRACT

Privacy is an important issue in data mining. In this paper we described a specific privacy preserving data mining problem. In electronic voting system, for the voter to cast his vote to prove the authentication voter needs to answer for some questions and sends back the answers to the authorities of the voting system. However, the questioner contains sensitive questions not every voter feels comfortable to disclose his/her answers to those questions.

We propose to use the randomised response techniques to conduct the data collection. To enhance the privacy level, in this paper we propose a multi-group and multi authority scheme in which the voters participating all their answers divided into multiple groups and the authorities are partitioned multiple authorities and for different groups and different authorities' data randomisation done separately. We present a method to build decision tree classifiers from disguise data based on multi-group/multi-authority scheme.

* Department of Computer Science, S V University, Tirupati.

KEY WORDS: Privacy, data mining, randomized response technique, ID3 algorithm.

INTRODUCTION

Data Mining refers to extracting or mining knowledge from large amounts of data. We extract gold from the rocks or sand is referred to as gold mining. The world wide Computerisation of many Transactions (Business or organisational transactions) and online availability created mountains of data which contains potentially valuable knowledge. Many People treat data mining as a synonym for knowledge discovery in databases.

In Modern days Organisations are extremely dependent on data mining in their every day activities and paybacks include providing better service and achieving greater profit and better decision-making.

PPDM Problem

People think of Privacy as protecting individual data. One way to privacy to use anonymous techniques, which allow users to disclose their identities. The biggest problem of using anonymous techniques is that there is no guarantee on the quality of data set. A malicious user (eg: computing company) could send a great deal of information to the database and render the database useless or a company could send a lot of made up information to the database with the goal of making their products the most favourable ones. These potential attacks could all render the database useless. If the communication is really anonymous it is difficult for the database owner to control the quality of data. To guarantee the quality it is for the database owner to verify the identities of the data contributors.

Another way to achieve privacy is to let each user disguise or randomise their data, such that the data collector cannot derive the truthful information about a user's private information. The challenge is how to conduct data mining from the disguised data? To address this challenge, we first propose the following computing model: The model consists of a data collection step and a computation step. In the data collection step, each user utilises certain techniques to disguise his/her data, then sends the disguised data to the central place; the central place authority should not be able to find out any user's actual data with probabilities better than a pre-defined threshold. In the computation step, the central place constructs a database using the disguised data, and conducts data mining computations on this database. The goal of the central place is to derive useful information (or knowledge) out of this disguised database. In this paper, we particularly focus on a specific data mining computation, the decision-tree based classification, namely we want to find out how to build decision tree classifiers when the data in the database are disguised.

OVERVIEW OF THE PAPER

In this paper we propose to use the *Randomised Response* techniques to solve the privacy-preserving data mining problem. The basic idea of randomised response is to scramble the data in such a way that the central place cannot tell with probabilities better than a pre-defined threshold whether the data from a customer contain truthful information or false information. Although information from each individual user is scrambled, if the number of users is significantly large, the aggregate information of these users can be estimated with decent accuracy. Such property is useful for decision-tree based on classification since it is based on aggregate values of a data set, rather than individual data items. One solution was proposed to solve the privacy-preserving data mining problem using the *Randomised Response* techniques.[1] We call this solution the one-group scheme, in which, users either send the truthful answers to all those questions or send the answers that are exactly opposite to their truthful answers for all the questions are send. The answers that are exactly opposite to their truthful answers for all questions. Namely, if the value for one attribute in a record is true, then the values for the other attributes in the same record are also true. Thus, once an adversary somehow knows whether data provider tells a truth or not for only one attribute for some record, he/she can obtain all the true values about this record. This is not a desirable property because in practice, due to the hints from other sources, the probability of obtaining the values of some attributes is very high. To further preserve data's privacy, we propose a multi-group multi-authority scheme, in which we partition the

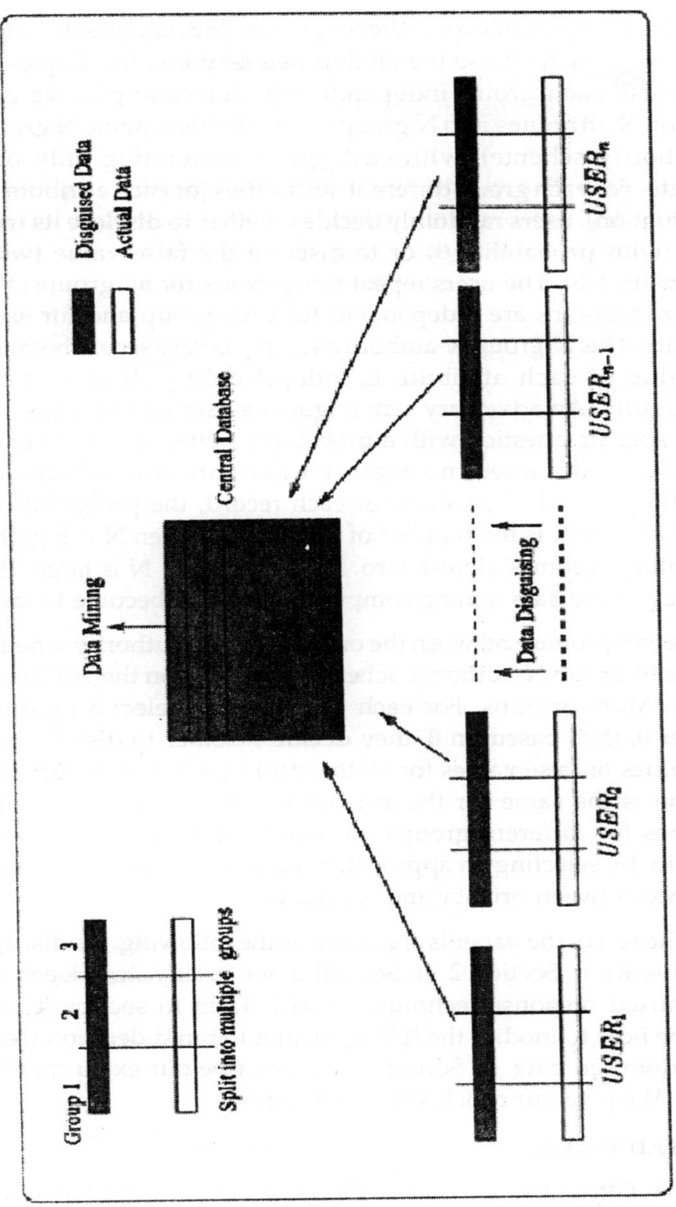

Fig 3.1: **Privacy Preserving Data Mining**

set of the attributes into a number of groups (the model is depicted in Fig. 3.1.); we then use the randomised response techniques to randomise each group independently. For example, we can partition N attributes into N groups (we call this scheme N group N authority scheme), with each group containing only one attribute. For each group different authorities (or each attribute in this situation), users randomly decide whether to disclose its true value (with probability θ) or to disclose the false value (with probability 1-θ). The users repeat this process for all groups; the random decisions are independent for each group and for each authority. This N-group N-authority scheme is very secure because the value of each attribute is independently disguised by N-Authority. An adversary cannot guess a user's correct answer to any specific question with a probability better than θ. Even if one value is disclosed, none other values are still hidden. To correctly guess all the values for each record, the probability is $\theta^N \times \theta^N$ (where N is the number of attributes). When N is big, the probability becomes almost zero. However when N is large, the accuracy of the data mining computations might become to low.

A compromise between the one-group one-authority scheme and the N-group N-authority scheme is to partition the attributes to $M(1<M<N)$ groups. For each group, users select a random number θ, then based on θ, they decide whether to disclose the true values or false values for all the attributes in this group (the decision is the same for the attributes in the same group, but decisions for different groups are independently). Take by N-authority by selecting an appropriate value of M, we can achieve a balance between privacy and accuracy.

The rest of the paper is organised as the following: we discuss related work in Section 2. In Section 3, we briefly describe how randomised response technique works. Then in section 4, we describe how to modify the ID3 algorithm to build decision trees on randomised data. In Section 5, we describe our experimental results. We give our conclusion in Section 6.

RELATED WORK

The concept of privacy-preserving data mining has been proposed recently. There have been two broad approaches. The randomisation approach focuses on individual privacy and reveals randomised information about each record in exchange for not having to reveal the original records to anyone. In the privacy preservation data mining using multi-group multi-authority approach the goal is to build a data mining model across the multi-group, multi-authority on the multiple databases without revealing the individual records in each data base to the other data bases and different records are verified by the different authorities.

Agarwal and Srikant proposed a scheme for privacy-preserving data mining using random perturbation.[2] In their scheme, a random number is added to the value of a sensitive attribute. For example, if x_i is the value of a sensitive attribute, x_i+r rather than x_i, will appear in the database, where r is a random value drawn from some distribution. The paper shows that if the random number is generated with some known distribution (e.g., uniform or Gaussian distribution), it is possible to recover the distribution of the values of that sensitive attribute. Assuming independence of the attributes, the paper then shows that a decision tree classifier can be built with the knowledge of distribution of each attribute.

When the number of attributes becomes large, the data quality will degrade very significantly. To address this problem, we propose a group-oriented randomisation scheme, in which we divide all the attributes to a number of groups, and attributes in a group are disguised in the same way, but attributes from different groups are disguised independently. Our goal is to achieve a better balance between data quality and privacy.

RANDOMISED RESPONSE

Randomised Response (RR) techniques were developed in the statistics community for the purpose of protecting surveyees' privacy. We briefly describe how RR techniques are used for single-attribute databases. In the next section, we propose a multi-group multi-authority scheme to use RR techniques for multiple-attribute databases. *Randomised Response* techniques were first introduced by Warner[3] in 1965 as a technique to solve the following survey problem: To estimate the percentage of people in a population that has attribute A, queries are sent to a group of people. Since the attribute A is related to some confidential aspects of human life, respondents may decide not to reply with incorrect answers. Two models, *Related-Question Model* and *Unrelated-Question Model,* have been proposed to solve this survey problem. In this paper, we can only describe the first one i.e. related question model.

Related Question Model

In *Related-Question Model,* instead of asking each respondent whether he/she has attribute A, the interviewer asks each respondent two related questions, the answers to which are opposite to each other.[3]

For example, the questions could be like the following. If the statement is correct, the answer of the respondent is "yes"; otherwise the respondent answer is "no".

1. I have the sensitive attribute A.
2. I do not have the sensitive attribute A.

Respondents use a randomising device to decide which question to answer, without letting the interviewer know which question is answered. The randomising device is designed in such a way that the probability of choosing the first question is θ , and the probability of choosing the second question is 1 - θ. Although the interviewer learns the responses (e.g., "yes" or "no"), he/she does not know which question was answered by the respondents. Thus the respondents' privacy is preserved. Since the interviewer's interest is to get the answer to the first question, and the answer to the second question is exactly the opposite to the answer for the first one, if the respondent chooses to answer the first question, we say that he/she is telling the truth; if the respondent chooses to answer the second question, we say that he/she is telling a lie.

To estimate the percentage of people who has the attribute A, we can use the following equations:

$$P^*(A=yes) = P(A=yes).\theta + P\ (A=no).\ (1-\theta)$$

$$P^*(A=no) = P(A= no).\theta + P\ (A=yes).\ (1-\theta)$$

Where P*(A=yes) (resp. P*(A=no) is the proportion of the "Yes" (resp. "no") responses obtained from the survey data, and

P(A=yes) (resp. P (A=no) is the estimated proportion of the "yes" (resp. "no") responses no the sensitive questions. Getting P(A=yes) and P(A=no) is the goal of the survey. By solving the above equations, we can get P (A=yes) and P (A=no) if $\theta \neq ½$. For the cases where $\theta = ½$ we can apply Unrelated questions Model where two unrelated questions are asked with the probability for one of the questions is known.

PROPOSED SCHEME FOR BUILDING DECISION TREE CLASSIFIERS USING MULTI-GROUP MULTI-AUTHORITY RANDOMISED RESPONSE TECHNIQUES

The randomised response techniques discussed in Section 3 consider only one attribute. However, in data mining, data sets usually consist of multiple attributes; finding the relationship among these attributes is one of the major goals for data mining. Therefore, we need the randomised response techniques that can handle multiple attributes while supporting various data mining computations. Work has been proposed to deal with surveys that contain multiple questions.[3, 14] However, their solutions can only handle very low dimensional situation (e.g., dimension = 2), and cannot be extended to solve data mining problems, in which the number of dimensions is usually high. We have developed a multi-group multi-authority, randomised response technique (MRR) to deal with multiple attributes corresponding multiple authorities.

Notations

In this work, we assume data are binary, but the techniques can be extended to categorical data. Suppose there are N attributes (A_1 ...... A_N) in a data set. Let E represent any logical expression based on those attributes (e.g., E=A_1=1)^(A_2=0) let $\overline{E}$ denote the logical expression that reverses the 1's in E to 0's and 0's to 1's; we call $\overline{E}$ the opposite of E . For example, for the E in the previous example, $\overline{E}$ (A_1=0)^(A_2=1).

Let P*(E) be the proportion of the records in the whole *disguised* data set that satisfy E = true. Let P(E) be the proportion of the records in the whole *undisguised* data set that satisfy E= true (the undisguised data set contains the true data, but it does not exist). P*(E) can be observed directly from the disguised data, but P (E), the actual proportion that we are interested in, cannot be observed from the disguised data because the undisguised data set is not available to anybody; we have to estimate P (E). The goal of MRR is to find a way to estimate P(E) and P*(E).

In our multi-group multi-authority scheme, we also divide each expression E to multiple sub-expressions. For example, in a three-group scheme, we write $E=E_1E_2E_3$, contains only the attributes in the group i . Several SMC-based privacy-preserving data mining schemes have been.[4,5,6,7]. These studies mainly focused on two-party distributed computing, and each party usually contributes a set of records. Although some of the solutions can be extended to solve our problem (party problem), the performance is not desirable when/becomes large. In our proposed research, we focus on centralised computing, and each participant only has one record to contribute. All records are combined together into a central database before the computations occur. In our work, the larger the value of/is, the more accurate the results will be.

Classification is one of the forms of data analysis that can be used to extract models describing important data classes or to predict future data. It has been studied extensively by the community in machine learning, expert system, and statistics as a possible solution to knowledge discovery problems. Classification is a two-step process. First, a model is built given the input of training data set which is composed of data tuples described by attributes. Each tuple is assumed to belong to a predefined class described by one of the attributes, called the class label attribute. Second, the predictive accuracy of the model (or classifier) is estimated. A test set of class-labeled samples is usually applied to the model. For each test sample, the known class label is compared with predictive result of the model.

The decision tree is one of the classification methods. A decision tree is a class discriminator that recursively partitions the training set until each partition entirely or dominantly consists of examples from one class. A well known algorithm for building decision tree classifiers is ID3.[8] In our paper we enhance the ID_3 algorithm as a method to build decision tree classifiers from disguised data for multi-group, multi-authority scheme.

Now we extend EID_3 (S, AAL) algorithm for our multi-group, multi-authority scheme. We describe the algorithm below where S represents the training samples and AAL represents attribute authority list and TAA represents the Test Attribute Authority.

EID3 (S, AAL, TAA)

1. Create a node V.
2. If S consists of samples with all the same class C then return V as a leaf node labeled with class C.
3. If AAL is empty then return V as a leaf mode with the majority class in S.
4. Select test attribute (TAA) among the AAL with the highest information gain.
5. Label node V with TAA.
6. For each known value of a_i of TAA.
   (a) Grow a branch from the node V for the condition TAA = a_i
   (b) Let s_i be the set of samples of S for which TAA = a_i.
   (c) If s_i is empty then attach a leaf labelled with the majority class in S.
   (d) Else attach the node returned by EID3(S_i, ALL-TAA)

According to EID3 algorithm, each non-leaf node of the tree contains a splitting point, and the main task for building a decision tree is to identify an attribute for the splitting point based on the information gain. Information gain can be computed using *entropy*. In the following, we assume there are m classes in the whole training data set. Entropy (S) is defined as follows:

$$\text{Entropy (S)} \quad -\sum_{j=1}^{m}\sum_{i=1}^{m} Q_{ij} \log Q_{ij} \tag{9}$$

where Q_{ij} is the relative frequency of class j authority i in S. Based on the entropy, we can compute the information gain for any candidate attribute A, for the corresponding authority AA if it is used to partition S:

$$\text{Gain (S, AA)} = \text{Entropy (S)} - \sum_{v \in A} \left(\frac{|S\,v|}{|S|} \text{Entrophy}(S\,v) \right) \quad (10)$$

where υ represents any possible values of attribute AA; S υ is the subset of S for which attribute A corresponding to the authority A has value υ ; $|S\,\upsilon|$ is the number of elements in is the number of elements in $|S\,\upsilon|$, $|S|$ is the number of elements in S. To find the best split for a tree node, we compute information gain for each attribute for each authority. We then use the attribute corresponding to the authority with the largest information gain to split the node.

When the data are not disguised, we can easily compute the information gain, but when the data are disguised using the multi-group randomised response techniques, computing becomes non-trivial.

CONCLUSION

In this paper, we have presented a multi-group, multi-authority scheme for building decision tree classifiers, based on randomised response techniques. Our method consists of two parts: the first part is the multi-group data disguising technique used for data collection; the second part is the EID_3 algorithm for decision tree building, which is used for building a classifier from the disguised data, based on our proposed multi-group multi-authority scheme.

REFERENCES

1. W. Du and Z. Zhan. Using Randomised Response Techniques for Privacy-preserving Data Mining. In Proceedings of the 9th ACM SIGKDD *International Conference on Knowledge Discovery and Data Mining*, Washington, DC, USA, August 24-27, 2003.

2. R. Agarwal and R. Srikant. Privacy-preserving Data Mining. In *Proceedings of the 2000 ACM SIGMOD on Management of Data*, pp. 439-450, Dallas, TX USA, May 15-18, 2000.

3. S.L. Warner, *Randomised Response: A Survey Technique for Eliminating Evasive Answer Bias*. The American Statistical Association, 60(309); 63-69, March, 1965.

4. W. Du and Z. Zhan. Building Decision Tree Classifier on Private Data. *In Workshop on Privacy, Security, and Data Mining at the 2002 IEEE International Conference on Data Mining* (ICDM'02), Maebashi City, Japan, December 9, 2002.

5. Y. Lindell and B. Pinkas. *Privacy Preserving Data Mining. In Advance in Cryptology—Crypto 2000*, Lecture Notes in Computer Science, Volume 1880-2000.

6. J. Vaidya and C. Clifton. Privacy Preserving Association Rule Mining in Vertically Partitioned Data. *In Proceedings of the 8th ACM SIGKDD International Conference on Knowledge Discovery and Data Mining*, July 23-06 2002.

7. J. Vaidya and C. Clifton. Privacy Preserving k-means Clustering over Vertically Partitioned Data. In *Proceedings of the 9th ACM SIGKDD International Conference on Knowledge Discovery and Data Mining*, 2003.

8. J. Han and M. Kamber. *Data Mining Concepts and Techniques*, Morgan Kaufmann Publishers, 2001.

4

Data Mining
CRM in Business Applications

V.Venkata Narayana*
Mrs. A. Kanaka Durga**

ABSTRACT

Data Mining is an effective tool and systematic method of knowledge discovery using patterns or behaviours within the data that lead to profitable business action. Data Mining needs large volumes of data in the past as well as in the current scenario, which can also be extrapolated to take the toughest, yet the most profitable decisions by the top managements of Organisations.

The Paper explains Data Mining as a concept, several insights of the concept of DM and stages /Life Cycle, how information be filtered for Business Information (certain classic examples who made effective use of Data Mining).

***CRM** stands for **Customer Relationship Management**, is a process or methodology used to learn more about customers' needs and behaviours in order to develop stronger relationships with them.*

* Marketing Manager-ITC LTD (Ph.D. in Management)
E-mail: durgapallavi@rediffmail.com; Mobile: 98491 60142

** Associate Professor CSE&IT, GNEC (Ph.D. in CSE)
E-mail: durgapallavi@yahoo.com; Mobile: 9849384247

The current paper touches elaborate aspects of CRM (using Data Mining), success and failure parts of CRM, turnaround strategy for CRM and need for sustaining the Success Rate of CRM.

The various types of CRM Software are also touched upon.

It concludes that data mining and drilling and analysis of data to the effective use of organisations in implementation of CRM will contribute to the better lifestyles of the people with an enhanced economic stature of the nation in general and industries in particular.

INTRODUCTION

Data Mining is a set of processes related to analysing and discovering useful, actionable knowledge buried deep beneath large volumes of data stores or data sets. This knowledge discovery involves finding patterns or behaviours within the data that lead to some profitable business action. Data Mining requires generally large volumes of data including history data as well as current data to explore the knowledge.

Data mining is the essential process that helps companies better understand their customers. It creates an enormous competitive advantage. It also enables alignment of actions or customer initiatives with the company's overall objectives.

Data Mining helps companies to proactively offer products and services that meet the predicted needs and desires of specific customers.

Crucial Concepts in Data Mining:

- Bagging (Voting, Averaging)
  Boosting
  RISP
  Data Preparation (in Data Mining)
- Data Reduction (for Data Mining)
  Deployment
- Drill-Down Analysis
- Feature Selection
  Machine Learning
- Meta-Learning

DATA MINING IS A PROCESS

There is increased interest in a process or methodology for data mining. It is argued that such a formalised process will widen the exploitation of data mining as an enabling technology for solving business problems. It will allow people with varying expertise in data mining and from different business sectors to carry out successful data mining projects with a high degree of consistency.

There are a number of initiatives for the development of a formal/documented data mining process both in Europe and North America. It is reassuring to the data mining community that the processes emerging from all of these initiatives reveal a large degree of similarity. There is widespread agreement on the main steps (stages) involved in such a process and any differences relate only to the detailed tasks within each stage.

A summary of the major stages of a data mining process is:

- *Goal Definition:* This involves defining the goal or objective for the data-mining project. This should be a business goal or objective, which normally relates to a business event such as arrears in mortgage repayment, customer attrition (churn), energy consumption in a process, etc. This stage also involves the design of how the discovered patterns would be utilised as part of the overall business solution.
- *Data Selection:* This is the process of identifying the data needed for the data-mining project and the sources of this data.
- *Data Preparation:* This involves cleansing the data, joining/merging data sources and the derivation of new columns (fields) in the data through aggregation, calculations or text manipulation of existing data fields. The end result is normally a flat table ready for the application of the data mining itself (i.e. the discovery algorithms to generate patterns). Such a table is normally split into two data sets; one set for pattern discovery and one set for pattern verification.

- *Data Exploration:* This involves the exploration of the prepared data to get a better feel prior to pattern discovery and also to validate the results of the data preparation. Typically, this involves examining the statistics (minimum, maximum, average, etc.) and the frequency distribution of individual data fields. It also involves field versus field graphs to understand the dependency between fields.
- *Pattern Discovery:* This is the stage of applying the pattern discovery algorithm to generate patterns. The process of pattern discovery is most effective when applied as an exploration process assisted by the discovery algorithm. This allows business users to interact with and to impart their business knowledge to the discovery process. In the case of inducing a tree, users can at any point in the tree construction examine/explore the data filtering to that path, examine the recommendation of the algorithm regarding the next data field to use for the next branch then use their business judgment to decide on the data field for branching. The pattern discovery stage also involves analysing the ability of the discovered patterns to predict the propensity of the business event, and for verification against an independent data set.
- *Pattern Deployment:* This stage involves the application of the discovered patterns to solve the business goal of the data-mining project. This can take many forms:
    - ❖ *Patterns Presentation:* The description of the patterns (or the graphical tree display) and their associated data statistics are included in a document or presentation. This requires the data-mining tool to generate text reports and WMF (Windows Meta File) representations of the graphical decision tree.
    - ❖ *Business Intelligence:* The discovered patterns are used as queries against a database to derive business intelligence reports. This requires the data-mining tool to generate SQL representations of the decision tree.
    - ❖ *Data Scoring and Labelling:* The discovered patterns are used to score and/or label each data record in the

database with the propensity and the label of the pattern it belongs to. This can be done directly by the data-mining tool or through generation of SQL or C representation of the decision tree.

- *Decision Support Systems:* The discovered patterns are used to make components of a decision support system. This can be achieved by embedding the data-mining tool as a decision-making component, or a C module generated by the data-mining tool.
- *Alarm Monitoring:* The discovered patterns are used as 'norms' for a business process. Monitoring these patterns will enable deviations from normal conditions to be detected at the earliest possible time. This can be achieved by embedding the data-mining tool as a monitoring component, or through using SQL generated by the data-mining tool.

- *Pattern Validity Monitoring:* As a business process changes over time, the validity of patterns discovered from historic data will deteriorate. It is therefore important to detect these changes at the earliest possible time by monitoring patterns with new data. Significant changes to the patterns will point to the need to discover new patterns from more recent data.

DATA MINING LIFE CYCLE: FIND OUT THE BUSINESS PROBLEM

Consider a company's current year sales dropped by a percentage when compared to the previous year. By using LAP Tools, the exact sales fact can be determined across several dimensions like region, time etc.

- *Knowledge Discovery:* Given the business problem, various reasons for the decrease in sales have to be analysed utilising one or more of the Data Mining Techniques. Causes may include poor quality or service of the product or flaws in marketing schemes or less demand for the product or seasonal changes or regulations enforced by the Government or competitors pressure, and so on. The exact solutions have to be found out in order to resolve this sales drop, which we call it as the Knowledge Discovery here.

- *Implement the Knowledge:* Based on above discovery, proper actions should be taken in order to overcome the business problem.
- *Analyse the Results:* Once it is been implemented, results need to be monitored and measured to find out outcomes of that action.

OLAP Vs. DATA MINING

OLAP helps organisations to find out the measures like sales drop, productivity, service response time, inventory in hand etc. Data Mining can also be used to predict 'What will happen in the future' with the help of data patterns available within the organisation and publicly available data.

Information Filtering

Whether your application is designed to filter intrusive or non-intrusive information, the Rosette Linguistics Platform delivers the computational linguistics necessary to identify key words and phrases that trigger your filtering application's results.

Example applications include:

- *Call Center Software:* For applications that manage inbound inquiries from customers, Rosette can identify the language of incoming messages and let route them to the associated native language customer service representative. In a deeper application of Rosette for message routing, may want to be able to pick out key words or phrases from among the text, which will route the message to the native language speaker who handles, say, "laptops, " or "ovens."
- *Anti-Spam:* Critical to the process of filtering Spam is being able to identify words and phrases from among the incoming text that are germane to the type of spam you are filtering. Add to this challenge the complexities of different languages, and delivering an Anti-Spam product for global customers is difficult. Rosette provides the multi-lingual identification and tagging functions necessary to accurately identify and filter out unwanted messages. Rosette can process these messages based upon statistical analysis, or it can be trained to identify domain specific words or phrases to fine-tune your filters.

- *Market Intelligence:* Applications that comb the web looking for specific information about a company, its products, its competitors, its coverage, its reputation, must analyse text in many languages to extract the critical pieces of information that help this company make educated business decisions. By applying Rosette's linguistics, this application will identify the language and encoding of web content, break the text into its components and extract the important concepts to build its database of this company's metrics. From there, it can apply its analytics to deliver concise decision support information.

BUSINESS INTELLIGENCE AND KEY PERFORMANCE INDICATORS

Key Performance Indicators, commonly referred to as KPIs, are a list of measurements that are identified as critical factors in achieving the organisational goals or mission. KPIs are often identified in a business to help them drive a business towards its success and are associated with a number of business activities like Customer Relationship Management (CRM), Supply Chain Analytics or any other activity that is happening within the organisation.

Business Applications—Case Studies

- *Bank of America* has used data mining to sculpt detailed demographic views of the banking habits and financial assets of select groups of its customers. Querying their data warehouse averages at 30 seconds. The system here draws data from the entire bank and its 30 business units, making it a truly enterprise-wide database able to serve 1,2C0 users making over 2,500 complex queries daily.
- Gilman Securities has used data mining to differentiate how the financial market reacts to the volatility of different business sectors.

  Example: finding the relationship(s) between rate of changes between Japanese yen and the Government bond market.
- *The Toronto-based Canadian Imperial Bank of Commerce* has used data mining analysis extensively, including statistical

modelling and consulting with regard to customer traffic patterns at branches to aid in scheduling; time-stamped cash withdrawals at branches and automated banking machines to manage levels of currency holdings; traffic patterns; products sold, and the relative mix of products to plan marketing strategies and performance measures.

- One of the larger retailing operations in America, the Army and Air Force Exchange Service (known to military personnel as "the PX") has used automated data mining to predict how much a particular woman will spend annually, given the age, her dependents and her annual wage level to target advertising and sales towards the appropriate customer base.
- "*Wal-Mart,* MasterCard International processes, Metro Health Insurance Corp. of Roanoke, Va., have excellently explored the data mining for business applications.

This is so important because all too often data mining is seen as an analytical tool for gaining business insight, but is difficult to integrate into existing Customer Relationship Management (CRM) systems. Segmentations generated by data mining contain a large potential value for your business. However, this value is not realised unless the segmentations are integrated into your business and combined with actual scores on basis of the segmentations.

In the commercial environment, clustering and profile scoring are used in the following areas among many others:

— Cross-marketing;

— Cross-selling;

— Customising marketing plans for different customer types;

— Deciding which media approach to use;

— Understanding shopping goals;

— Reuse customer profiles and scores in the operational databases;

— Exploit customer profiles and scores and combine it using the end-user reporting tool;

— Trigger additional actions based on customer profiles and scores;

— Personalise any customer access based on these customer profiles and scores.

Business Scenario Deployment Examples:

- Real-time personalisation
- Fraud detection

Business Benefits:

- Up-to-date analysis on current data
- A system that adapts to change in undesirable behaviour
- Capture data mining expertise
- Enhance repeatable success
- Potential for enhanced communication
- Actionable result (ROI)
- Automation
- Calibration: New data = new model
- Fast and accurate
- Ready for the Web environment

To enable a comprehensive view of existing and potential customers, a centralised data repository is usually necessary to collect data from all appropriated operational systems, channels, and third-party sources. This repository should support a customer centric, cross-product view necessary to develop effective marketing campaigns.

Campaign Management

As competition grows in the industry, companies look more than ever toward increasing profitability from existing customers, rather than expecting new customers to account for growth. The focus is on retaining the profitable customers. The telecommunications industry has proven this extensively. They determine the customers and the markets that bring the most profit, and drop those that do not bring profit to your business model. Retaining existing customers is easier and less costly than attracting new ones. Naturally, that means that companies are keenly interested in cross-selling a variety of products and services to existing customers. Cross-selling can substantially increase customer profitability, especially if an organisation targets valuable customers who are likely to purchase multiple products. But identifying good potential customers and effectively cross-selling without cannibalising other product lines are not easy tasks. It is essential to efficiently monitor and act on marketing opportunities. Changes to customer profiles occur all the time. One-to-one marketing requires a responsive system and a large number of initiatives that can be managed only by a system that provides automatic event detection, comprehensive reporting, and support for multiple customer and product profiles.

Campaign Management Deals with Three Types of Campaigns:

- *Outbound:* The enterprise contacts the customer during a campaign. Outbound campaigns are usually targeted based on the customer profile.
- *Inbound:* The customer contacts the enterprise.
- *Triggered:* The enterprise contacts the customer when some new and important information becomes available.

With target marketing and triggered actions, the direct marketer is in charge of who, when, and how to contact a customer or prospect. With inbound interactions, the customer decides when to contact and the purpose of the action. Outbound and targeted campaigns address a target group of customers that are selected based on specific characteristics. One example of a targeted campaign is a credit card acquisition campaign. In this example, a company selects a group of prospects based on credit history and potential customer value to offer a pre-approved low interest rate product. Another example is a credit card company that decides to pursue customers who were not timely in paying bills (but eventually paid them). Significant profit was made on late fees with minimal losses.

Campaign Management Solution Examples

An inbound campaign is granted when a company wants to create different treatments for customers when they interact with its channels.

(a) Example, it may be how to perform real-time personalisation when the customer interacts with the enterprise using the Web. The main challenge here is to detect when the right time is to present the right offer or service.

(b) An important example of this type of campaign is customer complaint management. When a valuable customer calls a customer service hotline dissatisfied with the company's services or products, it is important that the call center specialist can deal with that complaint to avoid escalation of the problem or even customer attrition. Most of the time, a call center specialist is not prepared to deal with this kind of situation due to inexperience or lack of rules of engagement.

Triggered campaigns need to deal with decisions based on new information available for the system. There are two ways to implement a triggered campaign, using schedulers or triggers.

Scheduled campaigns can systematically verify the data changes in the database looking for patterns that qualify a customer to receive a new product offer, for example, or any other kind of marketing action. The problem with this approach is determining the right interval to check for new information in the databases. Intervals that are too long can lead to missed opportunities or customer attrition. Intervals that are too short may not be viable due to performance constraints. To run a campaign using triggers, they need to be enabled in the database system or in the application.

CRM stands for *Customer Relationship Management*. It is a process or methodology used to learn more about customers' needs and behaviours in order to develop stronger relationships with them. There are many technological components to CRM, but thinking about CRM in primarily technological terms is a mistake.

Customer Relationship Management (CRM) gained recognition in the mid-1990s, primarily driven by its perception as information technology (IT). However, not enough attention has been given to the fundamental drivers of CRM success: strategy, metrics and the organisation. The more useful way to think about CRM is as a process that will help bring together lots of pieces of information about customers, sales, marketing effectiveness, responsiveness and market trends. *CRM* helps businesses use technology and human resources to gain insight into the behaviour of customers and the value of those customers. Successful CRM is about competing in the relationship dimension—not as an alternative to having a competitive product or reasonable price—but as a differentiator.

CRM really works to improve chances of getting an ROI from "CRM initiative" by following three simple steps: (1) Understand the value customer wants; (2) deliver that value profitably; and (3) repeat.

To be brief:

- CRM can work as a differentiating business strategy.
- CRM delivers a return on investment for two out of three projects.
- CRM produces solid short-term returns but lags in providing full strategic benefits.
- CRM success starts with putting customer interests first. Period.

You can succeed with CRM by being SMART:

Strategy which is Customer-Centric

Metrics that are used appropriately

Align organisation with your objectives

Redesign work processes as needed

Technology tools as enablers are used appropriately

But it all starts by putting your customers first and creating a better relationship with them than your competitors offer.

Advantages of CRM

- Provide better customer service
- Increase customer revenues
- Discover new customers
- Cross sell/Up Sell products more effectively
- Help sales staff close deals faster

- Make call centers more efficient
- Simplify marketing and sales processes

Ingredients of CRM

Customer Relationship Management: A Guide to Getting Started—A well-executed CRM programme can improve customer satisfaction, increase staff productivity, slash operational costs and maximise the effectiveness of each customer interaction. However, simply installing much-publicised technologies won't achieve these results. Successful CRM requires a comprehensive understanding of the context in which the initiative takes place, careful analysis of the key improvement areas and rigorous planning and execution to ensure implementation of CRM best practices.

The rate of successful CRM implementations is around 30 per cent. That's an astonishing 70 per cent failure rate. So why are we pointing out this unflattering statistic? Because we can greatly improve our chances of a successful implementation by following the lessons of those companies that make up the winning 30 per cent. Many factors can influence the results of CRM initiative. Based on our extensive background and experience with CRM implementations, many software solution providers are providing compiled guides to ensure that CRM project starts off right and stays on track for success.

How to Embrace CRM and Make It Succeed in an Organisation: The concept of CRM (Customer Relationship Management) is not a new one. Slogans, such as "The customer is always right," and "The customer is king," have long permeated the culture of many companies cognisant of the importance of their customer, as sources of future business.

Metrics Cure for CRM: While substantial investments in customer level initiatives have been made, marketers have not always been able to create customer value frameworks to track success/failure within and across such initiatives. Several elements of dissatisfaction with CRM deployments are resolvable through a re-look at the essential metrics used to track these initiatives.

Real CRM/SFA Success: If we accept that the technology for the SFA solution is sound and the software does work then what can be the problem? It must be the people tasked with using the SFA. Who really wanted the SFA solution? Senior management faced with the tumultuous changes over the last decade have attempted to ensure higher profit margins in various ways: reengineering, downsizing, cutting costs, outsourcing, sweating assets and of course attempting to make their sales efforts more effective. The investment in the whole concept of CRM in the eyes of senior management is based on improving the bottom line and their own tenure.

- *Secrets of CRM Success Across a Network:* It gives a step-by-step process toward creating a long-term CRM solution that can evolve with changing business objectives and technologies.
- *The Bottom Line on CRM Success:* It happens time and again. With high hopes and great anticipation, a company sets out to implement a new CRM solution—one that promises to boost sales and customer service, while dramatically reducing costs. But a funny thing happens on the way to achieving these benefits. The implementation and acceptance process proves to be rockier than anticipated.

Capturing the RIGHT Requirements: Key to CRM Success Organisations in the process of implementing a CRM solution is concerned about success of their CRM initiatives. Unfortunately, many CRM initiatives recently have failed to achieve success and the failure has been attributed to poor requirements. In most of the cases the failure is not because the requirements were not captured in the *RIGHT manner,* but because *RIGHT Requirements* were not captured.

Complexity, Fragmentation, Uncertainty and Emergence in CRM: As the business world is beginning to see, implementing CRM solutions is difficult.

The real reasons for the difficulty can be grouped into three categories: (a) dynamic complexity; (b) fragmentation; and (c) uncertainty. Companies can succeed in CRM implementations by mastering the three skills: adaptive iteration; fluidity in anecdotal, correlated and causal measurement; and coherency through emergent yet directed corporate self-consciousness.

Cost and Effect Analysis for Successful CRM Implementation: When an organisation implements a new CRM solution there are several cost components that must be considered to get the new technology solution into production. To insure the success of the implementation the project team must have a detailed understanding of each of these components, it's cost, and it's effect on the organisation.

CRM Projects: A Framework for Success: It provides a framework for CRM project success. Regardless of where you are in planning and implementing your CRM initiatives, should assist in conducting a point check and taking the necessary steps toward a successful CRM implementation.

CRM Strategy: Is it Just Strategy or Does the Customer have something to do with it? It will define the fundamental elements of putting together the strategy and will only define the most prevalent elements deciding whether to allocate capital to them.

CRM—Managing the Benefits: By identifying CRM as a strategic customer-centric approach to business, we can find the linkage to strategy planning and the necessary concomitant elements: portfolio and programme management.

Enhancing Customer Relations — The Secret of Sustaining Success Organisations today are still focussed on building brands and products, when their focus should be on building customer relationships. This can only be achieved through an effective CRM/ knowledge management strategy.

How to Avoid Post-Implementation Perils: Support Environment and Training Plan are Key: All too often, sales personnel are not comprehensively taught how to use CRM software after its company-wide implementation, resulting in inefficient use of the platform. The solution: web-based training.

Mapping CRM for Success—Start CRM Working Backwards: Many writers and researchers have offered their views and many say start with the end in mind and work backwards is best! This is a rather frightening approach as the journey can be long and costly.

Secrets for Internal Adoption: CRM implementations can still fail even with the proper vision, strategy, and technology. Use these guidelines to ensure adoption of the change that accompanies any CRM initiative.

Why CRM Isn't Working: Many enterprises find it hard to measure a return on their often-heavy investment in CRM, and have not enjoyed the level of business benefit that has been promised by their CRM solution provider. Why? In many cases the CRM implementation has been almost entirely IT-led, and as a result its technology has not been harnessed to the company's sales-based, commercial customer relationship strategy and market activity. There is an ample scope for Research on finding how-to guide to successful CRM project implementation.

Customer Relationship Management—A Diffusion Snapshot: Among those watching and waiting, or ignoring CRM, a number do not see CRM as presently important to their industry. The question arises as to whether CRM diffusion will slow unless the concept is reinvigorated, by being extended to relationship management more broadly.

Can CRM Project be Saved? - Something's gone terribly wrong with your promising CRM project. Pull the emergency brake, reset expectations, and focus, focus, focus. This is only possible but for the effective usage of Data Mining Concepts.

Is Your CRM System Destined to Fail?- CRM software is only as good as the information it contains. As the old programmers motto goes 'garbage in, garbage out'. So how can you avoid incomplete, incorrect, irrelevant or out-of-date and generally unfit-for-use data from permeating your CRM software? You need to gather your key CRM users together and write a standard guideline document, defining the CRM system rules of use. Data mining plays an effective role in the success/failure of CRM.

Pain-Free CRM: By taking the time to integrate data for its online CRM system, a regional health plan has succeeded where other large insurers have stumbled.

Successful CRM Hinges On Data Quality: With increased competition in online and offline marketplaces, organisations are turning to CRM to attract and retain customers.

What Others Have Learned While Implementing CRM: One of the best ways to achieve superior ROI from CRM is to employ the key practices of companies that are already reaping the benefits of CRM success.

You Can Succeed in Your CRM Sales Rollout: The rewards of CRM enable to forecast accurately, reproduce best practices and more easily scale your sales organisation.

CRM Software

- Sales Force Automation
- Contact Management
- Lead Management

Enterprise Lead Management Software

- eCRM or Web Based CRM
- Self Service CRM
- Self Service CRM (eCRM)
- Survey Management Software

Customer Service

- Call Center Software
- Help Desk Software

Partner Relationship Management

- Contract Management Software Contract Management Software enables an enterprise to create, track and manage partnerships, contracts, and agreements.

  Example: Upside Software, Accruent Software, diCarta, I-Many.
- Distribution Management Software

The Types of Data CRM Projects Collect

- Responses to campaigns
- Shipping and fulfillment dates

- Sales and purchase data
- Account information
- Web registration data
- Service and support records
- Demographic data
- Web sales data

CONCLUSION

With thorough knowledge spanning most major application areas, Data Mining and CRM may be readily adapted for virtually any business or industrial modelling challenge. While Data Mining helps in drilling the most apt and reliable data for effective use of the data, CRM helps in effective utilisation of this data in gaining and retaining the Customer for the long-term benefit of the organisation.

CRM has become a key business initiative for organisations of all sizes—making it an excellent business case, as it is both a vertical and horizontal market application.

"Successful customer relationship management" is the competitive advantage of the Information Age and is the bottom line for market leadership. These aspects together bring in a further positive change in the economic stature and better life style of the people of our country in general and people in the industrial segment in particular.

REFERENCES

1. Dr.V.Venkata Ramana and G. Somayajulu-"CRM—A Key To Corporate Success".
2. CRMGuru.com
3. Customer Relationship Management: A Guide to Getting Started-Unisys Corporation.
4. IT Toolbox CRM.
5. Enhance Your Business Applications: Simple Integration of Advanced Data Mining Functions: IBM Corp. 2002.
6. Putting the Brakes on Runaway CRM- *eCustomerServiceWorld.com*

5

Application of Data Mining Techniques to Earth Science Data

Dr. M. Usha Rani*
R.J. Ramasree**

ABSTRACT

Data mining techniques have the promise to aid by discovering interesting patterns in the earth science data that capture complex interactions among ocean temperatures, land surface meteorology, and terrestrial carbon flux. To explore earth science data, various data mining techniques, such as association rule mining for texture features in satellite images, classification of land cover types, and clustering of storm path trajectories are to be used. Improvements in data mining techniques made during the investigation of Earth Science data may have potential applications in other domains, such as transportation, business logistics, public health, and public safety.

INTRODUCTION

The remote sensing data, combined with historical climate records and predictions from ecosystem models, offers new opportunities for understanding how the Earth is changing, for determining what factors cause these changes, and for predicting future changes. Data mining techniques [BDGHNS] have the

* Associate Professor in Computer Science, SPMVV, Tirupati.

** Associate Professor in Computer Science, Rashtriya Sanskrit Vidyapeet, Tirupati.

promise to aid this undertaking by discovering interesting patterns that capture complex interactions among ocean temperatures, land surface meteorology, and terrestrial carbon flux.

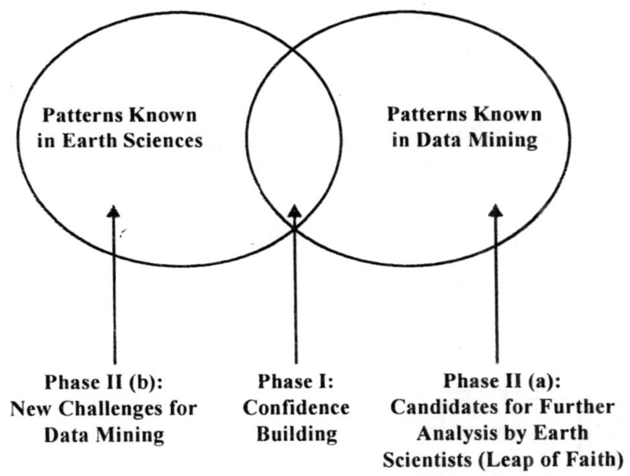

Fig. 5.1: **Using Data Mining to Find Earth Science Patterns**

Collaboration between Earth Scientists and data mining researchers has developed in two phases as illustrated by Figure 5.1. In the first phase, data mining techniques are applied to discover some well known patterns in Earth Science in order to build confidence in the use of data mining techniques. As an example, consider the El Nino climate pattern and its well known effects on temperature and precipitation [Tay98]. The second phase includes the exploration of novel patterns found by data mining, but not well known by Earth scientists. To explore Earth Science data, researchers have applied various data mining techniques [BDGHNS], such as association rule mining for texture features in satellite images [RRHG], classification of land cover types [KGC02], and clustering of storm path trajectories [ScPa99]. Table A.1 shows some data mining techniques that can be used to address basic Earth Science questions.

Table 5.1: Connection of data mining techniques to earth science questions

Earth Science Question	*Example of Data Mining Techniques*
How is the Earth changing?	Principal Component Analysis (PCA), Cluster Analysis, Anomaly Detection, ARIMA time Series modelling, Trend Detection, Change Point Detection
What factors cause these changes?	Correlation, Canonical Correlation Analysis, Association Analysis, Causal Analysis
Can we Predict Future Changes?	Regression, correlation.

DATA DESCRIPTION AND DATA SOURCES

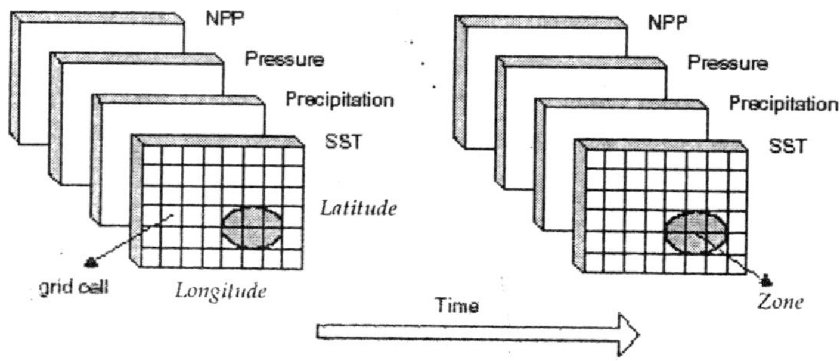

Fig. 5.2: **A Simplified View of the Problem Domain**

Earth Science data consist of a sequence of global snapshots of the Earth taken at various points in time, as shown in Figure 5.2. Each snapshot consists of measurement values for a number of variables (e.g., temperature, pressure, and precipitation) collected globally. All attribute data within a global snapshot is represented using spatial frameworks. A spatial framework is a partitioning of the surface of Earth into a set of mutually disjoint regions which collectively cover the entire surface of Earth. Examples of spatial frameworks for land include the political boundaries of countries and latitude longitude spherical grids at different resolutions, e.g., $0.5^0 X 0.5^0$ or $1^0 X 1^0$. Variables derived from global satellite data, e.g., Net Primary Production (NPP), are available at a resolution of 0.5^0 X 0.5^0. (NPP is the net assimilation of atmospheric carbon dioxide into organic matter by plants.) Global snapshots, i.e., values of variables for each location in a spatial framework, are available for periodic, discrete points in time that span a range of twenty to one hundred years. These variable values can either be observations from different sensors, e.g., precipitation and sea surface temperature (SST), or the result of model predictions, e.g., NPP from the NASACASA model.

DATA PREPROCESSING

Patterns derived from Earth Science data are often dominated by the presence of seasonal variations in the data. Although yearly patterns such as spring, summer, fall, and winter, or rainy season/ dry season are important, they are already well known. Earth Scientists are primarily interested in patterns that represent deviations from normal seasonal cycles. Examples of such patterns include anomalous climate events such as droughts, floods, heat waves, etc. Such anomalous events become apparent only if the seasonal components of the climate time series are removed. In the following, we describe a technique known as the "monthly" Zscore transformation for removing these components.

This transformation takes the set of values for a given month, e.g., all Januarys, calculates the mean and standard deviation for that set of monthly values, and then standardises each value by calculating its Zscore, i.e., by subtracting off the mean and dividing by the standard deviation. Put another way, we express each data value in the time series in terms of its deviation from the mean value for its corresponding month, scaled by the volatility factor for that month. The month by month rescaling used in this transformation causes seasonal fluctuations to disappear. Figure 5.3 shows the result of applying the monthly Zscore to a sample SST time series.

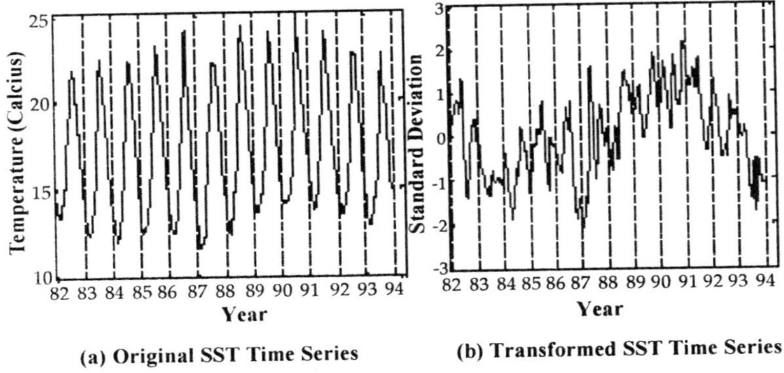

(a) Original SST Time Series (b) Transformed SST Time Series

Fig. 5.3: **Monthly Z-score Transformation Applied to Deseasonalize a Sample SST Time Series**

CLUSTERING

It is well known that ocean, atmosphere, and land processes are highly coupled, i.e., climate phenomena occurring in one location can affect the climate at a far away location. Indeed, understanding these climate teleconnections is critical for finding the answers to questions such as how the Earth's climate is changing and how ecosystems respond to global environmental change.

A common way to study such teleconnections is by using climate indices [W3cg] [W3cd], which distill climate variability at a regional or global scale into a single time series. As a result, Earth Scientists have devoted a considerable amount of time to developing/discovering climate indices, such as NINO 1+2 and the other indices described in Table 5.2.

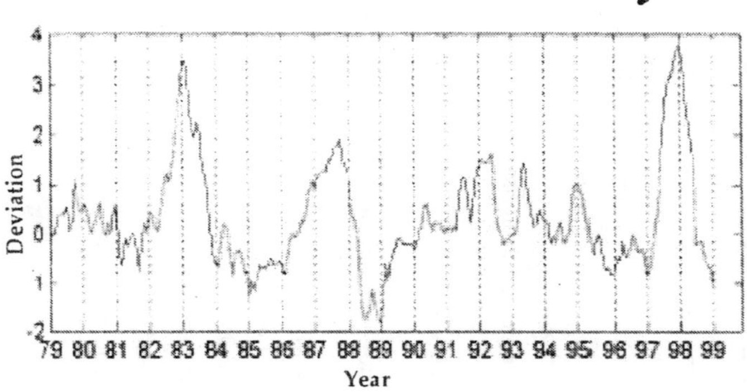

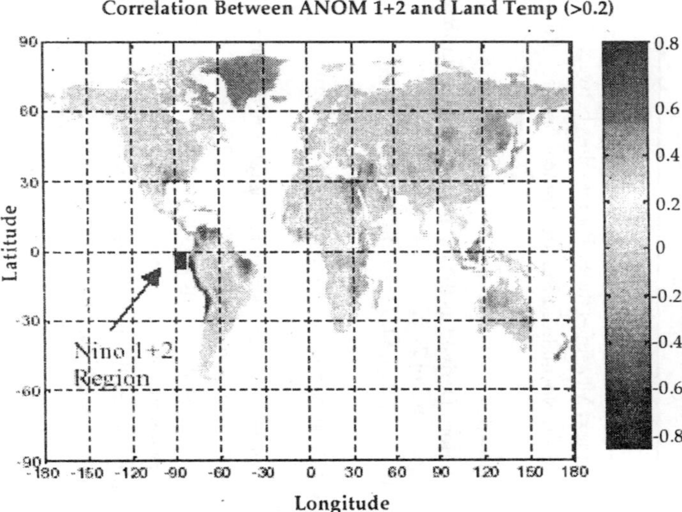

Fig. 5.4: **The NINO 1 + 2 Climate Index and its Correlation to Land Temperature Anomalies**

Table 5.2: Description of well-known climate indices

Index	*Description*
SOI	(Southern Oscillation Index) Measures the SLP anomalies between Darwia and Tahtti
NAO	(North Atlantic Oscillation) Normalised SLP differences between Posta Deigoda, Azores and Stykkisholmur, Ice land
AO	(Arctic Oscillation) Defined as the First Principal component of SLP poleward of 20°N
PDO	(Pacific Decadal Oscillation) Derived as the leading principal component of monthly SST anomalies in the North Pacific Ocean, poleward of 20°N
QBO	(Quasi-Biennial Oscillation Index) Measures the regular variation of zonal (i.e. east-west) stratospheric winds above the equator
CTI	(Cold Tongue Index) Captures SST variations in the cold tongue region of the equatorial pacific ocean (6°N 6°S, 180°-90°W)
WP	(Western Pacific) Represents slow frequently temporal function of the 'zonal dipole' SLP spatial pattern involving the Karnataka Peninsula, southeastern Asia and far western tropical and subtropical North pacific.
NINO 1+2	Sea surface temperature, anomalies in the region bounded by 80°W-90°W and 0°-10°S.
NINO 3	Sea surface temperature anomalies in the region bounded by 90°W-160°W and 6°S-6°N
NINO 3, 4	Sea surface temperature anomalies in the region bounded by 120°W-170°W and 6°S-6°N
NINO 4	Sea surface temperature anomalies in the region bounded by 160°W-160°W and 6°S-6°N.

As shown in Figure 5.5, SNN found 107 clusters or candidat indices. Note that many grid points from the ocean do not belon to any clusters (these are the points belonging to the whit background), as these points come from regions that are n relatively uniform and homogeneous.

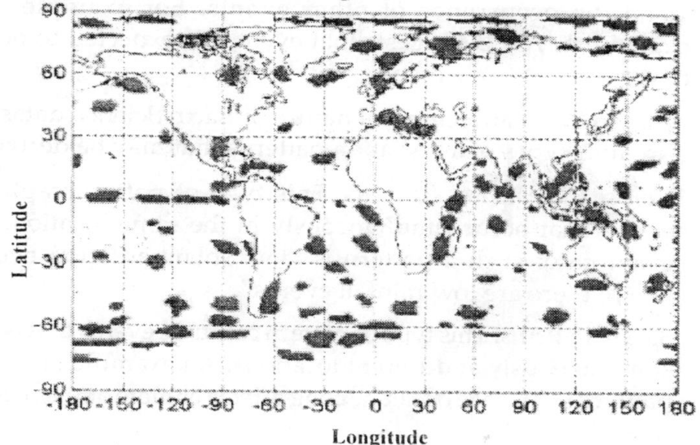

Fig. 5.5: **107 SST Clusters**

Some of the cluster centroids, i.e., candidate indices, that w found are very highly correlated to known indices. Figure 5 shows clusters that reproduce some well known climate indice

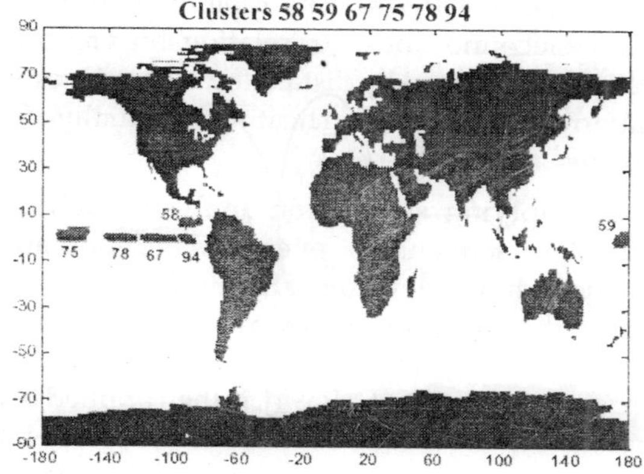

Fig. 5.6: **Clusters with correlation to known indices ≥ 0.8**

ASSOCIATION ANALYSIS

Association analysis can be used to derive spatiotemporal relationships hidden in Earth Science data. The goal of association analysis is to extract significant patterns, in the form of rules or sets of events, that will predict the occurrence of certain events based on the occurrence of other events. For example, the association rule A ¡! B suggests that event B is expected to occur whenever event A is observed.

Due to the spatiotemporal nature of Earth Science datasets, there are four types of association patterns that may be derived:

1. *Non-spatiotemporal Patterns*. This type of pattern captures events that occur simultaneously in the same location. An example of such a pattern is "low solar radiation events where there are low rainfall events".
2. *Spatial Patterns*. This type of pattern captures events that occur simultaneously at different locations. An example of such a pattern is "surface ocean heating affects climate at the nearby coastal areas".
3. *Temporal Patterns*. This type of pattern predicts events that are expected to occur in the future at the same location. An example of such a pattern is "low rainfall events eventually lead to an increase in wildfires."
4. *Spatiotemporal Patterns*. This type of pattern captures time lagged teleconnections, i.e., relationships among events that occur in geographically distant locations. An example of such a pattern is "surface ocean heating eventually affects regional wildfires and NPP."

Before applying association analysis, each time series is converted into a sequence of events. We define an event as an anomalously high or low value of the time series — specifically, if the value of the time series deviates by at least 1.5 standard deviations from its average. A standard association analysis algorithm, such as Apriori [RaRa94], is then applied to extract rules from the transformed data sets. The rules extracted by the Apriori algorithm are evaluated using the well-known support and confidence measures [RaRa94]. Rules with low support and low confidence tend to be statistically insignificant, and are pruned automatically by the Apriori algorithm. For example, some of the non-spatiotemporal patterns extracted by Apriori include:

R1: {FPARHI} → {NPPHI} (support = 4.6%, confidence = 51%)

QUERY PROCESSING

A spatial time series dataset [ZHSK03] is a collection of time series [BJR94], each referencing a location in a common spatial framework [Wor95]. NASA Earth observation systems currently generate a large sequence of global snapshots of the Earth, including various atmospheric, land, and ocean measurements such as sea surface temperature, pressure, and precipitation. These data are spatial time series data in nature. Queries that find highly correlated time series are frequently used to discover interesting relationships among observations in spatial time series data. For example, such queries are used to identify the land locations whose climate is severely affected by El Nino [Tay98]. However, correlation queries are computationally expensive due to large spatiotemporal frameworks containing many locations and long time sequences. Therefore, the development of efficient query processing techniques is crucial for exploring these datasets.

CONCLUSION

In this it is provided an overview of preliminary efforts to apply data mining techniques to the analysis of Earth Science data. It has been able to use clustering to find patterns that represent well known climate indices. Nonetheless, there are many tasks remaining both with respect to data mining and the application of data mining results. The main focus of the data mining work has been clustering and association analysis. More broadly, improvements in data mining techniques made during the investigation of Earth Science data may have potential applications in other domains, such as transportation, business logistics, public health, and public safety.

REFERENCES

[BDGHNS] J. Behnke, E. Dobinson, S. Graves, T. Hinke, D. Nichols, and P. Stolorz. *Final Report for NASA Workshop on Issues in the Application of Data Mining to Scientific Data*, 1999.

BJR94] G. Box, G. Jenkins, and G. Reinsel. *Time Series Analysis: Forecasting and Control*. Prentice Hall, 1994.

KGC02] S. Kumar, J. Ghosh, and M. Crawford. Hierarchical Fusion of Multiple Classifiers for Hyperspectral Data Analysis. *Pattern Analysis and Applications (Special Issue on Fusion of Multiple Classifiers)*, 5(2), 2002.

RaRa94] Rakesh Agrawal and Ramakrishnan Srikant. *Fast Algorithms for Mining Association Rules*. In Proc. 20th Int. Conf. Very Large Data Bases, VLDB, pp. 487-499, 1994.

RRHG] J. Rushing, H. Ranganath, T. Hinke, and S. Graves. Using Association Rules as Texture Features. *IEEE Transactions on Pattern Analysis and Machine Intelligence*, 23(8), 2001.

ScPa99] Scott Gaffney and Padhraic Smyth. Trajectory Clustering with Mixtures of Regression Models. In Proc. of the Fifth ACM SIGKDD *International Conference on Knowledge Discovery and Data Mining*, 1999.

Tay98] G. H. Taylor. *Impacts of the El Nino/Southern Oscillation on the Pacific Northwest*. Technical report, Oregon State University, Corvallis, Oregon, 1998.

W3cg] http://www.cgd.ucar.edu/cas/catalog/climind/.

W3cd] http://www.cdc.noaa.gov/USclimate/Correlation/ help.html.

Wor95] M. F. Worboys. GIS—A Computing Perspective. Taylor and Francis, 1995.

[ZHSK03] P. Zhang, Y. Huang, S. Shekhar, and V. Kumar. Correlation Analysis of Spatial Time Series Datasets: A Filter and Refine Approach. In the Proc. of the *7th PacificAsia Conference on Knowledge Discovery and Data Mining*, 2003.

6

Spatial Clustering Algorithms and Its Application to Geographic Databases

Dr. T.Sudha*
K.L. Mary Rani**

ABSTRACT

Spatial data mining is the discovery of interesting, implicit knowledge in spatial databases and is an important task for understanding and use of spatial data and knowledge bases. One of the techniques of spatial data mining is clustering. Though lot of research on clustering algorithms has been carried out, for application to large spatial databases minimal requirements of domain knowledge, discovery of clusters with arbitrary shape and good efficiency on large databases is required. The number and size of spatial databases, such as medical and geographic databases are growing rapidly because of the large amount of data obtained from satellite images and other scientific equipment. Efficiency of many data mining algorithms on spatial databases depends heavily on an efficient processing of neighborhood relationships. The database primitives required for processing of neighborhood relations, density based clustering algorithms is discussed in this paper. The application of these to geographic databases for spatial clustering is discussed.

* Head, Department of Computer Science, Sri Padmavathi Mahila Visvavidyalayam, Tirupati.

** Research Scholar, Department of Computer Science, Sri Padmavathi Mahila Visvavidyalayam, Tirupati.

INTRODUCTION

Data mining is the task of discovering interesting patterns from large amounts of data that is stored in databases, data warehouses or other information repositories. Data patterns can be mined from different kinds of databases such as relational, transactional, object oriented and information repositories like spatial, text, multimedia, world wide web etc. A pattern represents knowledge if it can be easily understood by humans and can be validated on text data with some degree of certainty and potentially useful, novel or validates a hypothesis. Measures of pattern interestingness, either objective or subjective can be used to guide the discovery process.

The number and the size of spatial databases are growing rapidly in applications such as geomarketing, traffic control and environmental studies. This growth by far exceeds human capacities to analyse the databases in order to find implicit regularities, rules or clusters hidden in the data. Therefore, automated knowledge discovery becomes more and more important in spatial databases. *Knowledge discovery in databases (KDD)* is the non-trivial extraction of implicit, previously unknown, and potentially useful information from databases. Though a lot of research has been conducted on knowledge discovery and data mining in relational databases, only a few works deal with knowledge discovery in *spatial* databases. The process of discovery in spatial data is more complex than in relational data. The reason is the efficiency of algorithms and also the complexity of possible patterns that can be found in spatial databases.

SPATIAL DATABASES SYSTEMS

Spatial Database Systems (SDBS) are relational databases, which include the concept of spatial location and spatial extension. The explicit location and extension of objects define implicit relations of spatial neighbourhood. Most KDD algorithms for *spatial* databases make use of those neighbourhood relationships, because it is the main difference between KDD in relational databases and in SDBS. Also, in SDBS, the attributes of the neighbours of some object of interest may have an influence on the object and therefore have to be considered as well.

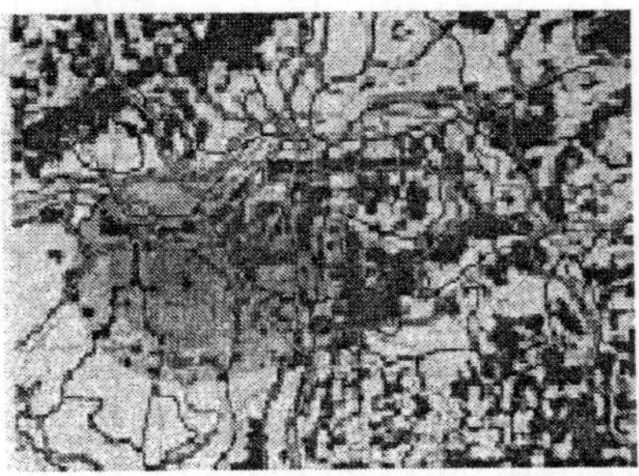

Fig. 6.1: **Regions of pollution around a planned industrial plant**

For instance, a new industrial plant may pollute its neighbourhood depending on the distance and on the major direction of the wind. Fig. 6.1 depicts a map used in the assessment of a possible location for a new industrial plant. The map shows three regions with different degrees of pollution caused by the planned plant. The influenced objects such as communities and forests are also depicted.

The efficiency of many KDD algorithms for SDBS depends heavily on an efficient processing of these neighbourhood relationships. There is a need to integrate these data mining algorithms into the existing commercial databases to obtain additional benefits for data mining applications such as efficient storage management, prevention of inconsistencies, index structures to support different types of database queries. Hence, a set of database primitives for mining spatial database is required, which express most of the algorithms for spatial data mining from the literature.

Neighbourhood Relations, Graphs, Indicies

Based on the neighbourhood relations between the objects, neighbourhood graphs and paths are defined and based on these graphs and paths the database primitives are defined. There are three basic types of spatial relations, namely, topography, distance and direction relation. These relations are combined with logical operators to form a neighbourhood relation that are useful in creating neighbourhood graphs and paths.

A neighbourhood graph $G^{DB}_{neighbour}$ = (N,E) is a graph with N nodes which are identified with object o ∈ DB and E edges , E ⊆ N x N where n_1 and n_2 ∈ N and are connected via some edge E iff n_1 and n_2 are neighbours.

A neighbourhood path is a sequence of nodes [n_1, n_2, ..., n_k] where n_i and n_{i+1} are neighbours for all $n_i \in N$, $1 \leq i < k$. The number k of nodes is called the length of the neighbourhood path.

Let DB be a set of spatial objects and let c and dist be real numbers. Let D be a direction predicate and T be a topological predicate. Then, the neighbourhood index for DB with maximum distance c, denoted by N_c^{DB} is defined as:

$N_c^{DB} = \{o_1, o_2, dist, D, T) \mid o_1 \; distance_{=dist} \; o_2 \wedge dist \leq c \wedge o_2 \; D \; o_1 \wedge o_1 \; T \; o_2\}$

CLUSTERING

Clustering is the task of grouping the objects of a database into meaningful subclasses (that is, clusters) so that the members of a cluster are as similar as possible whereas the members of different clusters differ as much as possible from each other. There has been a lot of research on clustering algorithms for decades but application of these to large spatial databases requires minimum knowledge of the domain to determine the input parameters, discovery of clusters with arbitrary shape and efficiency on large databases.

When looking at the sample sets of points depicted in Fig. 6.2, one can easily and unambiguously detect clusters of points and noise points not belonging to any of those clusters.

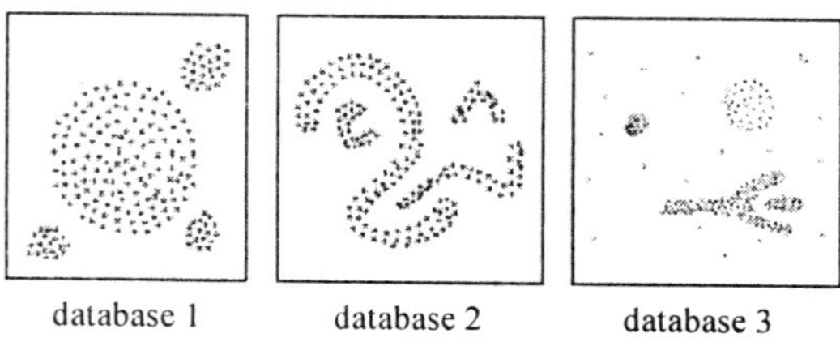

Fig. 6.2: **Sample databases**

The main reason why one recognises the clusters is that within each cluster there is a typical density of points, which is considerably higher than outside of the cluster. Further, the density within the areas of noise is lower than the density in any of the clusters.

Based on this intuitive notion of "clusters" and "noise" in a database *D* of points of some k-dimensional space *S*, a cluster is defined. This implies that for each point of a cluster the neighbourhood of a given radius has to contain at least a minimum number of points, i.e. the density in the neighbourhood has to exceed some threshold. The shape of a neighbourhood is determined by the choice of a distance function for two points p and q, denoted by *dist(p,q)*.

Density-based clusters can be generalised to density-connected sets by defining the neighbourhood, which can be anything instead of ε neighbourhood, if it is based on a binary predicate (*Npred*), which is symmetric and reflexive. The cardinality of the neighbourhood of these clusters is measured in terms of minimum weight.

Spatial Clustering Algorithms

DBSCAN Algorithm

The algorithm *DBSCAN* (*Density Based Spatial Clustering of Applications with Noise*) is based on the notion of density-based clustering. To find a cluster, DBSCAN starts with an arbitrary point p and retrieves all points density-reachable from p with respect to ε neighbourhood of p. The total number of points retrieved with respect to p should satisfy the minimum number of points required within the ε neighbourhood of p. The advantage of DBSCAN algorithm is that it requires only one input parameter and supports the user in determining an appropriate value for it. The algorithm is also effective in discovering clusters of arbitrary shape.

GDBSCAN Algorithm

The generalised algorithm—called GDBSCAN (*Generalised Density Based Spatial Clustering of Applications with Noise*)—can cluster point objects as well as spatially extended objects according to both, their spatial and their non-spatial attributes. To find a density-connected set, GDBSCAN starts with an arbitrary object *p* and retrieves all objects density-reachable from *p* with respect to *Npred-neighbourhood* and minimum weight *MinWeight* of respective results. If *p* is a core object, this procedure yields a density-connected set with respect to *Npred* and *MinWeight*, otherwise, *p* is assigned to *NOISE* since no objects are density-reachable from *p*. To construct a density-based decomposition of a dataset, this procedure is iteratively applied to each object *p* that has not yet been classified. Basic version of the algorithm GDBSCAN based on a neighbourhood graph with respect to the neighbourhood predicate *Npred* is given below (Fig.6.3):

GDBSCAN (DB, Npred, MinWeight)

// Precond.: for all objects *o* in DB: o.ClId = UNCLASSIFIED and *o*.Processed = FALSE

NpredGraph := createNeighbourhoodGraph(DB, Npred)

ClusterId := nextId(NOISE);

for i *from* 1 *to* DB.size *do*

Object := DB.get(i);

if not Object.Processed *then*

if ExpandCluster(Object,ClusterId,NpredGraph,MinWeight) *then*

ClusterId := nextId(ClusterId)

Fig. 6.3: **Algorithm GDBSCAN**

APPLICATION OF GDBSCAN ALGORITHM

GDBSCAN is used to extract density-connected sets of neighbouring objects having a similar value of the non-spatial attribute(s). To define the similarity on an attribute, its domain is partitioned into a number of disjoint classes and values in the same class are considered similar to each other. The sets with the highest or lowest attribute value(s) are most interesting and are called *influence regions*. For economic geography, the resulting influence region may be further analyzed by comparing them to a circular region representing the expected theoretical shape to obtain a possible deviation.

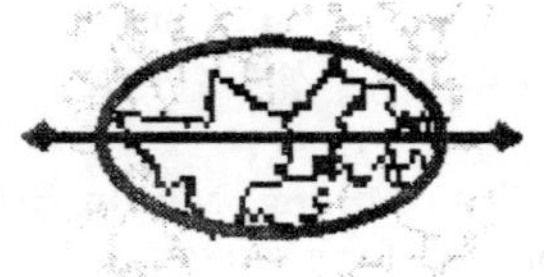

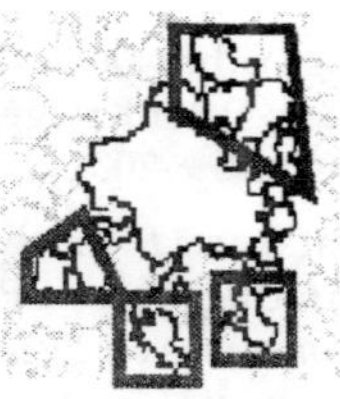

Fig. 6.4: **An illustration from the spatial database of Bavaria, of the influence regions of Ingolstadt (left) and Munich (right) and their deviation from the expected shape**

Different methods may be used for this comparison. A *difference-based method* calculates the difference of both, the observed influence region and the theoretical circular region, thus returning some region indicating the location of a possible deviation. An *approximation-based method* calculates the optimal approximating ellipsoid of the observed influence region.

If the two main axes of the ellipsoid differ in length significantly, then the longer one is returned indicating the direction of a deviation fig. 6.4.

In some spatial databases where the history of the relevant part of geographic data is stored for the purpose of analysis, further research on clustering techniques will enable to address the concept of time in such geographic databases.

CONCLUSION

A small set of basic operations on neighbourhood graphs and paths were defined as database primitives for spatial data mining. Further, techniques to efficiently support the database primitives by a commercial DBMS were presented. One of the main tasks of spatial data mining, spatial clustering was discussed with respect to DBSCAN and GDBSCAN algorithms. This application of GDBSCAN in the domain of geography was discussed and the need for including the aspect of time for historical spatial databases was indicated.

REFERENCES

1. *Data Mining: Concept and Techniques*—Jiawei Han and Micheline Kambler—Morgan Kaufmann Publishers.

2. Algorithms and Applications for Spatial Data Mining, Martin Ester, Hans-Peter Kriegel, Jorg Sander, *Geographic Data Mining and Knowledge Discovery*, 2001.

3. Database Primitives for Spatial Data Mining, Martin Ester, Stefan Gundlach, Hans-Peter Kriegel, Jorg Sander, *Proceedings of International Conference on Databases in Office*, Engineering and Science (BTW '99), Freiburg, Germany, 1999.

4. Spatial Data Mining: A Database Approach, Martin Ester, Hans-Peter Kriegel, Jorg Sander, *Proceedings of the Fifth International Symposium on Large Spatial Databases* (SSD '97), Berlin, Germany.

5. A Density-Based Algorithm for Discovering Clusters in Large Spatial Databases With Noise, Martin Ester, Hans-Peter Kriegel, Jorg Sander, Xiaowei Xu, *Proceedings of Second International Conference on Knowledge Discovery and Data Mining* (KDD 96).

7

Data Mining and Its Impact on Business

B. Indira*

ABSTRACT

In Today's Business world , information about the customer is a necessity for a business trying to maximise its profit. A new and important tool in gaining this knowledge is "Data Mining". Data Mining is primarily used by companies with a strong consumer focus. It enables these companies to determine the relationships among internal factors such as price, staff skills or external factors such as economic indicators, competition and customer demographics. And it also enables them to determine and analyse the impact on factors such as sales, customer satisfaction and corporate profit trends.

Data Mining is the non-trivial extraction of implicit, previously unknown and potentially useful information from the data. It uses machine learning, statistical and visualisation techniques to discover and present knowledge in a form which is easily understandable to human beings. Data Mining tools not only give business firms the distinct advantage of analysing the past and present data within their organisations but also allow to know the future trends and enable them to analyse its customer behaviour, which give business organisations an increased focus in the areas of customer relations and marketing in a more effective and efficient manner.

* **Lecturer, Department of Computer Science, Kasturba Gandhi Degree and PG College for Women, Secunderabad.**

INTRODUCTION

Advances in technology are making massive data sets common in many disciplines. Computerised systems collect data about everyday transactions: at super market checkouts, phone calls, bank cash machines(ATMs) etc. This accumulation of data has taken place at a dramatic rate.

"It is estimated that the amount of information in the world doubles every 20 months." The size and number of databases are increasing at an even faster rate. We are drowning in data but starving for knowledge. One solution to this data explosion problem is Data Mining. Data Mining is one way to extract predictive information from these large data bases. The main objectives of Data Mining is "Identification of data as a source of useful information" and "Use of this discovered information for competitive advantages when working in business environment". The focus of this paper is to define Data Mining, some important Data Mining technologies and to show how Data Mining may become a major tool for the business in decision-making.

DEFINITION OF DATA MINING

Data Mining is a useful tool , a new approach that combines discovery with analysis. It become an important tool for competitive business. Data Mining tools predict future trends and behaviours allowing business to make proactive, knowledge driven decision. Data mining tools can answer business questions that traditionally were too time consuming to resolve. They search data bases for hidden patterns, finding predictive information that experts may miss because it lies outside their expectations. Data Mining is a new interdisciplinary field merging ideas from statistics, machine learning, data bases and parallel computing.

Researchers have defined the term "Data Mining" in many ways:

1. Data Mining or Knowledge Discovery in Data Bases(KDD) is non-trivial extraction of implicit, previously unknown and potentially useful information from data;
2. Data Mining is the search for relationships and global patterns that exist in large data bases but are hidden among vast amounts of data;

3. Data Mining is a combination of powerful methods that help reducing costs and risks as well as increasing revenues by extracting information from the available data;

4. Data Mining is the exploration and analysis by automatic and semi-automatic means of large quantities of data in order to discover meaningful patterns and rules.

THE NEED OF DATA MINING

An increasingly competitive business environment drives the need for Data Mining. Data Mining is evolving as an essential segment in decision-support market place.

For the first 25 years of computing the emphasis was on automating existing business processes. During the last 10 years much of the emphasis has been on managing these automated processes better. Executive Information Systems(EIS), management reporting tools and more recently On Line Analytical Processing(OLAP) tools have allowed management to observe the performance of the business. Data Mining is the extension of EIS. It can be used to find patterns in data that optimise existing processes and better conduct of the business.

If Data Mining is understood and applied properly, it can generate new revenue, increased profits and have significant cost savings. Gartner Group Advanced Technology Research note listed Data Mining and Artificial Intelligence at the top of 5 key technology areas. Data Mining is emerging as a major solution to solve a series of critical and fast growing issues. In particular with the effects of globalisation and deregulation, major corporations are facing new pressure from increased competition on a world wide basis. Effectively responding to this challenge requires faster marketing cycles to produce a greater number of campaigns to attract and retain the best customers.

Data Mining offers a rich capability for modelling historical performance and then using this model to predict likely future outcomes. The only real prerequisite for Data Mining is a business problem plus relevant data. Collecting this data is the most time consuming part of Data Mining. Successful Data Mining requires both business knowledge and some analytical ability. The result of Data Mining is one or more decision models. Once tested these models can be deployed in many different places throughout the enterprise. For example, a model may be trained to recognise cases of bad credit risk and this would be deployed at sales transaction process.

The overall approach of Data Mining is first define a business goal, then deploy the Data Mining technology on the data and test models, then deploy the models to reap the benefit.

DATA MINING TECHNOLOGIES

The first name for Data Mining , beginning in 1960s was statistical analysis. The pioneers of statistical analysis were SAS, SPSS and IBM. All three of these companies are very active in Data Mining field today. Originally statistical analysis consisted of classical statistical routines such as correlation, regression, chi-square and cross tabulation. In late 1980s, classical statistical analysis was augmented with fuzzy logic, heuristic reasoning and neural networks. In late 1990s these statistical techniques were packaged with Decision Trees, Neural Networks, Rule Induction, Genetic Algorithms and other powerful techniques.

Decision Trees

A tree shaped structure that represents a set of decisions. From a business perspective decision trees can be viewed as creating segmentation of original data sets. Each branch of a tree is a classification question and leaves of the tree are partitions of the data set with their classification. i.e., segmentation of customers, products, sales regions etc. Segmentation is done for the prediction of some important piece of information.

The decision trees and algorithms that create predictive segments may be complex but the results are easy to understand and are useful to business user.

Decision tree algorithms are ID3, C4.5, Cart(Classification And Regression Trees), CHAID(Chi-Square Automatic Interaction Detector).

Advantages of Decision Trees

- ability to easily generate rules
- Clarity
- Can build complex and understandable models

- Able to handle numerical and categorical data
- Can indicate which fields are most important
- Used for both exploration and prediction

Decision trees can identify which variables should be used as inputs to Neural networks. Because they are very fast and can deal with thousands of independent variables.(Neural networks in general do not perform well with large number of inputs).

Neural Networks

Neural networks has an ability to deal with complicated or imprecise data and can be used to extract patterns and detect trends that are complex to be noticed by either humans or other techniques.

Neural networks are highly accurate, predictive models that can be applied to different types of problems like customer response prediction, sales forecasting, risk management, target marketing and fraud detection. Artificial neural networks can learn to detect the patterns in Data Bases and make better predictions similar to human beings. Neural networks can learn and improve over time while other techniques are static. A trained Neural network can be thought of as an expert and is used to provide projections given new situation and answers "what if" questions. But there are many important design decisions that need to be made in order to effectively use a Neural network such as number of nodes, connection of nodes, flow of information.

Advantages of Neural Networks

- Adaptive learning
- Self organisation
- Real time operation
- Fault tolerance

One of the key benefits of Neural network solutions is their capacity to save time, an important consideration in today's business world. Because of the adaptive nature of learning algorithms they are faster than traditional techniques. But understanding the data and clear definition of business problem to be solved are essential to ensure success.

Rule Induction

The extraction of useful if-then rules from data based on statistical significance. A Data Mining System has to infer a model from a data base. When classes are defined, the system should be able to infer the rules that govern classification. Production rules have been widely used to represent knowledge in expert systems and can be easily interpreted by human experts.

Rules induced by Data Mining tools are descriptions of patterns found in the data. They may be "explanations" which suggest some causal dependency.

Genetic Algorithms

Genetic algorithms initiated and developed in early 1970s by John Holland. They are unorthodox search and optimisation algorithms. Genetic algorithms are relatively new software paradigm inspired by Darwin's theory of evolution. A population of individuals, each representing a possible solution to a problem is initially created at random. Then pairs of individuals combine to produce offspring for next generation. A mutation process is also used randomly to modify genetic structure of some members of each new generation.Genetic algorithms are good at taking larger, potentially huge search spaces looking for optimal combinations of things and solutions.

DATA MINING AND NEURAL NETWORKS IN BUSINESS

Business is a diverted field. Data Mining and Neural Networks have broad applicability to real world business problems. They are well suited for prediction and forecasting needs including sales forecasting, customer research, risk management, target marketing, cross selling, quality control, competitive analysis, buying patterns, fraud detection, decision support etc. There is a strong potential for using Neural networks for Data Base Mining i.e., searching implicit patterns with in the stored information in Data bases. Any Neural network application would fit into any business area or financial analysis.

Marketing

A feed forward Neural network is integrated with AMT(Airline Marketing Tactician) and was trained using back propagation to assist the marketing control of airline seat allocations. The system is used to monitor and recommend booking advice for each departure. Such information has a direct impact on profitability of an airline and can provide a technological advantage for the users of the system.

BBC Case Study

SPSS Inc. developed a model for BBC that would predict the audience share of a proposed new TV Programme. This is one of the important applications of Data Mining, since BBC has years of historical data showing the audience share of each programme. To build this model the data that is considered was:

The proposed TV programme, time of show, audience type, preceding and following programmes on the same channel, programmes overlapping with the proposed programme on competitor channels, the weather, time of the year(winter, summer etc) anchor or star performer of the programme etc. The project was carried out with one year's viewing data between 6.00pm and 10.00 pm. A Neural network model was able to predict audience share within plus or minus 4%.

CONCLUSION

Data Mining is gaining wider acceptance in general business community. Data Mining provides significant çost savings in its day to day operations. The success of an enterprise can be measured in terms of increased profits, generating new revenue etc. Although Data Mining as a tool increases profitability for businesses, there are still some problems that need to be dealt. Understanding the data and preprocessing of data is an important task. Many businesses tend to ignore this vital aspect and start their analysis directly. The user's business knowledge is also essential to determine the factors responsible for a particular application and to ascertain how the various input factors that may need to be combined. Business or scientific expertise is always required on a continuous basis to determine whether the models put to use can be deployed safely or not for ensuring the overall success and sustained growth of the business ventures.

REFERENCES

1. *Data Mining Techniques*—Arun K. Pujari—Universities Press.
2. *Data Warehouse Lifecycle Tool Kit*—Ralph KimBall, Laura Reeves,Margy Ross, Warren — Wiley.
3. *Neural Networks, Fuzzy Logic and Genetic Algorithms Synthesis and Applications*— S. Rajasekaran, Vijayalakshmi Pai – PHI.
4. *Data Mining—An Introduction*—SPSS, White Paper.
5. *How Data Mining Can Help Advertising Management*—Seokmin Hong and John D. Leckenby —Austin, Texas.
6. *Data Mining in Economics, Finance and Marketing*—Hans C. Jessen, UK and Georgios Paliouras, Greece.
7. *Data Mining Techniques for Marketing, Sales and Customer Support*—Michael Berry and Gordon Linoff — Wiley, 1997.
8. *Building Data Mining Applications for CRM* by Alex BErson, Stephen Smith and Kurt Thearling.

8

Data Mining for Extraction of Knowledge from Spatial and Non-Spatial Database

I.V. Murali Krishna*

EXTENDED ABSTRACT

Data Mining is a process to search for relationships and patterns that exist in data but are 'hidden' among the vast amount of data. These hidden patterns and relationships represent valuable knowledge about the database and the objects in the database Data mining, or Knowledge Discovery in Databases (KDD) is extraction of implicit, previously unknown, and potentially useful information from data. This includes a number of different technical approaches, such as clustering, data summarisation, learning classification rules, finding dependency net works, analysing changes, and detecting anomalies. Knowledge discovery in databases (KDD) is the process of identifying a valid, potentially, useful and ultimately understandable structure in data. This involves sampling data from a data warehouse, cleaning or preprocessing it , transforming or reducing it (if needed), applying a data mining component to produce a structure, and then evaluating the derived structure.

* **PhD (IISc), FIE, MIEEE, Professor in Spatial Information Technology, Director (Research and Development), JNT University, Kukatpally, Hyderabad – 500072, ivm@ieee.org Mobile +91-98480 49624.**

Data mining has several applications. The tool has extensive application originally in banking finance and insurance sectors. After availability of the high resolution satellite data, data mining tools are increasingly finding scope for application in various domains related to image processing, medical informatics, drug search and biotechnology and natural resources and environmental management. Data mining is a step in KDD process concerned with the algorithmic means by which patterns or structure are enumerated from the data under acceptable computational efficiency limitations. Basically data mining is concerned with the analysis of data for finding patterns and regularities in sets of data. The idea is that it is possible to strike gold in unexpected places as the data mining software extracts patterns not previously discernable or so obvious that no-one has noticed them before. Data mining remains an important tool, irrespective of the forms or sources of data according to data mining problems. For different types of data there are of different categories.

Spatial data mining, i.e., mining knowledge from large amounts of spatial data, is important because huge amounts of spatial data have been collected in various applications, ranging from remote sensing, to geographical information systems (GIS), computer cartography, environmental assessment and planning, etc. Recent studies on data mining have extended the scope of data mining from relational and transactional databases to spatial databases. A spatial database stores spatial objects represented by spatial data types and spatial relationships among such objects. Spatial data carries topological and/or distance information and it is often organised by spatial indexing structures and accessed by spatial access methods. These distinct features of a spatial database pose challenges and bring opportunities for mining information from spatial data. Spatial data mining, or knowledge discovery in spatial database, refers to the extraction of implicit knowledge, spatial relations, or other patterns not explicitly stored in spatial databases.

Data mining potential can be enhanced if the appropriate data has been collected and stored in a data warehouse. A data warehouse is a Relational Database Management System (RDMS) designed specifically to meet the needs of a specific or general data analysis systems. Data warehousing is a new powerful technique making it possible to extract archived operational data and overcome inconsistencies between different legacy data formats. A Spatial data warehouse is a subject oriented ,integrated, time-variant , and non-volatile collection of both spatial and non-spatial data in support of spatial data mining and spatial data related decision-making process. Spatial Clustering, Spatial Characterisation, Spatial Classification and Spatial Trend Detection are the spatial data algorithms that are useful for detection of spatial relationships. In data mining for knowledge discovery, various kinds of rules can be discovered from databases. For example, characteristic rules, discriminant rules, association rules, or deviation and evolution rules can be mined. A *spatial characteristic rule* is a general description of spatial data. Thematic maps present the spatial distribution of a single or a few attributes. There are two ways to represent thematic maps: *raster* and *vector*. In the raster image form, thematic maps have pixels associated with the attribute values. In the vector representation, a spatial object is represented by its geometry, most commonly being the boundary representation along with the thematic attributes.

These are special kind of spatial databases where data almost entirely consists of images or pictures. Image databases are used in remote sensing, medical imaging, etc. They are usually stored in form of grid arrays representing the image intensity in one or more spectral ranges. Some studies have been done using Poly Analyst software package for agriculture, crime and forest fire data mining and knowledge discovery. PolyAnalyst is one of the powerful multi-strategy data mining system that implements a broad variety of mutually complementing methods for the automatic data analysis. It works with data extracted from flat files or relational databases, and can work with numerical (floating-point), integer, yes/no (binary), date, and discrete (categorical or string) variables. The studies carried by the author as a part of research work[1] are the basis for the paper. As the specific goal of any data mining this study aims at discerning trends in agriculture production with reference to the availability of inputs. The following are the details of software/Platform and tools used. in the study:

- Data Mining Software:-Poly Analyst 4.6
- GIS Software: Arc GIS
- Front End:-Visual basic 6.0, Map Objects 2.0
- Back-end:- ARC Shape files and MS-ACCESS
- Platform:- Windows XP

Definition of the task., mapping the task, Data pre-processing, Data evaluation and selection of data mining technique are the major steps of the knowledge extraction task. As in many cases the non-availability of a data warehouse increases the effort for data mining as in the present study. An evaluation or visual inspection of the data is the next important step. This requires many times browsing the input data with visualisation tools. After evaluation or visual inspection of data, selection of best suited mining technique for the given task is the next step. This step not only includes defining the appropriative technique or mix of techniques to use but also the way in which the techniques must be applied.

In general data mining technique can be divided into two broad categories viz ., Discovery data mining and Predicting data mining . Discovery data mining applies to range of techniques whose primary objective is to find patterns inside the data without any prior knowledge of what pattern exists. For example Clustering., Link analysis., Sequence analysis. Find Laws. The Predicting data mining is applied to a range of techniques that find relationship between specific variables (called the target variables) and the other variables in data. For example: Classification: Decision Tree. Neural Network.

Here the data Mining helps to find the relevant and useful information from databases. Data mining scours databases for hidden patterns, finding predictive information that experts may miss. The screen view of the Visual Basic interface provided for querying and data access are shown in Fig. 8.1. (*See on page 82)* A typical example of world data set prepared for the study is in Fig. 8.2. (*See on page 83)* The pattern of knowledge discovery through Decision tree algorithm is shown in Fig. 8.3. (*See on page 84)* A set of rules are formed based on the attributes as given below:

Field Name	*Source of Data*	*Data Type*	*Field Size*
Year-wise	Statistics/tables	Number	Long Integer
District-wise	Administrative data	Text	20
Utilised land (in Hect)	Remote sensing data	Number	Long Integer
Unutilised land (in Hect)	Remote sensing data	Number	Long Integer
Supplyof_water (in%)	Administrative data	Number	Long Integer
Demandof_water (in%)	Irrigation scheduling	Number	Long Integer
Supplyof_fertiliser (in%)	Irrigation scheduling	Number	Long Integer
Demandof_fertiliser (in%)	Irrigation scheduling	Number	Long Integer
Supplyof_pesticides (in%)	Irrigation scheduling	Number	Long Integer
Demandof_pesticides (in%)	Irrigation scheduling	Number	Long Integer
Seed Quality	Irrigation scheduling	Yes/no	

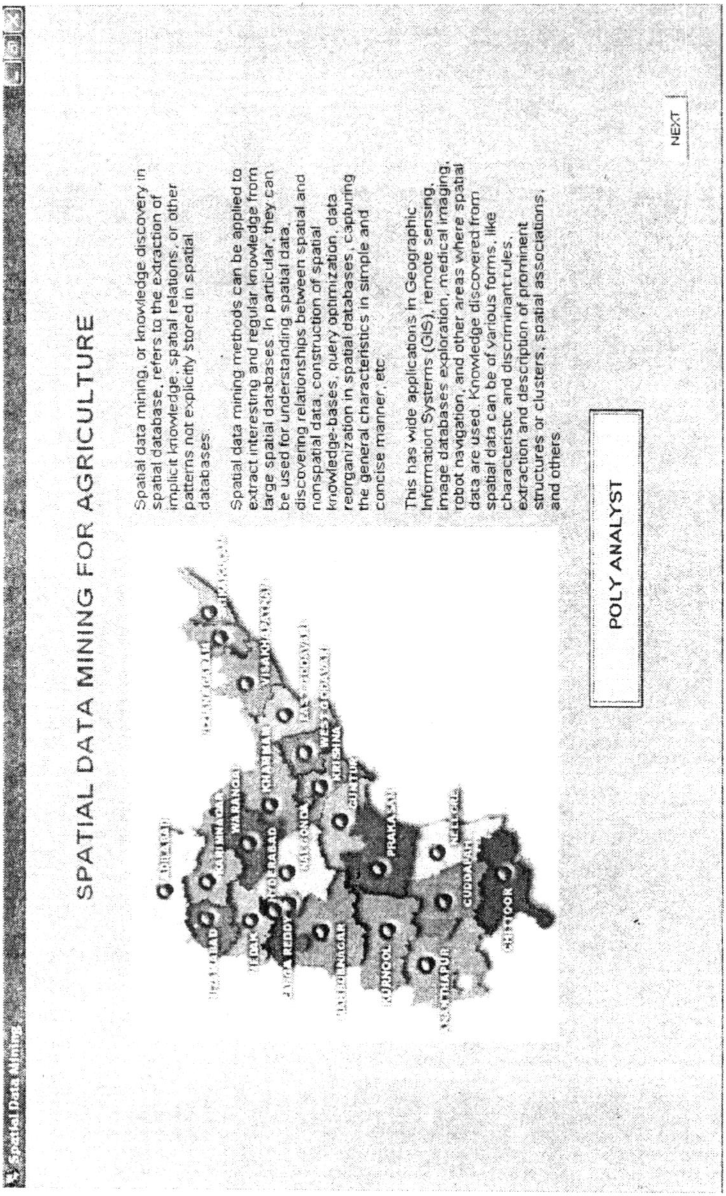
Spatial Data Mining
SPATIAL DATA MINING FOR AGRICULTURE
Spatial data mining, or knowledge discovery in spatial database, refers to the extraction of implicit knowledge, spatial relations, or other patterns not explicitly stored in spatial databases.
Spatial data mining methods can be applied to extract interesting and regular knowledge from large spatial databases. In particular, they can be used for understanding spatial data, discovering relationships between spatial and nonspatial data, construction of spatial knowledge-bases, query optimization, data reorganization in spatial databases, capturing the general characteristics in simple and concise manner, etc.
This has wide applications in Geographic Information Systems (GIS), remote sensing, image databases exploration, medical imaging, robot navigation, and other areas where spatial data are used. Knowledge discovered from spatial data can be of various forms, like characteristic and discriminant rules, extraction and description of prominent structures or clusters, spatial associations, and others.
WARANGAL
KHAMMAM
KRISHNA
PRAKASAM
CUDDAPAH
KURNOOL
CHITTOOR
MEDAK
POLY ANALYST
NEXT

Fig. 8.1: **Data Access in Visual Basic**

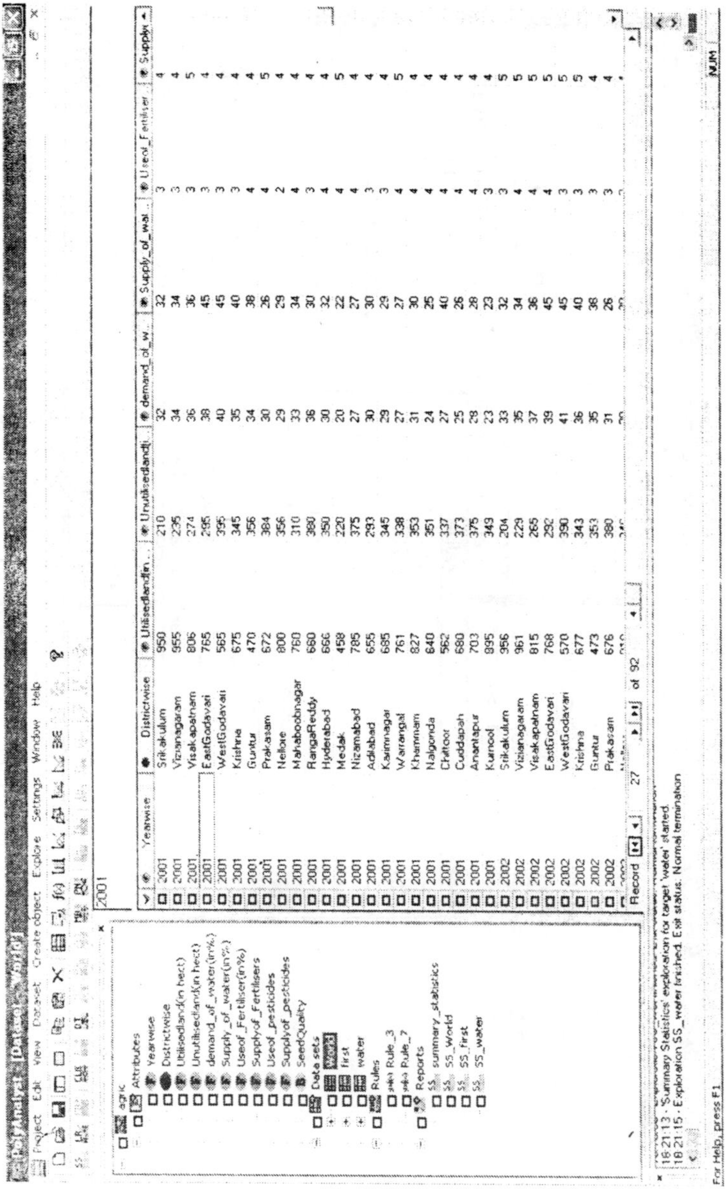

Yearwise	Districtwise	Utilisedland(in...	Unutilisedland(i...	demand_of_w...	Supply_of_wat...	Useof_Fertiliser...	Supply...
2001	Srikakulum	950	210	32	32	3	4
2001	Vizianagaram	955	235	34	34	3	4
2001	Visakapatnam	806	274	36	36	3	5
2001	EastGodavari	765	295	38	45	3	4
2001	WestGodavari	565	395	40	45	3	4
2001	Krishna	675	345	35	40	3	4
2001	Guntur	470	356	34	38	4	4
2001	Prakasam	672	384	30	26	4	5
2001	Nellore	800	356	29	29	2	4
2001	Mahaboobnagar	760	310	33	34	4	4
2001	RangaReddy	660	380	36	30	3	4
2001	Hyderabad	666	350	30	32	4	4
2001	Medak	458	220	20	22	4	5
2001	Nizamabad	785	375	27	27	4	4
2001	Adilabad	655	293	30	30	3	4
2001	Karimnagar	685	345	29	29	3	4
2001	Warrangal	761	338	27	27	4	5
2001	Khammam	827	353	31	30	4	4
2001	Nalgonda	640	351	24	25	4	4
2001	Chittoor	562	337	27	40	4	4
2001	Cuddapah	680	373	25	26	4	4
2001	Anantapur	703	375	28	28	4	4
2001	Kurnool	895	349	23	23	3	4
2002	Srikakulum	956	204	33	32	3	5
2002	Vizianagaram	961	229	35	34	4	5
2002	Visakapatnam	815	265	37	36	4	5
2002	EastGodavari	768	292	39	45	4	5
2002	WestGodavari	570	390	41	45	3	5
2002	Krishna	677	343	36	40	3	5
2002	Guntur	473	353	35	38	3	4
2002	Prakasam	676	380	31	26	3	4

Record 27 of 92

18:21:13 - 'Summary Statistics' exploration for target 'water' started.
18:21:15 - Exploration SS_water finished. Exit status: Normal termination

Fig. 8.2: Example of Data Set

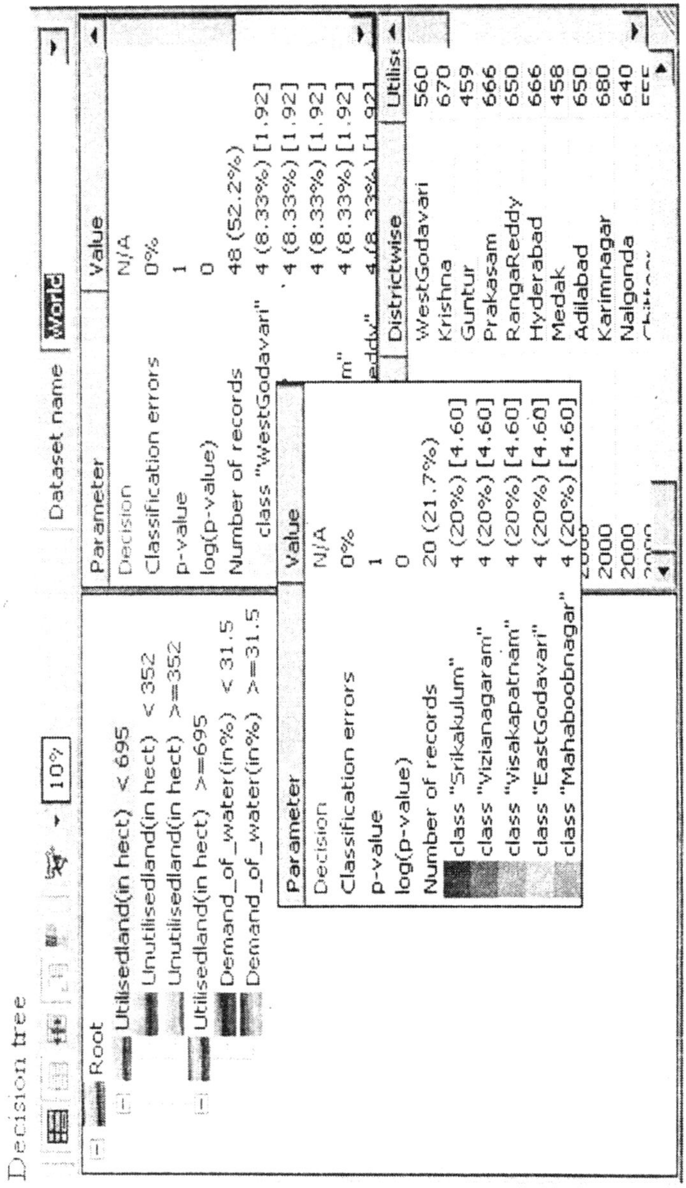

Fig. 8.3: **Knowledge Extraction Based on Decision Tree Algorithm**

REFERENCES

1. Muralikrishna I.V. and Kiranmai C, *Data Mining for Crime Analysis Map*, Middle East Conference, Dubai, April 2005.

2. Kiranmai C, Muralikrishna I.V. and Venugopala Reddy A, *Data Mining of Geospatial Database for Agriculture Related Application*, IEEE International Conference, IGARSS 2005, August 2004.

9

Social Impact of Data Mining

Dr. J. Katyayani*

WHAT IS DATA MINING?

Data Mining Means mining of data and finding the facts from large databases. Facts are hidden relations in the existing data bases.

SOCIAL IMPACT OF DATA MINING ON BUSINESS

Data Mining is Essential Tool for Organisations

➢ **Data Mining is Helping Decision**

Data Mining is helping decision-makers to think nationally and intuitively about the future. It is reducing the complexity in making decisions however the mined facts to be provided to the right person at right time. It is influencing the phases of decision-making process. According to Simon the model of decision-making has the three phases as shown below:

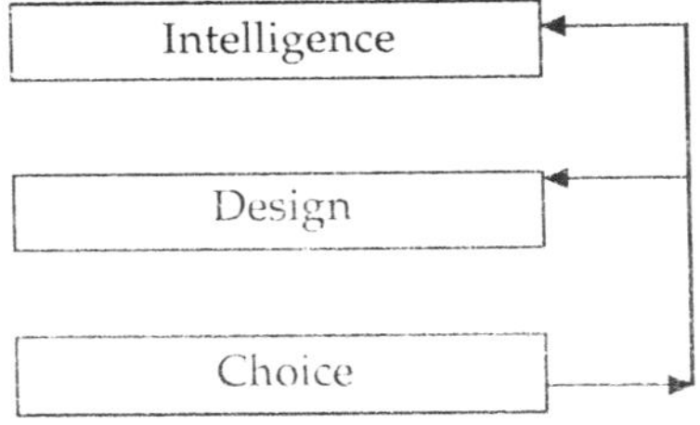

* Associate Professor, Department of Business Management, SPMVV, Tirupati.

Data mining technique is improving the efficiency of every phase of decision-making. In the intelligence phase the environment is scanned and the problem to be considered is defined. In this phase the data mining is helpful in scanning the environmental factors in multi dimensional and defining the problem crispy. Without data mining there are chances of defining fuzzy problems.

During the analysis and design of alternative data mining provides the facts which are helpful in the designing of correct alternations. It also helps in formulating correct hypotheses for the problem and in producing relevant production rules for the problem.

Thus data mining helps decision maker in recognising the needs identifying appropriate objectives by which the successful resolution of an issue in measured. It also helps in generating alternative course of action that will resolve the needs and satisfy objectives. It also provides support in enhancing the abilities of the decision-maker to obtain the possible impacts on needs of the alternative courses of action and to understand systems behaviour this analysis capability must be associated with providing the ability to study the response or changes in the existing situation due to potential interventions, so as to enhance the ability of the D.M to provide an interpretation of these impacts interns of predefined and evolving objective measures. The interpretation capability will have to evaluation of the alternatives and situation of preferred option. Associated with these must be the ability to acquire, represent and utilise information or knowledge and the ability to implement the chosen alternative courses of action. All of this must be accomplished with due consideration given to the particular rationality perspective that is used for decision-making.

The reasoning perspectives invoked at the cognitive process level of problem resolution depend upon the task requirements, the experiential familiarity of the D.M with the task, and the rationality perspectives that are used for task resolution.

How one can make himself/herself institutive. When one step into the present he/she step beyond tension. The body stops producing alternatives. Time-bound awareness is mass and solid.

No time-bound awareness in pure energy, liquid, dynamic, bubbling and creative. Once — one can step out of their boundaries he/she can become free and intuitive.

When one's thought stop their present vision extends into the past and future. They become free of time and space constraints.

➢ **Data Mining Helps—Corporate to Build Excellence**

It also helps in defining the role of corporate governance to make corporate excellent. That's how data mining is becoming one of the important technology in designing knowledge management system.

Data Mining is a technology. Like any other technology, data mining will require time and effort to research, to develop, and to mature, and its adoption, will likely go through a life cycle consisting of the following stages:

- *Innovators:* The new technology starts to take form as researchers begin to realise the need for methods to solve a particular (possibly new) problem;
- *Early Adopters:* Interest increases as more an more methods for the technology are proposed;
- *Chasm:* This represents the "hurdles" or challenges that must be met before the technology can become widely accepted as mainstream;
- *Early Majority:* The technology becomes mature and is generally accepted and used;
- *Late Majority:* The technology is well accepted, but interest in it declines as the initial problem either becomes less important or is replaced by other needs;
- *Laggards:* Use of the technology starts to die out, as it becomes old and outdated.

Business conducted on the Web, or e-commerce, is an obvious venue for data mining, as more and more companies collect large amounts of data from e-stores set up on the Web (also called Web stores). We will therefore examine how to provide domain—specific data mining solutions for e-commerce applications. Some of the case studies are described below:

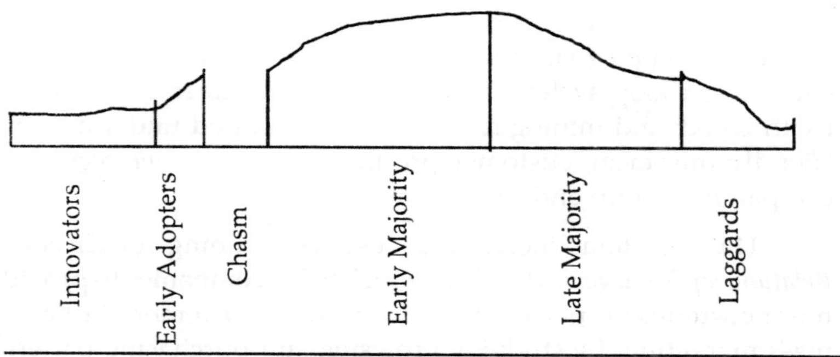

Fig. 9.1

➤ **Data Mining for Financial Data Analysis**

Financial data collected in the banking and financial industry are often relatively complete, reliable, and of high quality, which facilitates systematic data analysis and data mining. Here are few typical cases. *Design and construction of data warehouses for multidimensional data analysis and data mining, loan payment prediction and customer credit policy analysis. Classification and clustering of customers for targeted marketing,* Detection of money laundering and other financial crimes;

➤ **Data Mining for the Retail Industry**

The retail industry is a major application area for data mining since it collects huge amounts of data on sales, customer shopping history, goods transportation, consumption and service records, and so on. Retail data mining can help identify customer buying behaviours, discover customer shopping patterns and trends, improve the quality of customer service, achieve better customer retention and satisfaction, enhance goods consumption rations, design more effective goods transportation and distribution policies, and reduce the cost of business.

➤ **Data Mining for the Telecommunication Industry**

Fraudulent pattern analysis and the identification of unusual patterns can be discovered by multidimensional analysis, cluster analysis, and outlier analysis. The discovery of association and sequential patterns in multidimensional analysis can be used to promote telecommunication services.

Currently, more tailored systems are required that facilitate marketing campaign management (*often called e-marketing*). Ideally, such closed-loop systems bring together customer data analysis (with OLAP and mining technologies embedded under a user – friendly interface), customer profiling (*or one-to-one segments),* campaign roll-out, and campaign analysis.

These systems increasingly use data mining for *Customer Relationship Management (CRM),* which helps companies to provide more customised, personal service to their customers in lieu of mass marketing. By studying browsing and purchasing patterns on Web stores (e.g., by analysing *clikstreams,* the information that consumers provide by clicks of the mouse), companies can learn more about individual customers or customer groups. This information can be applied to the benefit of both the company and the customer involved. For example, by having more accurate models of their customers, companies should gain a better understanding of customer needs. Serving these needs can result in greater success regarding *cross-selling of related products, up-selling, one-to-one promotions, product affinities, larger baskets,* and *customer retention.* By tailoring advertisements and promotions to customer profiles, customers are less likely to be annoyed with unwanted mass mailings or junk mail. These actions can result in substantial cost savings for companies. The customer further benefits in that she is more likely to be notified of offers that are actually of interest to her, resulting in less waste of personal time and greater satisfaction. Customer-tailored advertisements are not limited to company mail-outs or ads placed on Web stores. In the future, digital television and on-line books and newspapers may also provide advertisements that are designed and selected specifically for the given viewer or viewer group based on customer profiling information and demographics.

From the above discussion one can identify that data mining is a essential tool for business and future business executives shall identify the right information to discover the business knowledge and use it for business excellence.

The algorithms used for creating business intelligence are:

Analytical problem	*Examples*	*Microsoft algorithms*
Classification: Assign cases to predefined classes such as "Good" vs "Bad"	• Credit risk analysis • Churn analysis • Customer retention	• Decision Trees • Naïve Bayes • Neural Nets
Segmentation: Develop a taxonomy for grouping similar cases	• Customer profile analysis • Mailing campaign	• Clustering • Sequence Clustering
Association: Advanced counting for correlations	• Market basket analysis • Advanced data exploration	• Decision Trees • Association Rules
Time Series Forecasting: Predict the future	• Forecast sales • Predict stock prices	• Time Series
Prediction: Predict a value for a new case (such as a new customer) based on values for similar cases (such as existing customers)	• Quote insurance rates • Predict customer income • Predict temperature	• All
Deviation Analysis: Discover how a case or segment differs from others	• Credit card fraud detection • Network infusion analysis	• All

HANDLING PRIVACY AND DATA SECURITY IN DATA MINING

Despite its benefit in a wide range of applications, data mining techniques also have raised a number of ethical issues. Some such issues include those of privacy, data security, intellectual property rights, and many others. One of the privacy problem is unauthorised secondary use of information. This can be addressed by using a family of Geometric Data Transformation Methods (GDTMs) which ensure that the mining process will not violate privacy up to a certain degree of security. This primarily focus on privacy preserving data clustering, notably on partition-based and hierarchical methods. This methods distort only confidential numerical attributes to meet privacy requirements, while preserving general features for clustering analysis. This experiment provides acceptable values in practice for balancing privacy and accuracy.

CONCLUSION

Data mining is an essential tool for organisations. But it has to tailored to be effective tool by choosing right information and right mining model for multi dimensional analysis for discovering the knowledge with good privacy and security maintenance.

10

Computer Aided Semi-Product Selection and Design

D. Subramanyam*
Dr. K. Ravindranadh**
Dr. G Krishnaiah***
Dr. S.V.K. Varma****

ABSTRACT

The selection and design of a semi-product are an essential element of a really complicated and multistage operation of process planning designing. The choice of the correct form of a semi-product, its design, selection, and finally its production depend on many factors. This paper presents factors which are influence the selection and design of semi-products and trends of semi-product design automation. The paper also presents a test of the expert system used for computer aided semi-products design and selection.

INTRODUCTION

Fast technological progress and industrial development cause continual improvement of constructional solution and

* Department of Mechanical Engineering, S.V. University College of Engineering, Tirupati.

** Department of Mechanical Engineering, S.V. University College of Engineering, Tirupati.

*** Department of Mechanical Engineering, S.V. University College of Engineering, Tirupati.

**** Department of Mathematics, S.V. University, Tirupati.

introduction of changes into production technology. New materials, and their practical application induce continuous development of construction, which, in turn, leads to technological progress. The introduction of a new materials is often connected with a change of the semi-product and of the way it is produced. Changes of the semi-product forms and of the ways of their production are necessary to reduce manufacturing costs while maintaining at least the same quality of the product. Correct form of the semi-product has a significant influence on costs of production and operating costs. Proper choice of the semi-product and production methods and correctly designed allowances are essential problems in industry. These problems require new and better solutions. The automation of computer aided semi-product selection and design is becoming of great importance.

SEMI-PRODUCT PLANNING

Starting materials (raw materials) are materials in such a form, in which one they leave ironworks' and other works' departments of raw material. They are for instance steel bars and metal plates, chemical materials, etc., they are further converted in the manufacturing process.

Semi-products (blanks, semi-manufactures) are starting materials, which have been converted in the manufacturing process of preparatory departments. They are casts, forgings, draw pieces and die stampings. Semi-products are also half-finished products, which undergo further change of the form, dimension, the state of surface and/or mechanical properties. Thus the required part is obtained.

The choice of starting materials can be divided into two phases:

(a) Choice of a semi-product's form, e.g. castings, forgings, draw pieces, die stampings, starting materials from metallurgic materials, sheared blanks, welded semi-products, etc.;

(b) Choice of the production method, e.g. forging or die forging, etc.;

One can split the factors which are necessary to make a design of semi-product correct, into three main groups:

1. *Constructional* – the material must be compatible with technological circumstances;
2. *Technological* – labour consumption ought to be minimal;
3. *Economical* – the cost of production ought to be minimal;

The main factors, which have an influence on selection of the for, of a semi-product, are:

1. The rate of production
2. The form of a work piece
3. The material of work piece or special recommendation for technical specifications.

The first two factors mentioned above have a crucial influence on the selection of a semi-product. The rate of production and the form of a work piece are the factors, which should be considered together. Often the material of a work piece established by the designer has a decisive influence on the choice of a semi-product. It would mean that the process engineer's potential, as far as the choice of a semi-product is concerned, has been strongly limited, because the decision is made by the designer who designs a certain part and works out technical specifications. It seems that the best solution to this problem is a continuous co-operation between process engineers and design engineers starting from the early stages of design. The application of Concurrent Engineering rules enables the proper choice of the semi-product. It also enables taking into consideration the demands of specified technology according to which this semi-product will be manufactured.

The choice of an optimum manufacturing process is really complicated. To solve this problem it is necessary to make advanced projects of manufacturing process automation and the automation of design process. There is a high correlation between a semi-product and the manufacturing process, especially when the potential of industrial plants, plants equipment, instrumentation, the state of technology and organisation, and staff experience are taken into consideration.

Semi-Product Selection in the CAPP

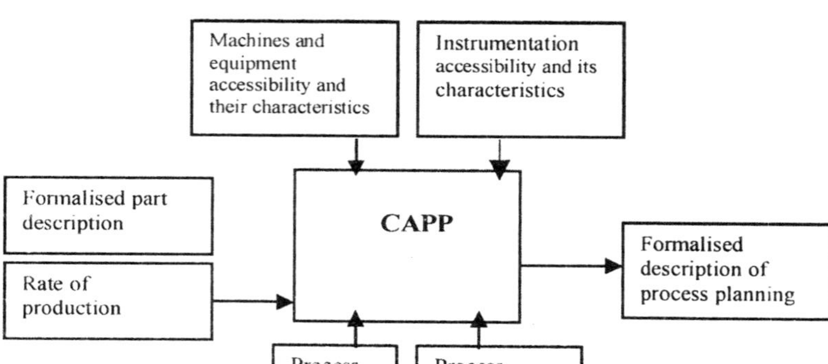

Fig. 10.1: **Semi-product and Starting Materials with Rules of Their Selection and Design**

If a design engineer has not imposed the form of a semi-product, it means, that the material, its shape and manufacturing process have not been stated. In this case a process engineer can choose the most popular form of the semi-product-black rolled bars or bright ground bars. It mainly concerns round bars, which are delivered by steelworks in the ready-made form of normalised measurement. The solutions, which have been used so far, treated semi-products, starting materials and rules of selection and design as one of elements (data, information) delivered to the CAPP system. Because of that the process of semi-product selection and design has not been automated; moreover, it has been frequently ignored. In the proposed system of he computer aided semi-product selection and design he process of semi-products design and selection is the integral part of the CAPP system.

Computer Aided Semi-Products Design

Since the choice of a semi-product the calculation its weight, the choice of the production method and material consumption standards are required many laborious calculations and analysis, the use of computers and computer programmes seems especially justified. It is necessary to make databases, which will contain allowances, tolerances and standards of manufactured programme, which can manage these data and use the knowledge needed to select and design a semi-product. The expert system can serve as this programme. Additionally the expert system can carry out the cost analysis of alternative projects (Design for Assembly and Manufacturing) and the analysis of alternative projects, which take potential of industrial plants into consideration. Depending on the detail level, the computer aided design solves the following problems.

— defining basic dimensions of a designed semi-product; these dimensions are necessary for correct designing of work piece process planning;

— determining design and construction data, such as: forging drafts, casts' edges roundings, parting lines, etc.

Defining dimensions which are necessary to design the semi-product process planning with needed tools specified.

The role part of a design engineer in the computer aided semi-product selection and design does not change. However, the process engineer is aided by the computer or he can even be replace by the computer during the process of designing. So, all algorithms on the basis of which a computer programme works must include all possible decisions, which could be made by the process engineer designing a semi-product. These algorithms must be additionally supplemented with appropriate databases containing data necessary to design a semi-product, for example: a database of allowances, a database of casts, forgings, draw pieces and die stamping standards.

1. The automated design of a semi-product can be realised as an independent system or as part of a larger system of the computer aided process planning. In both cases a formal description is necessary, thus for the whole system unified representation must be worked out. To recapitulate, data needed to design a semi-product can be defined.

2. Manually, i.e. the project is made by the process engineer on the basis of his own experience and data stored in books, tables and standards; the result is loaded in the computer for the needs of manufacturing process designing.

3. With partial automation of calculation; the process engineer selects the form of a semi-product, e.g. steel bard, forging or cast, and dimensions are calculated by the programme created on the basis of algorithms, databases and data delivered by the user.
4. With full automation; the computer automatically select the form of a semi-product, calculates its dimensions, conducts, economical analysis, makes the optimum choice and, as final results, delivers the ready project of the semi-product in the form of numerical technical documentation. This documentation makes the instant production of a semi-product possible. The obtained result may be also used to the automated designing of process planning.

Depending on the detail level, the computer aided semi-product selection and design can be divided into:

1. Determining basic dimensions, which are needed to design the manufacturing process;
2. Determining all of the more important dimensions, which are needed to design the manufacturing process and tools necessary to make a semi-product;
3. Determining all constructional data for a semi-products, e.g. for a cast the data are: dimensions, draft, parting lines, a gating system, etc.

It is also possible to design collective semi-products. The correct semi-product is selected from a group of similar parts. This procedure concerns mainly small lot production and it can be realised in the following ways:

1. By the automated analysis of database of similar parts, and then designing one common semi-product for these parts;
2. By the automated analysis of database of semi-products, which are applied in an industrial plant or in the entire branch and by choosing this semi-product whose dimensions are equal or bigger in specified limits (this approach is applied mainly with references to various kinds of forgoing).

The Economical Basics of Semi-Product Selection

A significant number of methods and manner of semi-product manufacturing together with diversity of applied material cause problems in the correct selection of a semi-product. The cost of the manufacturing process depends, among other things, on the material of a semi-product and production accuracy. Therefore it is necessary to take into consideration the entire issue during the choice of a semi-product or material. One has to consider not only the cost of a semi-product but also the costs of further machining in the conditions of the proper rate of production. The total cost of making a work piece is the basis of economical analysis. The economical analysis of semi-product selection can cause many difficulties, but it can be crucial especially in questionable cases.

This analysis is particularly useful when a few solutions are possible, the rate of production is significant and other methods do not give clear-cut answers. There is currently a trend to select such a semi-product whose shape is similar to the work piece's shape, or the semi-product has even finished same surfaces. It results in lower machining costs, but the costs of semi-product production are definitely higher. In that case the economical analysis of semi-product production and work piece machining should be decisive.

CONCEPTION OF SOLUTION

As a solution the following computer aided semi-product selection and design system has been proposed *(See Fig. 10.2 on page 100)*.

Knowledge Bases

In the proposed system of the computer aided semi-product selection and design the knowledge necessary to solve the task is stored in knowledge bases. It is suggested to show the structure of the knowledge base in the form of the decisive tree (*See Fig. 10.3 on page 101*). Colon dotted lines mean successive decision layer P_0, P_1, ... P_{N+1}. Transition from P_1 to P_{i+1} layer means transition from the state of knowledge W_{i-1} to the state of knowledge W_i, that is enriching W_{i-1} knowledge from P_{i-1} layer with the partial information q_i included in the layer P_i. The foregoing is shown by the formula (1).

$$P_i \rightarrow P_{i+1} \Rightarrow W_{i-1} \xrightarrow{Q_i} W_i \qquad (1)$$

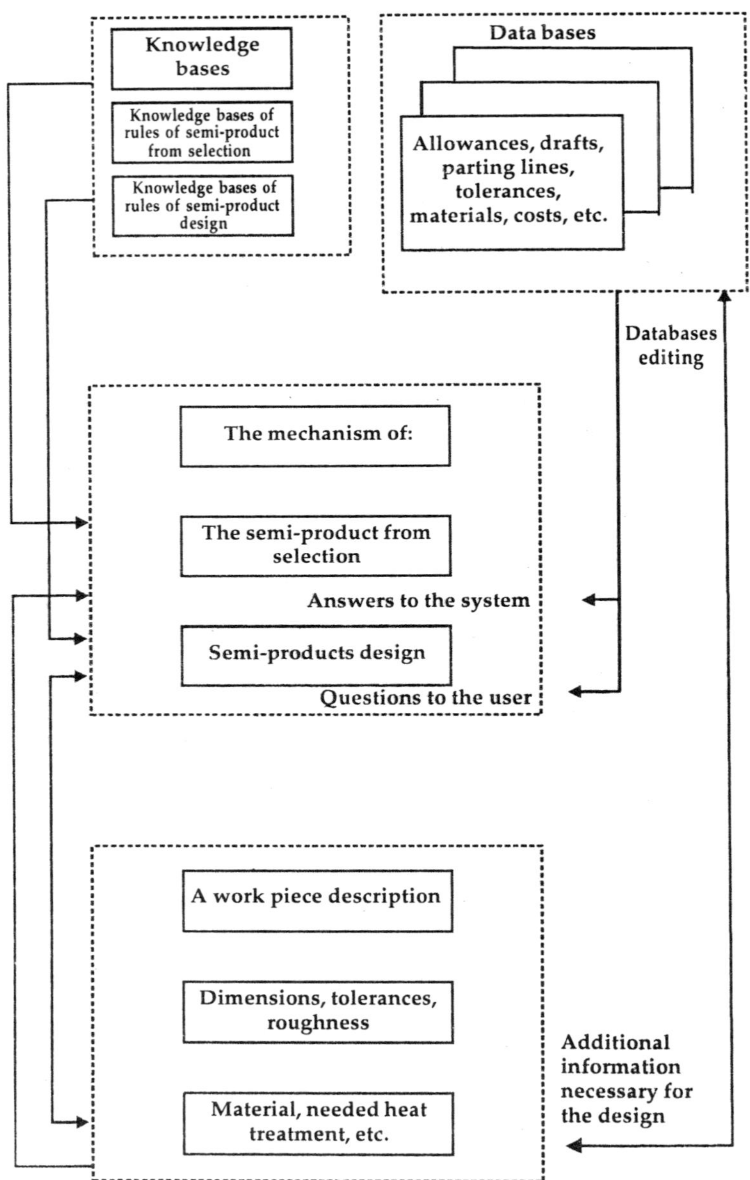

Fig 10.2: Diagram of the conception of the computer aided semi-product selection and design system

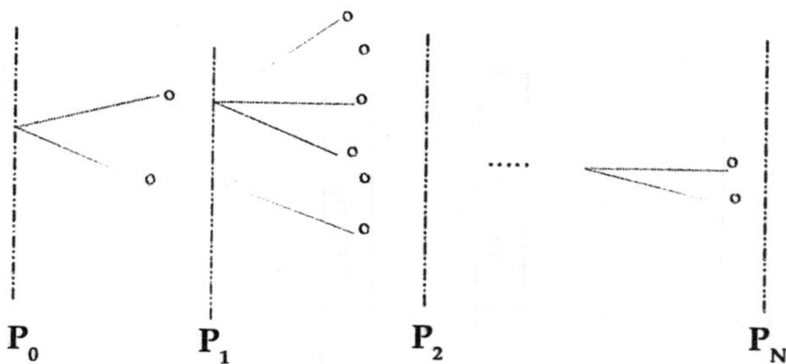

Fig. 10.3: **Diagram of the structure of the knowledge base in the form of the decisive tree**

Finally, in the layer P_{N+1} the entire knowledge W is accumulated; it is necessary to solve the task. This knowledge is the sum of all partial information q_i according to the formula (2).

$$W = \sum_{i=1}^{N} q_i \qquad (2)$$

Partial information q can come from three various sources: from databases, from the user or can be a result of different computer programmes. The information stored in the knowledge base concerns the choice of:

1. The form of a semi-product; a cast, forgoing or a die forging, a bar (peeled, black rolled, etc.), a draw piece and die stamping, others like: a double extra strong pipe, a welded semi-product, etc.;
2. Semi-product allowances which are estimated using the computational-analytic method.

Databases

The automation degree depends on the amount of data, which are stored in databases. Accumulating a significant number of data in databases enables acceleration of the design process and relives the process engineer from the necessity of manual searching for data in tables and standard brochures. Because the relation database has been built, a huge number of data has been arranged in the proper order and the stored data are simple in editing. A diagram of the suggested database is shown in Fig. 10.4.

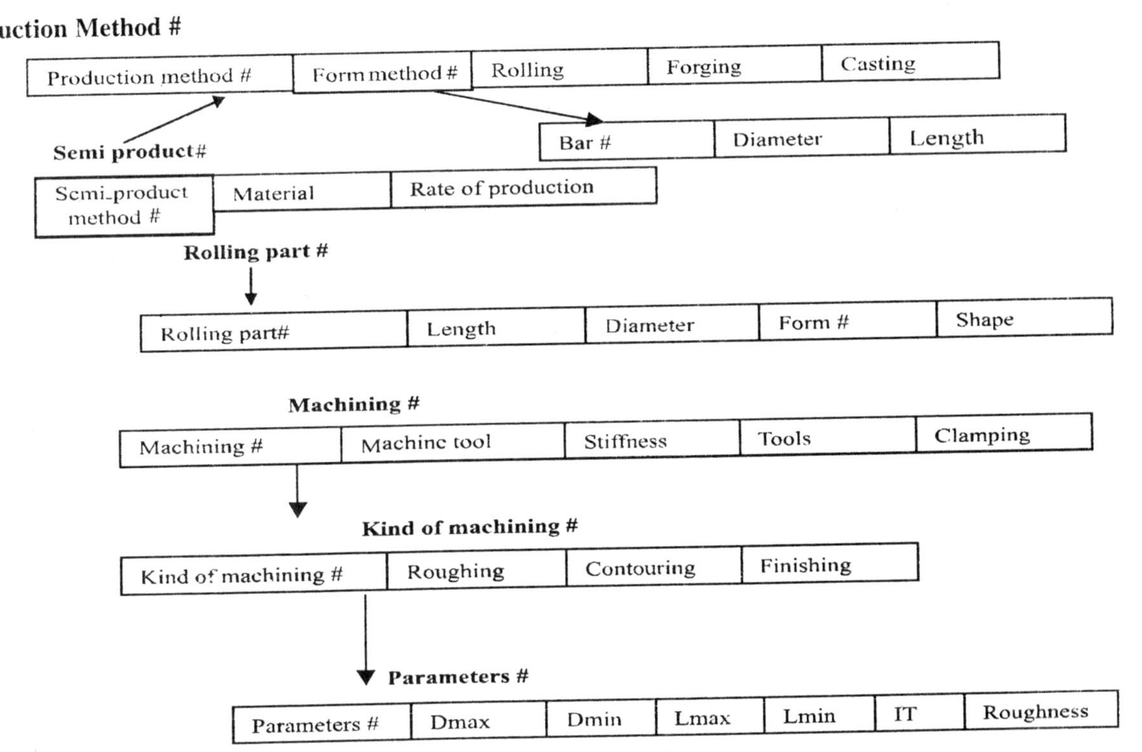

***Fig. 10.4*: Diagram of the database**

As a result of selection, the data needed for transition to the state of knowledge W_i are extracted from the database. It is shown in formula (3).

$$R(A_1, A_2 \ldots, A_m) \xrightarrow{\text{Selection}} (d_1, d_2, \ldots\ldots, d_p) \equiv q_i \qquad (3)$$

$R(A_1, A_2, \ldots, A_m)$ – attributes $A_1, A_2, \ldots, A_m$ of relation R,

$D_1, D_2, \ldots, D_p$ — extracted data.

Mechanism of Making a Decision

The computer aided semi-product selection and design system must be equipped with the mechanism of decision-making. This mechanism has to fulfil two tasks:

1. Processing the knowledge collected in knowledge bases; collecting data from databases and answering the question of what is the proposed form of a semi-product on the basis of given algorithms;
2. Designing the semi-product, i.e., allowances, calculation, and selection of other quantities, which are necessary to make, for example, the engineering drawing of a semi-product or digital technical documentation.

To fulfil these aims one can build a big independent computer programme of semi-product selection and design using a computer programme language. Unfortunately, due to the high degree of complication, such execution of the programme requires a lot of work and programming knowledge.

Since the system, which consists of the mechanism of decision-making and data and knowledge bases, is similar to the expert system structure, the other way of solving the task is to use a frame expert system. The frame expert system is a computer application enabling making an expert system by storing the decision rules in this system.

A Workpiece Description

The proposed system is open to co-operation with the external computer aided design (CAD) programme. To make this co-operation possible it is necessary to use the proper interface between the system and CAD programme. This interface should allow sending data from CAD programme to the computer aided selection and design system and in the opposite direction. This kind of communication enables immediately and automated introduction of changes into the project. It is necessary to mention a formalised of description a workpiece. This description allows a univocal interpretation of data, which are sent from the system to CAD programme and in the opposite direction. Missing information is completed by the user. Additionally the information which is obtained through the interface can be used in other programmes, for example in those oriented towards producibility, assembly, disassembly, recycling, cost, environmental protection, and others included in concurrent engineering.

CONCLUSION

1. The realisation of the computer aided semi-product selection and design system is possible with the use of existing and accessible software; this realisation depends on programming skill and available computer programmes.
2. The application of the expert system allows unification of the semi-product form selection; it leads to such simplification of decision process that the experience of the process engineer is not necessary and the significant part of technological knowledge is stored in knowledge bases. This fact causes that using of data is simple and all the rules are applied.
3. If usually a computational-analytic method of allowance estimating is used in industry in large-lot and mass production, then in the piece and small lot production it is different. The computational-analytic method is rather rarely used in small plants because of the high complication level and complex algorithms, especially when time is limited. In these cases the values of allowances are approximated and then are often much too big. The use of the proposed computer aided semi-product selection and design system is instrumental in small plants because it enable fast and correct designing of the semi-product form and dimensions.

REFERENCES

1. Gawlik, E. *The Analysis of Methods for Computer Aided Process Planning.* Workshop CA Systems and Technologies. Zilina 1998.
2. Grower, *Computer Aided Design and Manufacture.*
3. Grower, *Computer Integrated Manufacture.*
4. Hebrahimzeed, *Computer Aided Design and Manufacture.*
5. Radhakrishna, *Computer Aided Design and Manufacture.*
6. P.N Rao, *Computer Aided Design and Manufacture.*

11

Data Mining for Business Competitiveness

Prof. CSG Krishnamacharyulu*

Modern business has to strike a balance among the three forces that impact productivity and profitability-Relationship, Strategy and Technology. (Fig. 11.1)

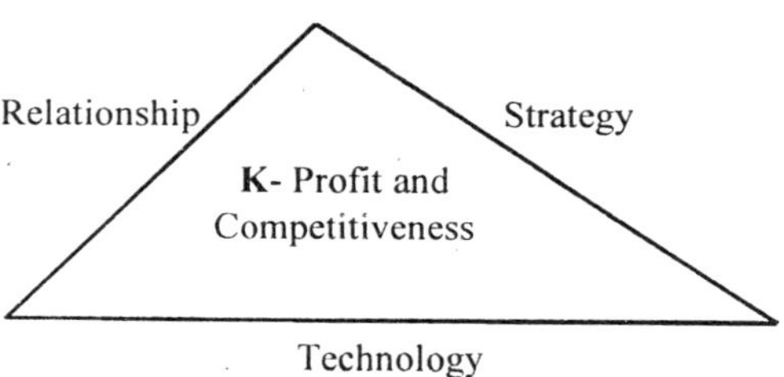

Fig. 11.1: **Business Triangle**

KNOWLEDGE—THE KEY COMPETENCE

Winston Churchil has once remarked that the empires of the future would be empires of the mind. This prophecy has turned out to be more than true in today's business world. Thomas Stewart (1977) rightly observed:

* School of Commerce, Management and Information Sciences, SV University, Tirupati.

> "Knowledge has become the primary ingredient of what we make, do, buy and sell. As a result, managing it – finding and growing intellectual capital, storing it, selling it, sharing it – has become the most important economic task of individuals, business, and nations.

Manasco (1997) asserted:

> "the global economy is becoming ever more transparent-and, as a result, capital will seek out intelligent enterprises with increasing precision."

Many other observers voiced similar views. For instance Allee, (1997) said:

> "When many companies must innovate or die, their ability to learn, adapt and change becomes a core competency for survival. Every business is a knowledge business, every worker is knowledge worker".

The fortunes of companies therefore can rise or fall meteorically, depending on how well they create, capture and leverage their knowledge. Businesses are therefore, moving from simple, transaction oriented processes to knowledge-oriented, multi-dimensional integrated activities. As shown in Fig. 11.2 higher levels of interactivity and knowledge intensity demand new approaches to Business Stakeholder Relations Management (BSRM). In other words, business can reap an immediate pay off when a key solution makes it easier for employers to reach out to employees, customers and partners.

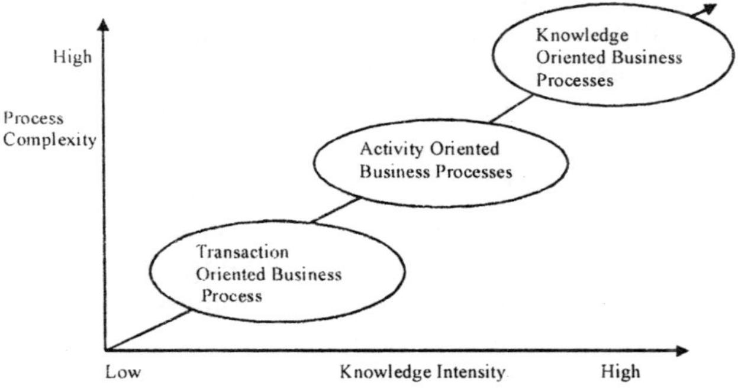

Fig. 11.2: **Knowledge orientation for relations management**

IT ADOPTION

Since information and knowledge sharing is guiding competitiveness, IT capability will be the single most effective weapon in the era of information economy. Arie de Geus, in his best selling book "The Living Company"[2], has given a very persuasive logic as to why Information Technology (IT) can be termed as the most potent competitive weapon for present day organisations. Most important aspect guiding competitiveness in current turbulent market is how a company gathers, analyses, and uses information to its advantage.

Thus, IT capability- that processes and manages information in a corporate—will be the single most effective weapon in the era of information economy. The road map for IT diffusion and adoption can be presented Table 11.1. (*See on next page)*

PROBLEM—NOT DATA, RELATIONSHIPS

Today, the secret of success of many profitable businesses lies in their ability to transact but in their ability to establish relationships; not in storing data but in processing the data using advanced analytical methods. By and large, organisations do not have any problem of not having enough data because most organisations are rich with data. They need analysis for new found relationships and establish enduring relationships with stakeholders.

For example, a typical report is able to identify the best-selling product in a supermarket. However, a report aided by data analysis or business intelligence, is not only able to identify the best-selling product in a supermarket but the report is also able to explain the reasons why the product is the best. This ability of knowing 'why will therefore empower the organisation to make the necessary strategic changes. For example, the organisation should capitalise on the new found knowledge by building a stronger, one-to-one relationship with its customers (Anonymous, 1999).

Table 11.1 Road Map for IT Adoption and Diffusion

IT Phase	*Technology*	*Data related stages*	*Business questions*
1. IT diffusion & automation (1960)	Computers tapes, disks	Data collection Retrospective static data delivery	What was total revenue over the last five years?
2. Acclimatisation (1980)	RDBMS, SQL Integration tools and protocols	Data access Retrospective, dynamic data delivery at one level	What were unit sales in central zone last March?
3. Assimilation (1990s)	Data warehouse—multi dimensional data bases. On-line analytical process; DSS	Data navigation Retrospective, dynamic data delivery at multiple levels.	What were unit sales in New Delhi last March? Drill down to districts and cities?
4. Enabling (200)	Advanced algorithms, multiprocessor computers, massive data bases; KM technology	Data mining Prospective, proactive information delivery	What is likely to happen in New Delhi unit sales next year?

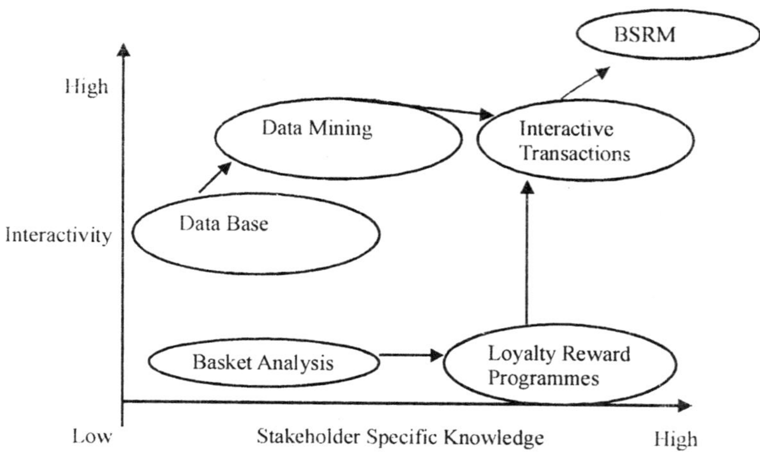

Fig. 11.3: **Business Relationship Management and knowledge**

DATA MINING GROWING

Obviously, the business of information management encompasses more than just storing the data. It also covers data 'mining' or acquiring information by processing data using a new form of business intelligence (Anonymous,1999a). Hence, organisations need to invest in data mining techniques (aided by statistical analysis, visualisation and neural networks) to uncover hidden patterns, discover new knowledge, and as a consequence gain more insight into the current business situation.

What is It?

Data Mining is application of statistical tools to predict events with a certain degree of accuracy."

Data mining is:

1. *Detective:* It goes on relentless *search* for finding data.
2. *Integrative:* It aggregates data from different spaces.
3. *Analytical:* Do "what if" analysis. For instance, what if I reduce the interest rates by 50 basis points? What is the probability of getting 25% more or less responses?

4. *Predictive:* Analyze past transactions to predict success or failure attributes. What will be the future sales if environmental factors change?

Who Have Taken It?

The application of data mining is wide-ranging, from financial analysis to fraud detection (credit card business) to product development (say, pharmaceutical industry). All the functional areas of business now embrace data mining.

Industry-wise, it is being adopted by one and all. In the financial industry, insurance companies and banks use data mining for risk analysis. For example, an insurance company may search its own databases to uncover relationships between personal characteristics and claim behavior (Basu, 1997). Usually the company is interested in the characteristics of insurants with a highly deviating claim behaviour. According to META Group, Inc. a Connecticut-based market research firm, data mining application is expected to grow one hundred fifty per cent from 1999 to 2000 (Bauer,2000). Additionally, the report suggests that applications of data mining in insurance industries will grow at a steady rate of six per cent during that period.

DATA MINING FOR A FUNCTION—DIRECT MARKETING

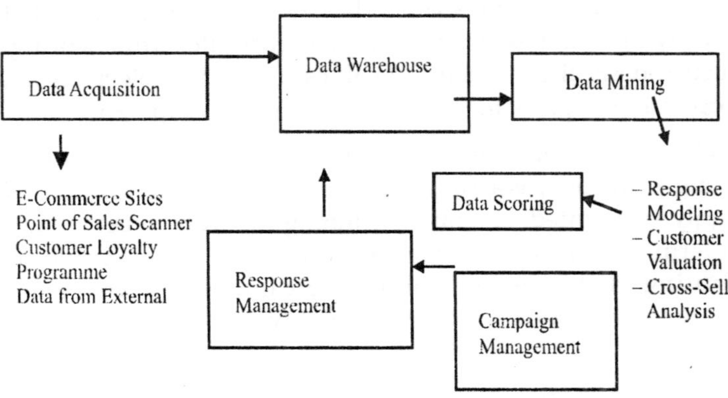

Fig. 11.4: **Direct Marketing Process**

The direct marketing chain involves the steps of data acquisition, storage, modelling and scoring, followed by campaign management and customer response measurement. The Direct Marketing chain starts with capturing data about prospective customer. The most common sources of such information are e-commerce websites, point of sale scanners in stores, and customer loyalty programmers. And the e-business/commerce also can purchase data from external database vendors such as supplementary or even a primary data source. In order to analyse capture data, the e-business should be transfer transactional data to a data warehouse. After that, OLAP tools are used to create use of data suitable for further analytical analysis.

A sample of historic data for analysis and machine learning has to be imported from the existing storage architecture, to a selected data mining application. Then the best strategy for data analysis has to be selected. Finally the developed model needs to be exported back to the direct marketing application in order to score the new data and identify the best business opportunities.

The prediction provided by a model is called a score. A score is assigned to each record in the database and indicates the likelihood that the customer whose record has been scored will exhibit a particular behaviour. For example, if a model predicts customer attrition, a high score indicates that a customer is likely to leave while a low score indicates the opposite. After scoring a set of customers, these numerical values are used to select the most appropriate prospects for targeted marketing campaign.

Campaign management automates and integrates the planning, execution, assessment and refinement of ten to hundreds of highly segmented campaigns running monthly, weekly, daily are intermittently. By tracking responses and following rules for attributing customer behaviour, the campaign management software can help measure the profitability and ROI of all ongoing campaigns.

Database marketing software enables companies to deliver to customers and prospects timely, pertinent and coordinated messages and value propositions. Today's campaign management software manages and monitors customer communication across multiple touch points, such as direct mail, telemarketing, customer service, point of sale, e-mail and web, branch office, etc. the software can also run campaigns with multiple communication points triggered by time or customer behaviour—such as the opening of a new account.

The closer data mining and campaign management work together, the better the business results. Today, campaign management software uses the score generated by the data mining model to sharpen the focus of targeted customers or prospects, thereby increasing response rates and campaign effectiveness. Unfortunately, the use of a model with in campaign management today is often a manual, time intensive process. The solution to this problem is the tight integration of data mining and campaign management technologies.

Integration is crucial in two areas:

- The campaign management software must share the definition of the define campaign segment with the data mining application. Through the integration of two applications, the data mining application can automatically restrict its analysis to data base records containing just those characteristics.
- Selected scores from the resulting predictive model must flow seamlessly into the campaign segment in order to form targets with highest profit potential.

DATA MINING IN ONE ORGANISATION

National Stock Exchange (NSE) has set up a data warehouse, with is acting as a giant 'storehouse' of information spanning various aspects of the capital market—from information on various trades undertaken, to membership, listing, clearing settlement related data—beginning from NSE 's inception. The warehouse will gradually be of the size of 500 giga bytes and will involve collation of information in multi-dimensional cubes. The end user (internal users of NSE) will thus have access to a multiple-source system, i.e. data analysis on top. The user can not only copy the data he requires, but can also hold data for analysis across different dimensions. As far as the business sense is concerned, action taken by the NSE shows that they are not only prepared for IT inclusion and absorption at a high rate but also pre-emptive in their strategies. No doubt then, that they have overtaken Bombay Stock Exchange (BSE) in terms of both volumes of shares transacted and market capitalisation.

EMPLOYEES' READINESS IN ADOPTING DATA MINING

Adopting a new technology is not an easy task. Foremost, the employees are humans who are naturally fearful of the uncertainty of change. This fear is often translated to resistance to change. Additionally, the design of high-tech products sometimes fails to account for the way the users adopt and react to the technology. As suggested by Eby et, al. (2000) understanding employees' readiness is crucial.

Objectives and Methodology

A study is undertaken with the following objectives:

1. What is the level of data mining readiners of the employees in the insurance industry in Malaysia?
2. What are the factors that may affect the employees' readiness level?

The Technology Readiness Index (TRI) is designed to identify the propensity of a customer, an employee or even a manager to adopt new technologies. Table 11.2 shows the parameters.

Table 11.2: Components of Technology Readiness Index (TRI)

Category	*Definition*
Optimism	The degree to which individuals believe that technology can benefit their lives and give them more control over their lives
Innovativeness	A natural desire to acquire and experiment with the newest technologies, as well as to be a thought leader
Discomfort	A feeling of lacking control over technology and lacking confidence in making it work properly
Insecurity	A need for assurance that a technology-based product, service or process will operate reliably and accurately

This study aims to understand the contextual factors in the insurance organisations that influence employees' Data Mining Readiness Index (DMRI). The theoretical framework is adapted from the Model for Building an Analytical Capability (Devenport et al., 2001), which states that the more analytically capable the individual, the higher the readiness. Fig. 11.5 illustrates the dependent variable (employees' DMR) and the independent variables (business strategy, users' skills and experience, data-driven culture, and data quality).

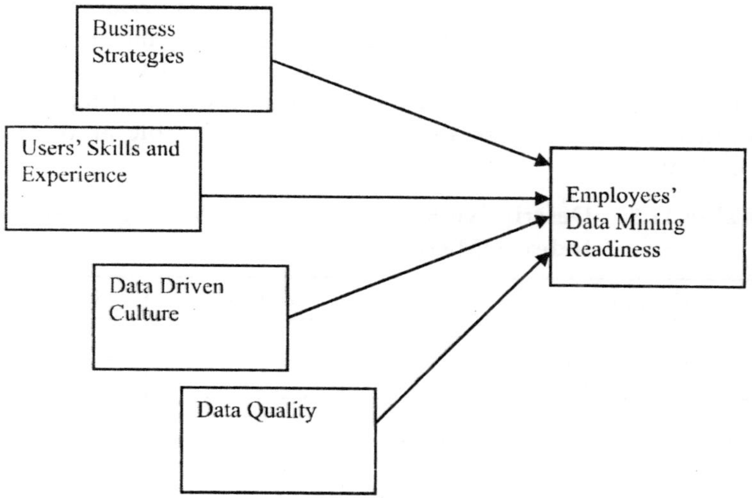

Fig. 11.5: **Factors Influencing Readiness**

The following four hypotheses are tested.

H1: The clearer the business strategy's definition, the higher the employees' DMR

H2: The better the users' skills and experience in analytic capabilities, the higher the Employees' DMR

H3: The higher the data-driven culture, the higher the employees' DMR

H4: The better the data quality, the higher the employees' DMR

Data is collected using e-mail questionnaire. The questionnaires are mailed to selected employees working in the insurance industry. A total of 200 questionnaire sets were mailed and distributed personally. A total of 114 employees from 12 insurance companies responded to this study.

A total of 103 employees of different insurance companies (based on the DMRI) indicate that generally they feel neutral when asked of their readiness in adopting data mining technology.

FINDINGS AND CONCLUSIONS

A DMRI mean of 3.27 explains this situation. Zooming in to the components of the data mining readiness, the mean of about 4.0 suggests that in general employees are optimistic about data mining. Nonetheless, from the mean discomfort of about 3.5 indicate that they also experience a considerable amount of discomfort.

Table 11.3: Descriptive Statistics for Data Mining Readiness Index (DMRI)

Components	*Mean*	*Standard Dev.*	*Skewness*
Optimism	3.91	.54	-.11
Discomfort	3.50	.62	-.20
Overall DMRI	3.27	.45	-.59

The DMRI value indicates that the employees are optimistic and yet experience discomfort in handling data mining. Parasuraman et al. (1993) highlight the feeling of technology-related anxieties experience by the employees who are optimistic about technology is similar to those experienced by those who are less enthusiastic. Indirectly, organisations need to identify who these people are and in which categories they belong to. Therefore, organisations should consider strategically, different sets of system or structure that needs to be in place to tackle the different levels of employees' readiness. The organisation may also need to establish a system or structure that can motivate the employees to adopt data mining technology. As a consequence, the relevant resources (such as human and budget) needed to be in place even before attempting to adopt the technology.

As skills and experience are identified to be positively correlated to employees' readiness, the insurance companies should focus on issues pertaining to the Human Resources Management (HRM), specifically on the quality of the current and future workforce. The implication here is on the IS and IT personnel regardless of whether the organisation uses the internal experts or outsource, because the IT personnel needs to acquire the necessary skills and knowledge of data mining in order to strategically and effectively manage the data mining technology in the organisation.

PRINCIPLES FOR DATA MINING TO SUCCEED

The following principles will be of help:

1. *Database Structuring:* Set up organisations database so that it can capture key information about organisations and its stakeholders. . For example, if your target audience is customers, the organisation needs more than just their name, address and phone. Other information includes e-mail address, ages of adults and children, income, occupation, denomination and position. It is also important to have their product purchase information and to maintain product purchase history such as date of last purchase, money spent, specific items purchased, etc.;
2. *Data Base Enhancement:* Determine what additional information would be beneficial in helping the business to establish relations with stakeholder. Incase of DM. work with vendors who have data and resources can use to append and update the information in files. Data can also be enhanced with more direct surveys;
3. *DataBase Maintenance:* Establish a plan to update organisations file on a regular basis;
4. DM tools are expensive and have long implementation timeframes;
5. DM may give patterns which are not really related;
6. DM succeeds only if a information strategy is developed and communicated;
7. A phased roll out is better than a time consuming, expensive, multi location, multi function roll out.

12

Data Mining Applications in Business Prospects and Problems

Dr. Lalitha Ramakrishnan*

This paper addresses the issue of a need to build data mining and data warehousing as complex adaptive systems with the business end user firmly in mind. This requires broadening the traditional meaning of data mining and data warehousing, to encompass information mining and knowledge retrieval. Companies will need to link the concept of data mining to equally sophisticated information retrieval tools that work on the basis of combined machine and human intervention in more intelligent ways than those presently offered.

INTRODUCTION

In the emergent competitive, knowledge economies, companies are looking for ways to excel in their practices. The emphasis is more on information and knowledge—on their creation, capture, sharing and application. In this context—the twins of IT innovation—data warehousing and data mining have gained popularity. Big business is betting more and more on a series of data mining tools to help them predict future trends based on an analysis of historical behaviour.

---

* Associate Professor, Department of Business Management, SPMVV, Tirupati.

PROSPECTS

In the book "Advances in Knowledge Discovery and Data Mining," published by the MIT Press, Dr. Usama M. Fayyad and his fellow editors stated that: "... in combining the two terms" data mining" and "data warehousing", they are attempting to build bridges between the statistical, database and machine learning communities and appeal to a wider audience of information systems developers. We think this approach is very helpful—in fact, we believe that the term "data mining" is actually on the cusp of appearing on the radar screens, for the first time, of millions of companies.

According to major research companies like Forester Research, the data mining industry is predicted to grow from its present 40 million dollar size today to over 800 million dollars by the turn of the century. One expert comments on opportunities for further growth:

Have just reached the end of a DM application in social policy studies. These social policy people seem to have quite a lot of complex data, but not much evidence of substantial DM inroads in this area.

KD Nuggets 2005 poll asked about successful applications (*See Table 12.1 on next page*). The applications are successful in very few companies only. This indicates two things:

- There is an opportunity for other companies to embrace data mining;
- There is a need to make data mining tools more users friendly.

BUSINESS EXPECTATIONS

In the construction of data warehouses to day, companies are pinning their hopes on being able to extract out from the data mined content stored in their data warehouses, information for sound decision-making.

Analytic Database Marketing Division at AT & T has implemented leading edge methodologies for targeting, segmentation and marketing strategy applications.

Table 12.1: Industries/fields where you *successfully* applied data mining in the past 3 years

2005 Survey (149 replies, 421 votes total)

Industry	*Number of respondents*	*Successful applications (%)*
Banking	29	13
Bioinformatics/Biotech	18	8
Direct Marketing/Fund Raising	19	9
eCommerce/Web	12	6
Entertainment/News	1	0
Fraud Detection	19	9
Insurance	15	7
Investment/Stocks	9	4
Manufacturing	9	4
Medical/Pharma	15	7
Retail	9	4
Scientific Data	20	9
Security	8	4
Telecommunications	12	6
Travel	2	1
Other	19	9

Business Geographic Information Systems

There are now millions of companies using 'business GIS' from their desktops and laptops to be able to both display and extract all kinds of information relating to such common problems as the location of a new shop or service store to help guarantee the largest "reservoir" of people in the surrounding area. In other words, GIS went from a very specialised status, known only to a small group of professionals working in such fields as the oil and gas industry, forestry, and mining, to being an enabling application that could also be used on the desktop. It proved to be a strategic business advantage to both small and large companies alike. A burst of new applications came on the market and names like Map Info and Strategic Mapping captured chunks of the global business GIS market. Interestingly enough, it was the GIS enabling capability of linking demographics with psycho-graphics that opened up the way for whole new suites of business applications to be built.

Consumer Research

There are many reasons why marketers want to go beyond an understanding of what consumers do and also understand *why* they do it. It is particularly useful to understand:

1. What product and brand attributes drive customer purchase and loyalty (product performance, reliability, brand status, price, etc.); and
2. How do consumers rank the products of your company and your competitors on these characteristics?

Clearly, an understanding of these factors would allow companies to identify new customers for products or services through the integration of existing customer account information with demographics and lifestyle data. Also it helps in many ways:

- Communicate with their customers in ways that emphasize the most valued attributes;
- Target the weaknesses of competitive products;
- Design new products that better meet the needs of customers;
- Target different products towards the customers that most value their attributes.

Consumer Research Application

Tremendous marketing advantage can be gained from data mining in huge transactional data sets. But it is worth remembering that traditional research and modelling can also add value. But it is limited. To prove the point, we will discuss "attribute importance and performance scores" method and what it can give and cannot give.

Attribute importance and performance scores are obtained using straightforward consumer surveys. Respondents are asked about a list of product or brand attributes and provide feedback about the importance of each attribute in their buying decision and their perception of how each product or brand performs against these attributes.

Let us say, the product is viewed as highly reliable, useful, fun and innovative. Also it is viewed as very high-priced, does not enhance status and has poor service support.

We will now look at preferences. Service is given low score and reliability is given high score.

Given the low importance given to service, it may not pay to invest in improving this score. However, given the strong scores in product functionality there seems to be a possibility of improving the product status through advertising. While the price is high, strong scores for other attributes may allow the company to maintain a high price.

A model based on the factors and outcomes can be drawn. What does it tell and what it does not tell?

First, it quantifies the size of the influence of each purchase driver on the actual probability of purchase. The survey captured responses on attribute importance, but could not link these directly to purchase intent.

Second, by using actual purchase behaviour as one indicator of purchase intent, it combines information from surveys and transaction data. This provides a more powerful overall model.

Third, it quantifies the variables that influence the purchase process. For example, is price perception driven mostly by price advertising or by the actual price differential?

These information gaps are critical sometimes. Companies need complete and accurate information. Advances in data technology have overwhelmed corporations with information, driving the urgent need to develop new tools that can help transform data into business advantage. The advent of the Internet and the World Wide Web has, in the matter of five years, made more information accessible to more individuals than at any other time in our history.

SHORTCOMINGS

The problems in data mining are worth the attention of the IT developers.

(i) Conceptual Confusion

Even today, there is confusion by many in business over the use of the term "data." Often that term is used to cover textual and other forms of information and not just transactional data. In fact the terms "data" and "information" are often used interchangeably by many business people as they go about their day-to-day data/information-gathering tasks.

(ii) Information Retrieval

(a) *Content:* We believe that in the very near future, the present suites of data mining tools will start coming with a complement of new information retrieval tools. These tools will have an in-built ability to help even an untrained user extract, from textual and other media formats, the kind of gold nuggets of information presently being pulled from a company's transactional data, by suites of data mining tools. It is important to bear in mind that a large chunk of any company's in-house information is to be found in textual form. That information, if retrieved from a data warehouse using advanced information retrieval tools, can be made to bring forth added value information, leading to better business decisions.

(b) *Search Words:* Information technology as offered to corporations today suffers from having yet to catch up with cyberspace, even in its current incoherent state. Corporate data is treated as a supermarket from which items are to be retrieved, or a pit from which data should be mined. "Search engines" on the Web are similarly crippled at a conceptual level. Users try to funnel their desires through keywords shot into the dark.

There are lots of well-known problems with keywords. For instance, very few recipes contain the word "recipe." The way to look for recipes is actually with such words as "teaspoon," "tablespoon," and "cuillere"! And then the same words can mean different things to different people. An architect looking for documents on computer-aided architecture might form the query -"computers AND architecture" - and arrive at the home page of Intel. Mapping cyberspace will solve these problems and the enabling technologies of data mining and data warehousing must figure out quickly how to pro-actively lead the business charge. If not, there will be then the risk of being trampled by a stampede of business users, who will quickly brand those terms as their own, inventing a broader meaning for those concepts than they currently have today.

(c) *Distributed Data* Companies know that their in-house databases contain untapped knowledge about themselves. This information, if properly stored, can then be retrieved and analysed. The outcomes can provide them with a competitive edge in a world of saturated markets. The single biggest problem is that so much of this information is distributed across networks, divisions, and often continents.

SUCCESS DRIVERS

The major initiatives necessary to make data mining attractive are:

(i) Intelligent Information Retrieval

In our opinion, corporate nirvana in the use of data mining tools and data warehousing will only be achieved when companies link the concept of data mining to equally sophisticated information retrieval tools. These tools will work on the basis of combined machine and human intervention in more intelligent ways than those presently offered in to day's information retrieval tools. Corporations will need to run two complementary data/ information retrieval processes. One process will literally mine data and allow software to detect hidden patterns. Another process will query information through the posing of specific questions and secure targeted answers.

(ii) Facilitating Human–Machine Interaction

Machine learning in its present state is nowhere near the capacities of a human. After 30 years of artificial intelligence research, we can no longer claim with a straight face that machines can replace humans. Instead, we are looking for ways by which the machine can aid in a specially integrated fashion, rather than replacing human intervention in information retrieval. We believe that the remedy is still for human and machine to work together in order to extract the most useful knowledge from a database.

(iii) Meta Data, Not Just Data

We recognise that there is a major difference between data and information. In data warehousing, there is a tremendous risk that what will be delivered from these warehouses will be vast quantities of data rather than quality information. This is where the importance of metadata comes in to play. There is no question that improving the quality of metadata automatically improves the quality of the information retrieved. And the amount of data retrieved is also reduced. Successful data warehouses invariably are individually small, heavily used by the target business unit organisation, are constantly changing in terms of their content based on changing market needs, and are controlled by the business unit of an enterprise.

(iv) Need Based Knowledge

The importance of providing all in-house company users with a single, uniform view of information throughout a corporation is key to a company's efficiency and ability to deliver a higher quality customer service. It is only through the complementary usage of data mining tools, and data warehousing, alongside with that of cutting-edge information retrieval tools and processes, that corporate nirvana in the area of knowledge extraction, can be achieved.

CONCLUSION

If data mining and data warehousing are to become corporate nirvana for the 21st Century, then they must be built as complex adaptive systems with the business end user firmly in mind. A complex, adaptive system is a social system, a physical system, and an artificial biological system, all at the same time. A think tank that particularly focuses on this kind of research is the Santa Fe Institute in Santa Fe, New Mexico.

As data mining companies work on adding complements of information retrieval processes and tools to their present suites of offerings, this will vastly speed up the adaptation of the data mining industry to the broader needs of the business end user. When the worlds of data mining and knowledge extraction expand to include information retrieval from alternative media formats and text based data, then "data mining" and "data warehousing" will become the hottest buzz words for businesses in the information age.

REFERENCES

1. David S.Coppock, *Data Mining and Modeling: Customer Motivation, DM Review. com*, March 28, 2003. Can be contacted at: *dcoppock@patmedia.net*.

2. Amrit Tiwana , *Knowledge Management Tool Kit* , Pearson Education Asia, New Delhi, 2005.

13

Data Mining for Library Services

Mrs. D. Prabhavathi*

ABSTRACT

The digitisation of libraries has greatly helped the universities and colleges to increase the scope of their education system. Users need not be physically present in the campus to utilise the library facilities. This has helped users to increase their skills. This in turn helps users in the highly competitive situation. In addition to the traditional services, a wide range of new functions and services have emerged to meet the challenges of digital information society. Among those new services data mining is of recent origin but has significant contribution. In the 1980s all the major organisations built infrastructural databases, containing data about their clients, competitors, and products. These databases form a potential gold mine which contains gigabytes of data with much hidden information which cannot be easily traced out using query facilities or SQL (Standard Query Language). Data mining algorithms can find optional clustering in databases. These algorithms zoom in on interesting sub parts of the data base, and establish new patterns of existing data that connects the world with networks.

INTRODUCTION

The Information Age we live in has rightly been characterised by a rapid explosion of information of bewildering size and complexity. Correspondingly, the traditional role of libraries as

* **Assistant Professor, University Library, Sri Padmavathi Mahila Viswavidyalayam, Tirupati – 517 502 A.P.,** *E-mail:* **prabha_dg@yahoo.com**

focal points of society's accumulated knowledge has also undergone a radical change. Today, libraries have evolved from being mere physical repositories of books to dynamic storehouses of information, incorporating novel approaches to traditional library practices, intensive use of electronic systems and networks and dramatic shifts in organisation, storage and retrieval of information. This transition from a print-based to a largely digitised environment, while maximising user satisfaction, has also given rise to unexplored issues. Libraries today are inundated with data, numerical and otherwise, which must be analysed and processed to convert them into information that informs, instructs or otherwise aids the potential user. Given this flood of information, effective and timely use of the results is no longer possible solely using traditional approaches, particularly where multidimensional data are concerned. Consequently, libraries have felt the need for specific data analysis techniques utilising more complex and sophisticated tools than those used in the past. This has led to the utilisation of the concept of data mining, a growing field finding increasing application in a variety of organisations worldwide.

DEFINITION OF DATA MINING

Data Mining is an interdisciplinary area focusing upon methodologies for extracting useful knowledge from data. Defined as "the non-trivial extraction of implicit, previously unknown, and potentially useful information from data", it draws upon a number of computational techniques from Statistics and Pattern Recognition to deliver information that would not be available otherwise. As a powerful tool for identifying patterns, trends, correlations and anomalies across large databases, data mining provides the solution to discover and model the relevant knowledge, especially patterns and relationships, residing in the data. It has been used successfully for several years in the scientific and business communities for tracking behaviour of individuals and groups, processing medical information and a number of other applications.

DATA MINING IN LIBRARY SERVICES

Till now, the use of data mining in libraries has been limited. However, exponential growth in information and the increasing need for libraries to provide relevant information speedily to geographically distributed users with inter and intra disciplinary subject interests at macro and micro level has necessitated the need for adopting automated access mechanisms such as data mining tools in a modern library.

We live in an expanding universe of data in which there is too much data and too little information. The development of new techniques to find the required information from huge amounts of data is one of the main challenges for software developers today. The quantity of data in the world roughly doubles every year, as a surprising consequence, the amount of meaningful information decreases rapidly. The very fact that the amount of information is growing is the reason it is increasingly difficult to find the meaningful facts we seek. This growth of information is due to the mechanical production of texts.

OPAC (Online Public Access Catalogue)/Searching

The OPAC serves as the primary means of searching for the documents/collection/records/works owned by the library. In addition to this most of the OPAC/s use a browser interface, users can access bibliographic databases, World Wide Web (WWW), and other online resources. Online searching is an active area of research in Library and Information Science for studying information seeking behaviour and human interaction with the computer.

Inter Library Loan (ILL)

This is unique service of the information seeking behaviour of users and the library staff. As we know, in most ILL cases, the user seeking a document/record contacts the ILL section, and the ILL staff members locate the material from another library and borrow the book/document/record. Once the requesting library receives the book, they lend it to their user. The cost for lending and the time it takes for delivery vary by the source selected. Most of the libraries have a number of consortium agreements, each with different response times and costs, which makes this a complex data source. The information tracked varies by library, but it contains information about the record requested, the user, the lending library, and the essential dates involved.

Circulation

When a user checks out a document the checkout date, due date, call number, and user identification is recorded. When the document is returned, borrower information disappears form the librarian's perspectives, but the borrowing record/document remain hidden in the database. A similar database is a hold/ request, where request for document either not in the library or already checked out are recorded. Again, once the hold/request has been dealt with, the user information is removed from the view of the librarian. In most of the cases the user identifiers are still kept in database in inaccessible tables.

PROBLEMS WITH DATA MINING

Unproven in Libraries

It is very unclear whether data mining techniques used on the Internet or for certain business and scientific applications can be successfully applied in a library setting. Most successful examples of data mining in the business and scientific communities involve short documents consisting of well-structured or statistically oriented data. Conversely, libraries work predominantly with large unstructured text documents from diverse sources. While a number of text-mining tools do provide access to minimally structured text documents, the total amount of information they provide access to is small in comparison with that found in a large library. Also, Web pages, e-mail, and corporate reports (the focus of most text-mining tools) tend to be relatively short, so the procedures used to index and search them might not work successfully with the larger information objects typically found in libraries.

Lack of Standards

There are no established standards for data mining storage and retrieval. Consequently, record sharing between libraries is impractical, and long-term access to materials is in doubt. In an electronic environment where database access in a library is determined by IP or password validation, record sharing may not be an important consideration, but information-sharing programmes such as interlibrary loan become complicated at best and impossible at worst. Because data mining increases library dependence on proprietary functions, libraries that invest heavily in data mining technologies increase the risk of incurring expensive and difficult conversions or severe data loss when vendors quit supporting their products. In the present environment, widespread use of the MARC format dramatically reduces data migration problems and greatly simplifies record sharing and inter library loan.

Big Technical Hurdles Remain

The third problem with data mining is that it faces the same difficulties as other searching mechanisms. The quality of data is critical for successful data mining, just as it is for successful searching by other methods. If information is not structured in a way that allows pattern discovery, the likelihood of extracting meaningful information from the data is greatly reduced. Data mining looks for patterns in data. It is very difficult for data mining tools to identify the relationships between different information objects when it is not possible to determine the meaning of the data.

Despite advances in technology, it is not practical to use all processing techniques on all documents in a given search, except when small sets of data are concerned. Unless all data can be stored in memory and there is sufficient processing power, heuristics must be used to determine the optimal searching strategy. Users may reveal information about themselves and the purpose of their searches in the way they phrase their queries, but it is difficult to glean enough information to identify techniques that will optimally serve the user.

Moreover, effective techniques for indexing and retrieving non-textual data are not yet available. As the number of multimedia information objects increases rapidly, so will the need for effective storage and retrieval mechanisms. When this problem is considered together with the lack of storage and retrieval standards even for text documents, libraries need to be wary of depending on particular data mining technologies that are not expected to provide long-term access to materials.

CONCLUSION

Libraries have gathered data about their collections and users for years, but have not often used those data for better decision-making. By taking a more active approach based on applications of data mining, data visualisation, and statistics, these organisations can get a clearer picture of their information delivery and management needs. At the same time, libraries must continue to protect their users and employees from misuse of personality identifiable data records. Libraries must compete against online booksellers, downloadable audio books and the vast supply of free information varying quality from the internet. Librarians must begin to take the initiative in using their systems and data for competitive advantage and to justify continued support and funding of libraries.

REFERENCES

1. Nicholson, S: *Bibliomining Data Mining for Libraries. http:// www.bibliomining.com*

2. Nicholson, S: *Bibliomining Process: Data Warehousing and Data Mining for Library Decision-making. http://www.ala.org/ala/lita/litapublications/ital/ 2204nicholson.htm*

3. *President's Information Technology Advisory Committee's Report,* Washington, http:// *www.ccic.gov/ac/interim/*, 1998.

14

A Data Mining System for Classifier Development Using CPAR
Classification Based on Predictive Association Rules

V.N.L. Mythili Gollapudi*

INTRODUCTION

Classification

Databases are rich with hidden information that can be used for making intelligent business decisions. Classification and prediction are two forms of data analysis that can be used to extract models describing important data classes or to predict future data trends. *Classification* predicts categorical labels whereas *Prediction* models continuous-valued functions. Data classification is a two-step process. In the first step, a model is built describing a predetermined set of data classes or concepts. The model is constructed by analysing database tuples described by attributes. Each tuple is assumed to belong to a predefined class, as determined by one of attributes, called the class label attribute. In the second step, the model can be used to classify future data tuples or objects for which the class label is not known.

* M.Tech-CST, Andhra University, Visakhapatnam.

Classification Based on Association Rule Mining

Recently, data mining techniques have been developed that apply concepts used in association rule mining to the problem of classification. There are three such methods:

1. ARCS, 2. Associative Classification, 3.CAEP

1. *ARCS:* The ARCS, or Association Rule Clustering System, mines association rules of the form $A_{quan1} \wedge A_{quan2} \Rightarrow A_{cat}$, where A_{quan1} and A_{quan2} are tests on quantitative attribute ranges, and A_{cat} assigns a class label for a categorical attribute from the given training data.
2. ***Associative Classification***: It mines rules of the form *condset* => *y*, where condset is a set of items (or attribute-value pairs) and y is a class label.
3. *CAEP:* CAEP, Classification by aggregating emerging patterns, uses the notion of itemset support to mine Emerging Patterns (EPs), which are used to construct a classifier. An EP is an itemset whose support increases significantly from one class of data to another.

CPAR, the Classification Based on Predictive Association Rules

Traditional rule-based classifiers, such as C4.5, FOIL and RIPPER are substantially faster, but they suffer from lack of accuracy. Later studies in Data Mining proposed a classification approach, called Associative Classification. It uses association rule mining algorithm, such as Apriori or FP growth, to generate the complete set of association rules. Then it selects a small set of high quality rules and uses this rule set for prediction. The experiments show that this approach achieves higher accuracy than traditional classification approaches such as C4.5. However, associative classification suffers from efficiency due to the facts that it often generates a very large number of rules in association rule mining, and also it takes efforts to select high quality rules from among them.

Later, a novel approach called CPAR (Classification based on Predictive Association Rules) has been proposed. CPAR inherits the basic idea of FOIL in rule generation and integrates the features of associative classification in predictive rule analysis. In comparison with associative classification, CPAR has the following advantages: (1) CPAR generates a much smaller set of high-quality predictive rules directly from the dataset; (2) to avoid generating redundant rules, CPAR generates each rule by considering the set of "already generated" rules; and (3) when predicting the class label of an example, CPAR uses the best k rules that this example satisfies. Moreover, CPAR employs the following features to further improve its accuracy and efficiency: (1) CPAR uses dynamic programming to avoid repeated calculation in rule generation; and (2) when generating rules, instead of selecting only the best literal, all the close-to-the-best literals are selected so that important rules will not be missed. CPAR generates a smaller set of rules, with higher quality and lower redundancy in comparison with associative classification. As a result, CPAR is much more time-efficient in both rule generation and prediction but achieves as high accuracy as associative classification.

CPAR ALGORITHM

Rule generation in CPAR uses Predictive Rule Mining Algorithm.

Predictive Rule Mining

Input: Training set D = P U N. (P and N are the sets of all positive and negative examples, respectively.)

Output: A set of rules for predicting class labels for examples

Procedure PredictiveRuleMining

set the weight of every example to 1

rule set R←ϕ

total Weight← TotalWeight(P)

A←Compute PNArray from D

while TotalWeight(P) > δ*totalWeight

N'←N, P'←P, A'←A

rule r←empty_rule

while true

```
find best literal p according to A¢
if gain(p) < min_gain then break
append p to r
for each example t in P' U N' not satisfying r's body
remove t from P' or N'
change A' according to the removal of t
end
end
R←R U {r}
for each example t in P satisfying r's body
t.weight←α*t.weight
change A according to the weight decreased
end
end
return R
```

Here gain(P) is calculated as:

gain(a) = WP' (log(WP'/WP'+NP') - log(WP/WP+NP))

where WP = totalWeight(P)

WN = totalWeight(N)

WP' = totalWeight(P')

WN' = totalWeight(N')

IMPLEMENTATION

To implement this algorithm, I have selected the "German" dataset. It consists of 1000 examples. Amongst, 700 belong to class 1, good category and the remaining belong to class2, bad category. There are 20 attributes among which 13 are categorical and the remaining 7 are numerical. The 20th attribute is class label attribute i.e., the class to which a particular tuple belongs. I have used JAVA language for implementation.

The implementation undergoes three phases:

1. Data Preprocessing
2. Rule Generation
3. Testing

Data Preprocessing

In the Data Preprocessing phase, the German dataset is preprocessed such that the 7 numerical attributes are categorised by calculating the Split points using the method of Gini Index. This process is being automated. The programme takes the raw dataset as input in the form of a file and it produces processed data in two files: the train dataset file and the test dataset file. The train dataset file is used for generating the rules and the test dataset file is used for testing the generated rules.

To illustrate this programme, let us take the loan default classification problem. Training set for predicting borrowers who will default on loan payments:

Tid	*Home Owner*	*Marital Status*	*Annual Income*	*Default Borrower*
1.	Yes	Single	125k	No
2.	No	Married	100k	No
3.	No	Single	70k	No
4.	Yes	Married	120k	No
5.	No	Divorced	95k	Yes
6.	No	Married	60k	No
7.	Yes	Divorced	220k	No
8.	No	Single	85k	Yes
9.	No	Married	75k	No
10.	No	Single	90k	Yes

Splitting of Continuous Attribute, the Annual Income:

55		65		72		80		87		92		97		110		122		230	
<=	>	<=	>	<=	>	<=	>	<=	>	<=	>	<=	>	<=	>	<=	>	<=	>
0	3	0	3	0	3	0	3	1	2	2	1	3	0	3	0	3	0	3	0
0	7	1	6	2	5	3	4	3	4	3	4	3	4	4	3	5	2	7	0
0.420		0.400		0.375		0.343		0.417		0.400		0.300		0.343		0.375		0.420	

The first row of the above table is the Split Positions, the second row is the number of records for Class "Yes", and the third row is for Class "No". That is, there are 0 records with Annual Income <=55 with class for both classes. And, there are 3 records of class "Yes" and 7 records of class "No" with Annual Income >55. The last row is the Gini Index Value. The formula for calculating the Gini Index is:

$$\text{Gini (t)} \quad 1-\sum_{i-0}^{c-1}[p(i/t)]^2$$

where c, the number of classes and t, the split position.

The Gini value for the split position t=55 is 0.420. The Split position with the smallest Gini Index is taken as the actual Split Position. So here, in this example, the Split position 97 (with the smallest Gini Value, 0.300) is taken as the Actual Split position. The records with Income less than 97 come under one category and the records with Income greater than 97 come under another category.

Rule Generation

In the Rule Generation phase, actual PRM algorithm is implemented. The programme takes the preprocessed train data file as input and generates the rules and produces the rules in another file.

Let us see how the algorithm works using a sample of a famous dataset, The Pima Indian Dataset.

Given the following data set (first 15 lines from the Pima Indian set):

1	*2*	*3*	*4*	*5*	*6*	*7*	*8*	*9*
2	9	13	17	21	28	32	38	42
1	8	13	17	21	27	31	36	41
3	10	13	16	21	27	32	36	42
1	8	13	17	21	28	31	36	41
1	9	12	17	21	29	35	37	42

(Contd...)

1	2	*3*	*4*	*5*	*6*	*7*	*8*	*9*
2	8	14	16	21	27	31	36	41
1	7	13	17	21	28	31	36	42
3	8	11	16	21	28	31	36	41
1	10	13	18	24	28	31	38	42
3	9	14	16	21	26	31	38	42
2	8	14	16	21	28	31	36	41
3	10	14	16	21	28	31	37	42
3	9	14	16	21	28	33	39	41
1	10	13	17	25	28	31	39	42
2	10	13	16	22	27	32	38	42

Initialisation:

Min_gain=0.5, α=1/3, δ=1/3.3

First we need to set the weight of every example to 1.0

2	9	13	17	21	28	32	38	42	{1.0}
1	8	13	17	21	27	31	36	41	{1.0}
3	10	13	16	21	27	32	36	42	{1.0}
1	8	13	17	21	28	31	36	41	{1.0}
1	9	12	17	21	29	35	37	42	{1.0}
2	8	14	16	21	27	31	36	41	{1.0}
1	7	13	17	21	28	31	36	42	{1.0}
3	8	11	16	21	28	31	36	41	{1.0}
1	10	13	18	24	28	31	38	42	{1.0}
3	9	14	16	21	26	31	38	42	{1.0}
2	8	14	16	21	28	31	36	41	{1.0}
3	10	14	16	21	28	31	37	42	{1.0}
3	9	14	16	21	28	33	39	41	{1.0}
1	10	13	17	25	28	31	39	42	{1.0}
2	10	13	16	22	27	32	38	42	{1.0}

We commence with class 41 and create the following P and N sets and an NP array. The first column numbers in the NP array gives the attribute label (1 to 40), the following two columns give the positive and negative total weightings for the P and N example sets respectively. On "start up" each attribute has a weighting of 1 associated with it, so attribute 1 occurs twice in P and four times in N.

PositiveExamples: P, P′

{1	8	13	17	21	27	31	36	41}	(1.0)
{1	8	13	17	21	28	31	36	41}	(1.0)
{2	8	14	16	21	27	31	36	41}	(1.0)
{3	8	11	16	21	28	31	36	41}	(1.0)
{2	8	14	16	21	28	31	36	41}	(1.0)
{3	9	14	16	21	28	33	39	41}	(1.0)

NegativeExamples: N, N′

{2	9	13	17	21	28	32	38	42}	(1.0)
{3	10	13	16	21	27	32	36	42}	(1.0)
{1	9	12	17	21	29	35	37	42}	(1.0)
{1	7	13	17	21	28	31	36	42}	(1.0)
{1	10	13	18	24	28	31	38	42}	(1.0)
{3	9	14	16	21	26	31	38	42}	(1.0)
{3	10	14	16	21	28	31	37	42}	(1.0)
{1	10	13	17	25	28	31	39	42}	(1.0)
{2	10	13	16	22	27	32	38	42}	(1.0)

total weight=Total weight(P)=6, δ*total weight=1.82

PN Array: A,A′

Literal	*P*	*N*	*Gain (Literal)*
Att 1:	2.0	4.0	-5.06
Att 2:	2.0	2.0	-3.56
Att 3:	2.0	3.0	-4.48
Att 4:	0.0	0.0	-
Att 5:	0.0	0.0	-
Att 6:	0.0	0.0	-
Att 7:	0.0	1.0	-
Att 8:	5.0	0.0	1.989
Att 9:	1.0	3.0	-0.204
Att 10:	0.0	5.0	-
Att 11:	1.0	0.0	0.398
Att 12:	0.0	1.0	-
Att 13:	2.0	6.0	-0.408
Att 14:	3.0	2.0	0.528
Att 15:	0.0	0.0	-
Att 16:	4.0	4.0	0.387
Att 17:	2.0	4.0	-5.06
Att 18:	0.0	1.0	-
Att 19:	0.0	0.0	-
Att 20:	0.0	0.0	-
Att 21:	6.0	6.0	0.581
Att 22:	0.0	1.0	-
Att 23:	0.0	0.0	-
Att 24:	0.0	1.0	-
Att 25:	0.0	1.0	-
Att 26:	0.0	1.0	-
Att 27:	2.0	2.0	-3.56
Att 28:	4.0	5.0	0.183
Att 29:	0.0	1.0	-
Att 30:	0.0	0.0	-
Att 31:	5.0	5.0	0.483
Att 32:	0.0	3.0	-
Att 33:	1.0	0.0	0.398
Att 34:	0.0	0.0	-

(Contd...)

Literal	P	N	*Gain (Literal)*
Att 35:	0.0	1.0	-
Att 36:	5.0	2.0	1.25
Att 37:	0.0	2.0	-
Att 38:	0.0	4.0	-
Att 39:	1.0	1.0	-1.78
Att 40:	0.0	0.0	-

Literal with the best gain is Att8 (with gain=1.989). So rule r←8. Now the tuples not satisfying r's body should be removed from P′ U N′ be removed. After removal, the set of P′ and N′ are:

PositiveExamples2 (copy):

{1	8	13	17	21	27	31	36	41}	(1.0)
{1	8	13	17	21	28	31	36	41}	(1.0)
{2	8	14	16	21	27	31	36	41}	(1.0)
{3	8	11	16	21	28	31	36	41}	(1.0)
{2	8	14	16	21	28	31	36	41}	(1.0)

NegativeExamples2 (copy):

Null

Now A′ is changed according to the removal of t. New A′ is

PN Array:

Literal	P′	N′	*Gain (Literal)*
Att 1:	2.0	0.0	-5.06
Att 2:	2.0	0.0	-5.06
Att 3:	1.0	0.0	-0.204
Att 4:	0.0	0.0	-
Att 5:	0.0	0.0	-
Att 6:	0.0	0.0	-
Att 7:	0.0	0.0	-
Att 8:	5.0	0.0	1.989

(Contd...)

Literal	*P′*	*N′*	*Gain (Literal)*
Att 9:	0.0	0.0	-
Att 10:	0.0	0.0	-
Att 11:	1.0	0.0	0.398
Att 12:	0.0	0.0	-
Att 13:	2.0	0.0	-5.06
Att 14:	2.0	0.0	-5.06
Att 15:	0.0	0.0	-
Att 16:	3.0	0.0	0.387
Att 17:	2.0	0.0	-5.06
Att 18:	0.0	0.0	-
Att 19:	0.0	0.0	-
Att 20:	0.0	0.0	-
Att 21:	5.0	0.0	0.581
Att 22:	0.0	0.0	-
Att 23:	0.0	0.0	-
Att 24:	0.0	0.0	-
Att 25:	0.0	0.0	-
Att 26:	0.0	0.0	-
Att 27:	2.0	0.0	-5.06
Att 28:	3.0	0.0	0.083
Att 29:	0.0	0.0	-
Att 30:	0.0	0.0	-
Att 31:	5.0	0.0	1.24
Att 32:	0.0	0.0	-
Att 33:	0.0	0.0	-
Att 34:	0.0	0.0	-
Att 35:	0.0	0.0	-
Att 36:	5.0	0.0	1.25
Att 37:	0.0	0.0	-
Att 38:	0.0	0.0	-
Att 39:	0.0	0.0	-
Att 40:	0.0	0.0	-

Now the literal with the best gain is Att36 (with gain=1.25). So the rule becomes r←8^36. As all the tuples here contain the literal Att36, there will not be any change in the PN Array. Now it is the time to come out of inner While loop. Now R contains r←8^36. Now for all the examples in P satisfying r's body, we change the weights according to the formula t.weight←α*t.weight. Then, the sets P and N will be:

PositiveExamples: P, P′

{1	8	13	17	21	27	31	36	41 }	(0.33)
{1	8	13	17	21	28	31	36	41 }	(0.33)
{2	8	14	16	21	27	31	36	41 }	(0.33)
{3	8	11	16	21	28	31	36	41 }	(0.33)
{2	8	14	16	21	28	31	36	41 }	(0.33)
{3	9	14	16	21	28	33	39	41 }	(1.0)

NegativeExamples: N, N′

{2	9	13	17	21	28	32	38	42 }	(1.0)
{3	10	13	16	21	27	32	36	42 }	(1.0)
{1	9	12	17	21	29	35	37	42 }	(1.0)
{1	7	13	17	21	28	31	36	42 }	(1.0)
{1	10	13	18	24	28	31	38	42 }	(1.0)
{3	9	14	16	21	26	31	38	42 }	(1.0)
{3	10	14	16	21	28	31	37	42 }	(1.0)
{1	10	13	17	25	28	31	39	42 }	(1.0)
{2	10	13	16	22	27	32	38	42 }	(1.0)

Now A is changed accordingly. Now the new A will be

PN Array: A, A′

Literal	*P*	N	*Gain (Literal)*
Att 1:	0.66	4.0	-0.135
Att 2:	0.66	2.0	0.024
Att 3:	1.33	3.0	0.325
Att 4:	0.0	0.0	-
Att 5:	0.0	0.0	-
Att 6:	0.0	0.0	-
Att 7:	0.0	1.0	-
Att 8:	1.65	0.0	0.424
Att 9:	1.0	3.0	-0.204
Att 10:	0.0	5.0	-
Att 11:	0.33	0.0	0.424
Att 12:	0.0	1.0	-
Att 13:	0.66	6.0	-0.408
Att 14:	1.66	2.0	0.528
Att 15:	0.0	0.0	-
Att 16:	1.99	4.0	0.387
Att 17:	0.66	4.0	-5.06
Att 18:	0.0	1.0	-
Att 19:	0.0	0.0	-
Att 20:	0.0	0.0	-
Att 21:	2.65	6.0	0.581
Att 22:	0.0	1.0	-
Att 23:	0.0	0.0	-
Att 24:	0.0	1.0	-
Att 25:	0.0	1.0	-
Att 26:	0.0	1.0	-
Att 27:	0.66	2.0	-3.56
Att 28:	1.99	5.0	0.183
Att 29:	0.0	1.0	-
Att 30:	0.0	0.0	-

(Contd...)

Literal	P	N	Gain (Literal)
Att 31:	1.65	5.0	0.483
Att 32:	0.0	3.0	-
Att 33:	1.0	0.0	0.643
Att 34:	0.0	0.0	-
Att 35:	0.0	1.0	-
Att 36:	1.65	2.0	0.544
Att 37:	0.0	2.0	-
Att 38:	0.0	4.0	-
Att 39:	1.0	1.0	-1.78
Att 40:	0.0	-	0.0

Now the total weight(P)=2.65 which is greater than the factor δ*total weight=1.82. So we repeat the outer While loop with the new Sets and PN Array.

Now the literal with the best gain is Att33. So the rule becomes r←33. Now we need to remove from P′ and N′ all the sets that do not satisfy r. So the new sets become positiveExamples2 (copy):

{3 9 14 16 21 28 33 39 41} (1.0)

negativeExamples2 (copy):

Null

Now we need to change the PN Array accordingly and then repeat the whole process. Lastly, we get the rule set, R:

r←8^36

r←33

r←11

Testing

In the Testing phase, the accuracy of the generated rules is tested using the test dataset. The programme takes the test dataset file and the rules file as input and the accuracy of the generated rules is calculated and displayed. In addition, the information regarding the number of examples that are correctly classified, the number of examples that are misclassified using the generated rules is also displayed.

RESULTS

Preprocessing Phase

The sample data from German dataset includes

A11	6	A34	A43	1169	A65	A75	4	A93	A101	4	A121	67	A143	A152	2	A173	1	A192	A201	1
A12	48	A32	A43	5951	A61	A73	2	A92	A101	2	A121	22	A143	A152	1	A173	1	A191	A201	2
A14	12	A34	A46	2096	A61	A74	2	A93	A101	3	A121	49	A143	A152	1	A172	2	A191	A201	1
A11	42	A32	A42	7882	A61	A74	2	A93	A103	4	A122	45	A143	A153	1	A173	2	A191	A201	1
A11	24	A33	A40	4870	A61	A73	3	A93	A101	4	A124	53	A143	A153	2	A173	2	A191	A201	2
A14	36	A32	A46	9055	A65	A73	2	A93	A101	4	A124	35	A143	A153	1	A172	2	A192	A201	1
A14	24	A32	A42	2835	A63	A75	3	A93	A101	4	A122	53	A143	A152	1	A173	1	A191	A201	1
A12	36	A32	A41	6948	A61	A73	2	A93	A101	2	A123	35	A143	A151	1	A174	1	A192	A201	1
A14	12	A32	A43	3059	A64	A74	2	A91	A101	4	A121	61	A143	A152	1	A172	1	A191	A201	1
A12	30	A34	A40	5234	A61	A71	4	A94	A101	2	A123	28	A143	A152	2	A174	1	A191	A201	2

The preprocessed data for the above 10 records:

A11	A21	A34	A43	A51	A65	A75	A84	A93	A101	A114	A121	A132	A143	A152	A162	A173	A181	A192	A201	1
A12	A22	A32	A43	A52	A61	A73	A82	A92	A101	A112	A121	A131	A143	A152	A161	A173	A181	A191	A201	2
A14	A21	A34	A46	A51	A61	A74	A82	A93	A101	A113	A121	A132	A143	A152	A161	A172	A182	A191	A201	1
A11	A22	A32	A42	A52	A61	A74	A82	A93	A103	A114	A122	A132	A143	A153	A161	A173	A182	A191	A201	1
A11	A21	A33	A40	A52	A61	A73	A83	A93	A101	A114	A124	A132	A143	A153	A162	A173	A182	A191	A201	2
A14	A22	A32	A46	A52	A65	A73	A82	A93	A101	A114	A124	A132	A143	A153	A161	A172	A182	A192	A201	1
A14	A21	A32	A42	A51	A63	A75	A83	A93	A101	A114	A122	A132	A143	A152	A161	A173	A181	A191	A201	1
A12	A22	A32	A41	A52	A61	A73	A82	A93	A101	A112	A123	A132	A143	A151	A161	A174	A181	A192	A201	1
A14	A21	A32	A43	A51	A64	A74	A82	A91	A101	A114	A121	A132	A143	A152	A161	A172	A181	A191	A201	1
A12	A21	A34	A40	A52	A61	A71	A84	A94	A101	A112	A123	A132	A143	A152	A162	A174	A181	A191	A201	2

Generation of Rules

The first 800 examples of 1000 are used for generating the rules and the remaining 200 examples are used for testing the data.

The Rules generated for the 800 records include:

A14 A34 A21 A51

A143 A201 A132 A181 A152 A173 A161 A191

Testing

Test Results for the accuracy of the Generated Rules with the 200 test data include:

Number of Examples: 200

Number of Rules: 2

Number of Records belonging to Class 1:139

Number of Records participated in Classification: 137

System's Accuracy is: 0.9856115107913669

Examples correctly classified with rule1: 119

Examples correctly classified with rule2: 118

Examples misclassified with rule1:0

Examples misclassified with rule2: 6

APPLICATIONS

One of the major applications of this classification is in the area of Text Mining. In Text Mining, we take different types of data that is, Biological data, Scientific data etc. Based on some of the key words that are present in the given text, the given text is classified to belong to one of the categories.

CONCLUSION

A new classification approach, called CPAR, is developed to integrate classification and association rule mining. CPAR represents a new approach towards efficient and high quality classification. It is interesting to further enhance the efficiency and scalability of this approach and compare it with other well-established classification schemes.

REFERENCES

1. Jiawei Han, Micheline Kamber, "*Data Mining Concepts and Techniques*", Morgan Kaufmann Publishers, 2002.
2. http://www.cs.uiuc.edu

15

Spatial Knowledge Management System with Web-based Architecture

M. Nagabhushana Rao*
A. Rama Mohan Reddy**
Dr. P. Govindarajulu***

ABSTRACT

This system uses geo-spatial data and applies spatial collocation rule to mine spatial patterns. These spatial collocation patterns are stored as knowledge database and subsequently provided to Disaster Management teams for rescue and management. A spatial collocation rule for epidemic is proposed. This system uses self-adaptive architecture for adapting different disaster components without developing a separate system for every new disaster from the scratch. This Disaster Management System (DMS) identifies disaster dynamically and adapts the appropriate commodity component in the web. The software architecture proposed is Web-based distributed system, which provides components for Self-adaptation.

* Associate Professor, CSE, S.V. Engineering College, Tirupati, mnraosir@yahoo.com.

** Associate Professor, CSE, S.V. Engineering College, Tirupati,. ramamohansvu@yahoo.com.

*** Professor, <pgovindarajulu@yahoo.com> Department of Computer Science and Engineering, Sri Venkateswara University College of Arts and Science/College of Engineering, Sri Venkateswara University, Tirupati – 517 502. A.P., India.

KEYWORDS: Data mining, web-based architecture, self-adaptive software, mining collocation.

INTRODUCTION

Geography is an integrative discipline and geographic data under analysis often span across multiple domains. The complexity of spatial data and geographic problems, together with intrinsic spatial relationships, constitute an enormous challenge to conventional data mining methods and call for both theoretical research and development of new techniques to assist in deriving information from large and heterogeneous spatial datasets.[1] Due to larger heterogeneity of spatial data, the providers of geographic data specify different models for same spatial objects. *Context Specific Semantics* (CSS) is one of the best approaches suggested which deals with provision of feature space derivations. An Ontological analysis need to be done on the fundamentals of the domain space. Spatial data mining becomes more interesting and important as more spatial data have been accumulated in spatial databases.[2] *Mining spatial co-location patterns* is an important spatial data-mining task with broad applications.

A hypothesis space is formed by all possible configurations of the tools used to detect patterns in a feature space.[3] Characteristically, however, the hypothesis space for a large and high dimensional geographic dataset has an extreme degree of complexity. Complexity is caused by several factors. First, each pattern may involve a different subset of variables from the original data, and the number of such subsets (hereafter subspaces), i.e., possible combinations of attributes, is huge. Second, inside a subspace, potential patterns can be of various forms (e.g., clusters can be various shapes). Third, for a specific Pattern form (e.g., cluster of a specific shape), its parameter space is still huge, i.e., there are many ways to configure its parameters. Fourth, patterns can vary over geographic space, i.e., patterns can be different from region to region.[4]

MINING COLLOCATION PATTERNS FROM SPATIAL DATA

Mining collocation patterns gives the standard of observing the generic characteristics of a given spatial zone with more relevant Boolean features with their *s (support)* and *c (confidence)*.[5]

The work of mining collocation patterns into spatial statistics and combinatorial approaches. The spatial co-location pattern-mining framework presented in the previous works has bias on popular events. It may miss some highly confident but "infrequent" co-location rules by using only *"support"*-based pruning. In a spatial database S, let $F = \{f_1,\ldots,f_k\}$ be a set of *Boolean spatial features*. Let $I = \{i_1,\ldots,i_n\}$ be a set of n instances in the spatial database S, where each instance is a vector consisting of [instance-id, location, spatial features]. ~ *Neighbourhood relation R over pair wise locations in S exists* ~ is assumed. The object of this collocation rule mining is to find rules in the form of $A \cup B$, where A and B are subsets of spatial features. A determines the set of spatial features that form the antecedent part of the rule and B defines the action and its consequential parts the support and the confidence. The rule indicates the coincidence of the spatial collocation rule absorbs the action of the rule in the *"nearby"* regions of the spatial objects that comply with the collocation rule. To capture the concept of the predicate *"nearby"*, the concept of neighbour-set L is a set of instances such that all pair-wise locations in L are neighbours. Neighbourhood relation R may be defined based on Euclidean distance and neighbouring instances are linked by edges. A *collocation pattern* C is a set of spatial features, i.e., $C \subseteq F$. A neighbour-set L is said to be a row instance of collocation pattern C if every feature in C appears in an instance of L, and there exists no proper subset of L does so. We denote all row instances of a collocation pattern C as *rowset(C)*. In other words, *rowset(C)* is the set of neighbour-sets where spatial features in C collocate. The conditional probability is the probability that a neighbour-set in *rowset (A)* is a part of a neighbour-set in *rowset* $(A \cup B)$. Intuitively, the conditional probability p indicates that, whenever we observe the occurrences of the spatial features in A, the probability to find the occurrence of B in a nearby region is p.[6]

History of Epidemic

The history of the epidemics has their own influence in the world history, which has taken many lives together. The epidemic is the result of an infection caused by any of the microbes. The microbe, following the indelible rules of evolution, strives to survive and reproduce, while the host's immune system mounts a warlike defense designed to find, destroy, and eliminate it. An agent that kills its host quickly cannot be expected to survive long enough to reproduce. Thus, excessive virulence is not selected for in evolution. Gels, which can reproduce and be passed from one host to another, are favored.

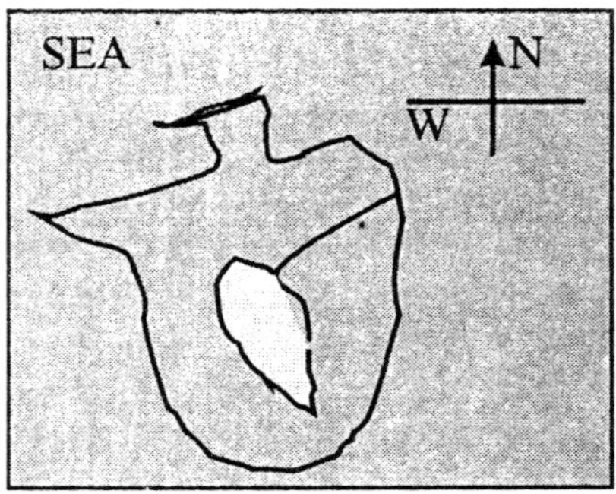

Fig. 15.1: **Imaginary Landscape**

Here we are concentrating on the world's most deadly disease Cholera that was not only an epidemic but also a pandemic, which shook the world with the fear of death. In 1947, nearly 20,000 to 30,000 people infected in Egypt and died. Despite modern medicine, cholera remains an efficient killer. This disease has swept the world in seven major pandemics, including a major outbreak in South America, particularly Peru, as recently as 1991. Cholera (also called Asiatic cholera) is an infectious disease of the gastrointestinal tract caused by the Vibrio cholera bacterium. These bacteria are typically (consume) ingested by drinking water contaminated by improper sanitation or by eating improperly cooked fish, especially shellfish. Symptoms include diarrhoea, abdominal cramps, nausea, vomiting, and dehydration. Death is generally due to the dehydration caused by the illness. When left untreated, cholera generally has a high mortality rate. Treatment is typically an aggressive dehydration regimen usually delivered intravenously, which continues until the diarrhoea ceases.

Example: In the imaginary, fig. 15.1 the landscape describes two important spatial marks, sea and lake. The lichens and mosses at the western zone of the lake afflict the water in the lake, as most of the water is stagnant and covered by marsh. The people utilising the water resources at this zone may be affected by so many kinds of fecal contamination in water and food. The water in the sea is contaminated with the high salts and the crude oil and base products, as the people cannot take the water for the domestic purposes, the climatic changes are affected by the water contents in the shores of sea. People breading their lives at the shores will have the indirect contamination of fecal material in the water and as well as in the form of moisture in the air. As the lake water is supplied into the agriculture lands surrounding in the adjacent zones, there people may be affected indirectly by the virulent characteristics.

Form of Collocation Rule for Epidemics

The term Collocation stands for features located together in different instances. The collocation rules are very useful in detecting the affected areas by finding the symptoms of a disease. The collocation rule *C*, we use is, *C:{cause of epidemic}→{causative agent, infection sources} in the"nearby" region with high probability.*

This typical confident co-location rule involves with both frequent and rare events because although infection is quite common and epidemic is rare the later factor implies the former one strongly. Assuming firstly, the *'b'* as the consequence of feature *'a'* is developed, forms a first level of collocation, which is identified by $a \rightarrow b$, secondly, if the consequence *'c'* from the feature *'b'* is developed, forms a collocation, which is identified by $b \rightarrow c$. As *'b'* already have an antecedent *'a'*, the consolidated version of collocation, $\{a, b\} \rightarrow c$ can be formed. If *'c'* becomes another feature that can lead to the consequence of *'d'*, then the notation wholly represents the cause of *'d'* as $\{a, b, c\} \rightarrow$d. Also implies to $\{a \cup b \cup c\} \rightarrow d$ representation.[7]

IMPLEMENTATION STRATEGY

Software Architecture is an emerging important discipline.[8,9] Dynamically modifiable at any point in system lifecycle can be achieved by knowledge-based approach in which adaptive behaviour is achieved through observations.[4] We are proposing an *architecture-based self-adaptable system* for various types of disaster. In case of epidemic disaster, the losses of related object in spatial are men, money, and animal. A considerable amount of populated area becomes an empty (no men's land) due to the migration of people from epidemic region to other locations. This system is also useful for damage surveys as earthquake, hurricane etc., provided some one could adapt the related software component quickly enough.[10, 11] The collocation rules which are proposed in this paper to predict the future disaster with sufficient assurance that the system would perform as intended. The collocation rules for various types of disasters are being supported as self-adaptable or commodity components. The system support an open adaptive behaviour and adaptation plans that can be introduced during runtime. Adaptation mechanism depends on change, Change management is a controlling component that identifies change, reasoning content for change, specifying and implementing change, preserves system integrity and risks create by runtime modification. Changes can include the addition, removal or replacement of components and connectors.[12] The next section discusses about the Epidemic Disaster Management System (EDMS) for particular epidemic disaster, and then we discuss a common architecture called Disaster Management System (DMS) for all disasters.

Epidemic Disaster Management System (EDMS)

The Epidemic Disaster Management System (EDMS) that we propose here is to manage the epidemic disaster and it is based on the spatial collocation pattern-mining model. This system contains four-components. First component is for collecting information related to epidemics from spatial knowledge using the collocation rule based algorithm. Second component is a conventional database system, which is responsible for populating the tables with the data. The third component is to mine collocation (Data Mining). The fourth component is Database of Spatial knowledge, Fifth component is for knowledge processing, and the sixth component has a report generation component and guidelines for the field staff. The field staff implements the results produced by EDMS as shown in Figs. 15.2 and 15.3.[13, 14]

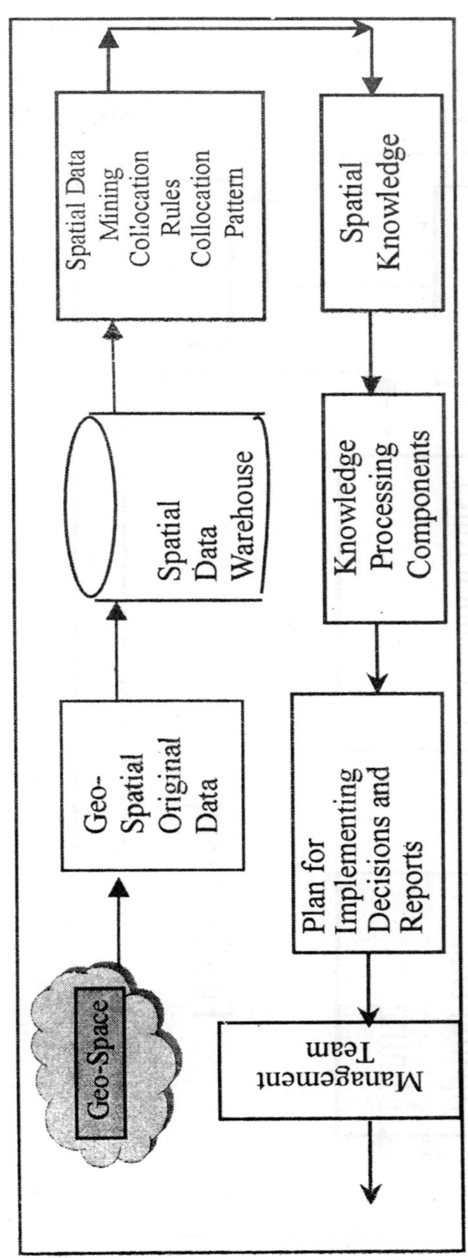

Fig. 15.2: **The Software Components Structure of Epidemic Disaster Management System (EDMS)**

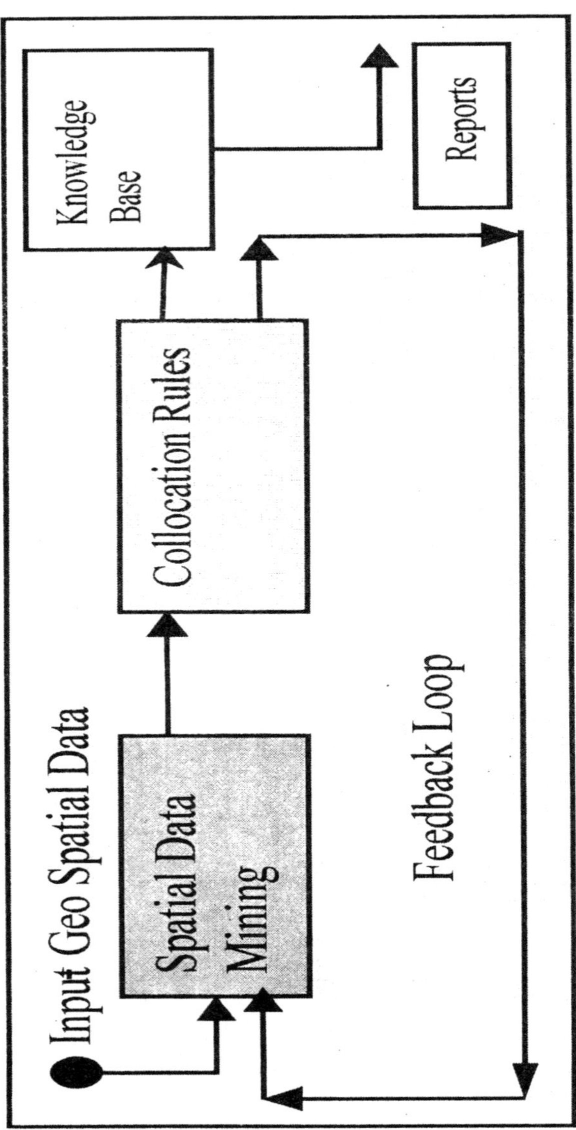

Fig. 15.3: **Simple Pipe and Filter Style Architecture for Implementing the disaster based on spatial collocation pattern mining.**

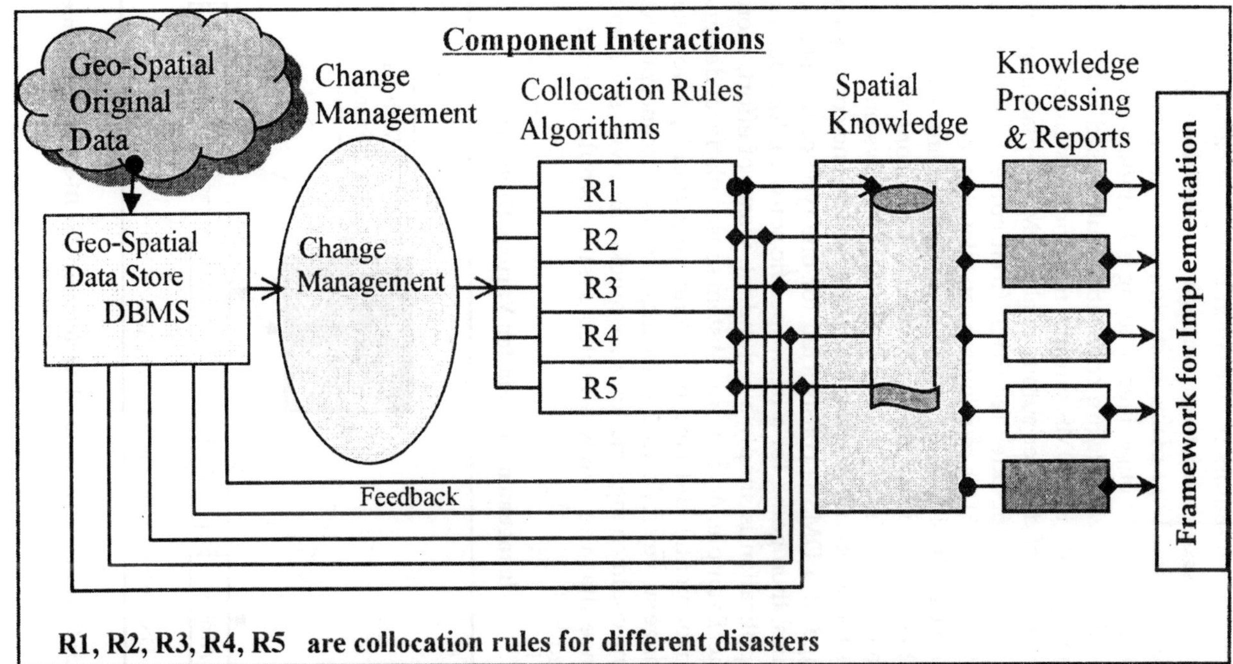

Fig. 15.4: **Proposed Software Architecture for Architecture-based Self-adaptable Disaster**

DISASTER MANAGEMENT SYSTEM (DMS) FOR DISASTERS

The DMS monitors the situation round the clock, identifies the type of disaster, shows the status and generates reports. The DMS autonomously re-plans its strategy, adapts it, and proceed to accomplish their objectives. During adaptation process, the system adapts new software collocation rule based component dynamically insert into DMS, without requiring system restart that detect the type of disaster automatically. DMS re-planning relies on analysis that includes feedback from current performance shown in fig. 15.3.[10] This re-planning can take place autonomously, can involve multiple, distributed, cooperating planners and when major changes are demanded by human approval or guidance can cooperate with mission analysts. Throughout, system integrity requires the assurance of consistency, correctness and coordination of change. If a DMS is constructed for one type of disaster i.e., epidemics, then going for a fresh specific software for each new DMS application is simply a redundant, waste of effort, money and time. Example, An airborne system sensor platform designed for environmental and land use monitoring could prove useful for damage survey following an earthquake or hurricane, provided some one could change the software quickly and with sufficiently assurance that the newly adapted system would perform as intended.[12, 15]

Management System for Various Disasters

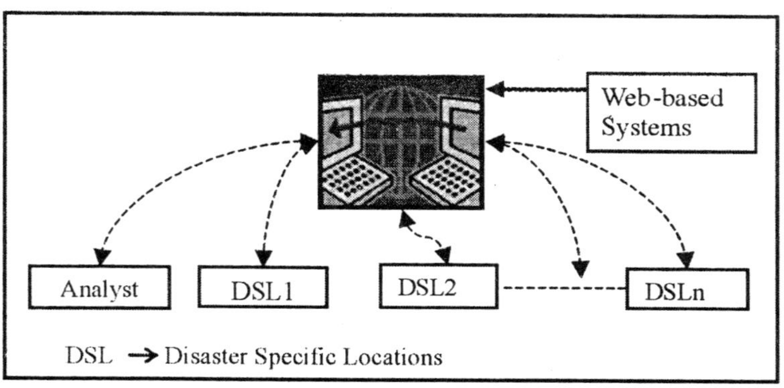

Fig. 15.5: **Overview of Web-based Architecture for Disaster Management**

CONCLUSION

This article examines the fundamental role of software architecture in web-based systems and outlines technologies we have considered for supporting the methodology. Spatial knowledge is extracted by applying one of the data-mining concepts called Collocation rule. This Collocation rule finds the Spatial Knowledge. Such Spatial Knowledge is mined for epidemic as an example. EDMS (Epidemic Disaster Management System) Architecture was proposed to help the disaster management team. A novel disaster management system with web Architecture was proposed.

REFERENCES

1. Alan T Murray, Ingrid McDuffie, John S Western and Patrick Mullins: *"Exploratory Spatial Data Analysis for Examining Urban Crime"*., 2001.

2. Martin Ester, Hans – Peter Kriegel, Jorg Sander., *"Spatial Data Mining: A Database Approach, Institute for Computer Science"*, University of Munich, Proc' of 5th Int. Symposium on Large Spatial Databases (SSD'97).

3. A.G. Ganak and T.A. Corbi, *The Dawning of the Autonomic Computing, Era, IBM Systems J.*, Vol. 42, No. 1, 2003, pp. 5-18.

4. John C. Georgas, *Knowledge Based Architecture Adaptation Management for Self Adaptive Systems*, ACM, 2nd MAY 2005.

5. Knorr and Ng., "Extraction Proximity Patterns by Concept Generalisation", Sponsored by *NSERC* Grants OGPO138055 and STR 0134419. IRIS -2 Grants HMI-5, and IC-5 and a CITR Grant on Distributed Continuous Media File Systems -1996.

6. Koperski and Han, Discovery of Spatial Association Rules in GI Databases, Sponsored by *NSERC* – 0GP003723 from the Natural Sciences and Engineering Research Council of Canada and an NCE/IRIS Research Grant from the Networks of Centres of Excellence of Canada -1995.

7. M.N.Rao [M.Nagabhushana Rao], P Govindarajulu, *Spatial Knowledge for Disaster Identification, ICSCI*, Hyderabad, Volume 2, Jan. 5, 2006.

8. David Garlan and Mary Shaw, *An Introduction to Software Architecture*, CMU-CS-94-166, January 1994.

9. Bass, L., Clements, P., and Kazman, R. (1998) *Software Architecture in Practice., Addison-Wesley*, Massachusetts.

10. Shaw M, and Garlan D., *"Software Architecture: Perspectives on an Emerging Discipline"*, Prentice-Hall (1996).

11. D.E. Perry and A. L. Wolf., Foundations for the Study of Software Architecture, *ACM* SIGSOFT SEN 17:40-52, 1992.

12. Peyman Oreizy, Michael M. Gorlick, Richard N. Taylor, Dennis Heimbigner, Gregory Johnson, Nenad Medvidovic, Alex Quilici, David S. Rosenblum, and Alexander L. Wolf. An Architecture-Based Approach to Self-Adaptive Software, *IEEE Intelligent Systems,* May/June 1999.

13. P Clements et al., *"Documenting Software Architecture: Views and Beyond",* Addison-Wesley, 2003.

14. D. Garlan, R. T. Monroe, and D. Wile, *Acme: Architectural Descriptions of Component-based Systems, Foundations of Component-based Systems,* G.T. Leavens and M. Sitaraman, eds., Cambridge Univ. Press, 2000, pp. 47-68.

15. P. Oriezy et al., "An Architecture-based Approach to Self-Adaptive Software, "*IEEE Intelligent Systems,* Vol. 14, No. 3, 1999, pp. 54-62.

16. David Garlan, Shang-Wen Cheng Huang Bradley Schmerl, Peter, Rainbow: Architecture-based Self-adaptation with Reusable Infrastructure. Carnegie Mellon University. Published by *IEEE Computer Society, 2004 IEEE.*

17. D Garlan, J Kramer, and A Wolf, eds: Proc. 1st *ACM SIGSOFT Workshop on Self-healing Systems (WOSS 02)",* ACM *Press,* 2002.

16

Data Mining Applications in Spectroscopy Using MATLAB

P. Narasimha Reddy*
A. Ashok Kumar**
K. Jagadeswara Reddy*** and
S. Venkatramana Reddy****

ABSTRACT

Data mining is a relatively new field emerging in many disciplines. Generally data mining is most often applied to extraction of useful knowledge from business data. However, it is also useful in all scientific applications where sufficient data is to be collected and analysed to extract specific information. The present paper describes the data mining techniques for the raw data collected from Deep Level Transient Spectroscopy (DLTS), which is an area in Microelectronics to characterise semiconductor devices. Data mining provides a very useful avenue for examining large amounts of data without yielding to the high cost of processing of complete data sets. The neural network method is a capable data mining method that is highly adaptable. The raw data has been analysed using Matlab with some neural network algorithms like adaptive linear filtering, pre and post processing methods, and histograms and are plotted using Matlab. This paper deals with the data collection and analysis to extract certain information in semiconductor materials and devices.

* **Electronics Division, Department of Physics, S.V.University, Tirupati – 517 502.**

INTRODUCTON

Knowledge Discovery in Databases (KDD) or data mining is not a new technique but rather a multi-disciplinary field of research; machine learning; statistics, database terminology, expert systems, and data visualisation all make a contribution[1]. The present paper describes the artificial neural network (ANN) design using Matlab and it's applications in microelectronics.

Neural networks are a highly promising, computational technology due to their capabilities in mathematical modelling of human brain and solving complex problems approachable with traditional methods such as statistical, pattern recognition, and conventional artificial intelligence. The main attractive features of this paradigm are the self-learning capability, non-linear mapping, and parallel processing to achieve the results fast. Neural networks offer a number of potential benefits for application in the field of control engineering particularly for modelling non-linear systems. Self learning approach of the neural network makes the system that does not depends on a prior knowledge and can approximate well for any arbitrary non-linear continuous function[2].

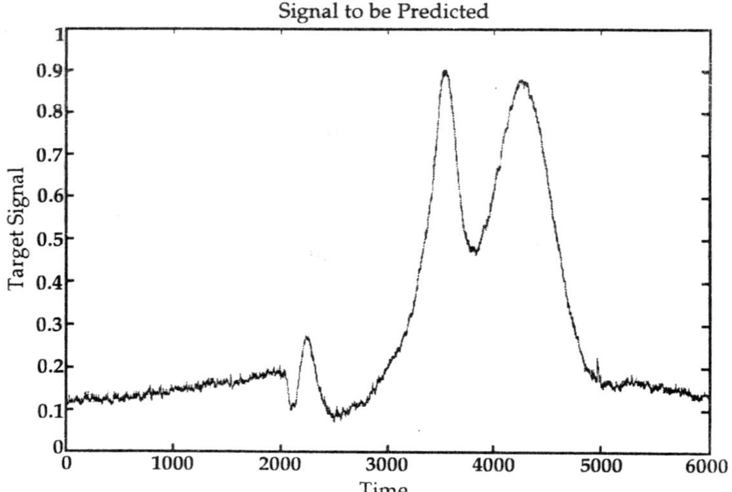

Fig. 16.1: **The DLTS Spectrum**

Deep Level Transient Spectroscopy has been widely used to characterise the semiconductor materials[3]. The semiconductor junction capacitance has been measured with change in sample temperature and is plotted in Matlab which is shown in fig. 16.1. This data set has been analysed using Matlab with some artificial neural network algorithms like Adaptive Linear Prediction, Pre and post processing methods and histograms to find which method is best suited for DLTS data analysis.

ADAPTIVE LINEAR PREDICTION

The DLTS data is adaptively filtered by using this method in ANN. In this method, the linear neuron is adaptively trained to predict the next value in a signal and is able to adapt the changes in the signal. NEWLIN is a function in the neural network toolbox of Matlab was used to generate a linear network with a learning rate of 0.1, and five delays in the input[4]. The resulting network will predict the next value of the target signal using the last five values. ADAPT in neural network toolbox of Matlab had been used to simulate the adaptive linear neurons[5]. It takes the initial network, an input signal (DLTS spectrum), and a target signal, and filters the signal adaptively. The output signal of the network and the error signal obtained with the new network are shown in Fig. 16.2 and fig. 16.3 respectively.

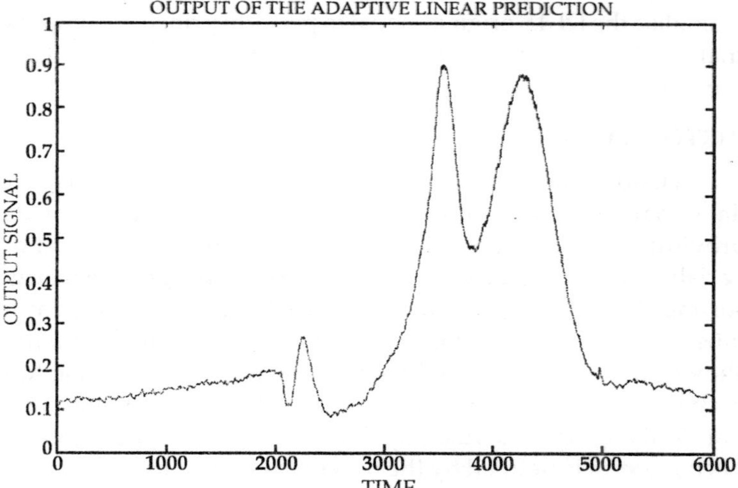

Fig. 16.2: **Output of the Adaptive Linear Prediction**

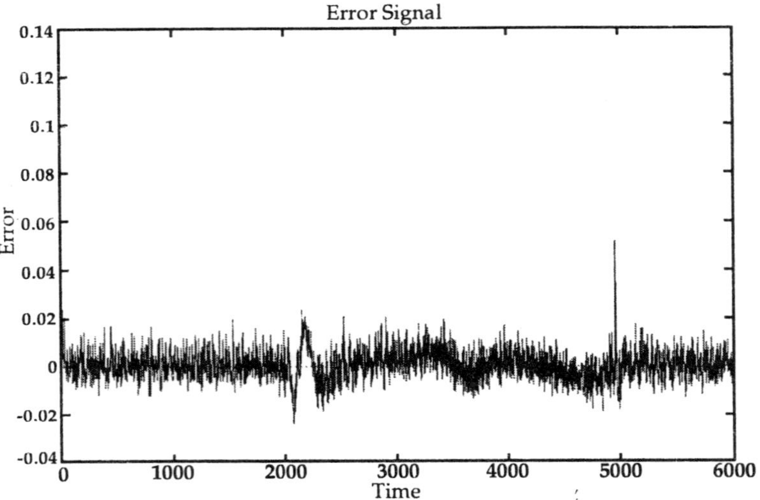

Fig. 16.3: **Error Signal**

PRE AND POST PROCESSING METHODS

The pre and post processing methods can be used to normalise the signals and they can also be used to determine mean and standard deviation of the signals. PRESTD and POSTSTD functions in the neural network tool box have been used to normalise the DLTS original signal to perform principle component analysis. Mean of the original signal from these functions is 0.27717 and standard deviation is 0.22767.

HISTOGRAMS

Histograms are one of the most used tools in exploratory data analysis. They present a graphical representation of data, providing useful information about the distribution of a random variable. The basic algorithm to construct histogram consists of sorting the values of the random variable and places them into bins. The histogram of the original signal plotted in the Matlab is shown in the fig.16.4. The height of the bar drawn on the top of each bin is proportional to the number of observed values in that bin. A histogram is defined by a set of non-overlapping intervals. Each interval is defined by the boundaries and a frequency count.

Discretisation of continuous attributes is an important task for certain types of machine learning algorithms. Bayesian approaches, for instance, require assumptions about data distribution. Decision Trees require sorting operations to deal with continuous attributes, which largely increase learning times.

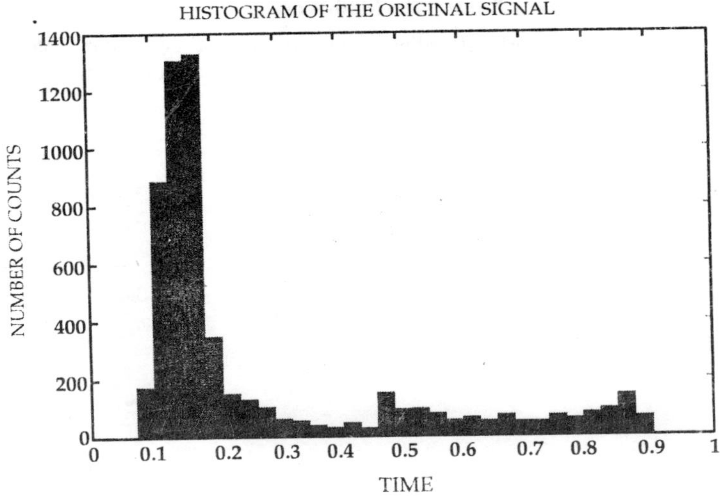

Fig. 16.4: **Histogram**

CONCLUSION

Matlab is very efficient and simple software to implement different algorithms that not only relates to signal processing but also applicable to neural networks. Different data mining techniques can be used with the flexible inbuilt data mining toolboxes in Matlab. Adaptive linear prediction technique can be useful to recover the original signal information in the noisy environments. Pre and post processing techniques are used in the area of principal component analysis of signals. Histogram algorithms have very important applications in the area of Bayesian approaches and decision Trees.

REFERENCES

1. *"Data Mining"*, Pieter Adriaans and Dolf Zantinge, Addison Wesley Longman Singapore Pte. Ltd. (1999).

2. *"Neural Network Fundamentals with Graphs, Algorithms, and Applications"*, N. K. Bose and P. Liang, McGraw-Hill Inc. (1996).

3. *"Semiconductor Material and Device Characterisation"*, D.K. Schroder, Wiley, New York (1990).

4. *"Matlab User's Guide"*, The MathWorks Inc., Version 6.5.1 (2004).

5. *"Neural Networks Algorithms, Applications, and Programming Techniques"*, James A. Freeman and David M. Skapura, Pearson Education, Singapore Pte. Ltd. (2001).

17

Role of Cryptography for Preserving Privacy in Data Mining

P. Vasudeva Reddy*
G. Anjan Babu*
B. Nagarajasri*
Prof. M. Padmavathamma*

ABSTRACT

Primary Considerations often constraing data mining projects. This paper addresses to demonstrate basic ideas from a large body of cryptographic research on secure distributed computation and their applications to data mining. Research in secure distributed computation, which was done as part of a larger body of research in the theory of cryptography, has achieved remarkable results. It was shown that non-trusting parties can jointly compute functions of their different inputs while ensuring that no party learns anything but the defined output of the function. These results were shown using generic constructions that can be applied to any function that has an efficient representation as a circuit. We describe these results, discuss their efficiency, and demonstrate their relevance to privacy preserving computation of data mining algorithms.

INTRODUCTION

Defining Privacy

The common definition of privacy in the cryptographic community limits the information that is leaked by the distributed

* Department of Computer Science, S.V. University, Tirupati.

computation to be the information that can be learned from the designated output of the computation. The cryptographic community aims at designing protocols that do not reveal any information except for their designated output, and in many case such protocols can in fact be efficiency constructed.

As an example for the definition of privacy, consider the following problem (described in.[4] Alice and Bob are both teaching the same class, and each of them suspects that one specific student is cheating. None of them is completely sure, though, about the identity of the cheater, and they would therefore like to compare the names of their two suspects. Since they care about their students privacy they wish that, (1) if they both have the same suspect, then they should learn his or her name, but (2) if they have different suspects then they should learn nothing beyond that fact. They therefore have inputs x and y, and wish to compute f (x, y) which is defined as 1 if x = y and 0 otherwise. (Note that if f(x, y) = 0 then each party does learn some information, namely that the other party's suspect is different that his/hers, but this is inevitable).

Adversarial Behaviour

Privacy preserving protocols are designed in order to preserve privacy even in the presence of adversarial participants that attempt to gather information about the inputs of their peers. There are, however, different levels of adversarial behaviour. Cryptographic research typically considers two types of adversaries namely a semi honest adversary and a malicious adversary.

It is of course easier to design a solution that is secure against semi-honest adversaries, than it is to design a solution for malicious adversaries. A common approach is therefore to first design a secure protocol for the semi-honest case, and then transform it into a protocol that is secure against malicious adversaries. This transformation can be done by requiring each party to use zero-knowledge prools to prove that each step that it is taking follows the specification of the protocol.

CRYPTOGRAPHIC RESULTS: SECURE FUNCTION EVALUATION

We describe here results of a body of cryptographic research that shows how separate parties can jointly compute any function of their inputs, without revealing any other information.

The Main Building Block-oblivious Transfer

Oblivious transfer is a basic protocol that is the main building block of secure computation. The notion of 1-out-2 oblivious transfer was suggested by Even, Goldreich and Lempel.[3] The protocol involves two parties, the sender and the receiver. The sender's input is a pair (x_0, x_1) and the receiver's input is a bit $\sigma \in \{0,1\}$. At the end of the protocol the receiver learns x_σ (and nothing else) and the sender learns nothing. In other words, if we use the notation (input_A, input_B) $\rightarrow$ (λ, x_σ), where λ is the empty output.

In the case of semi-honest adversaries, there exist simple and efficient protocols for oblivious transfer.[3, 5] One straightforward approach is for the receiver to generate two random public keys, a key P_σ whose decryption key he knows, and a key $P_{1-\sigma}$whose decryption key he does not know. The receiver then sends these two keys to the sender, who encrypts x_0 with the key P_0 and encrypts x_1 with the key P_1, and sends the two results to the receiver. The receiver can then decrypt x_σ but not $x_{1-\sigma}$. It is to show that the sender does not learn anything about σ. If we consider also malicious adversaries, then this oblivious transfer protocol must ensure that the receiver chooses the public keys appropriately. This can be done using zero-knowledge proofs that are used by the receiver to prove that he choose the keys correctly. Fortunately, there are very efficient proofs for this case, see e.g. [9]

Oblivious Polynomial Evaluation

The problem of "Oblivious Polynomial Evaluation" (OPE) involves a sender and a receiver. The sender's input is polynomial Q of degree *k* over some finite field F and the receiver's input is an element z$\in$ (the degree k of Q is public). The protocol is such that the receiver obtains Q(z) without learning anything else about the polynomial Q, and the sender learns nothing. That is, the problem considered is the private computation of the function $(Q,z) \rightarrow (\lambda,Q(z))$. This problem was introduced in.[8]

The Two Party Case

In[11], Yao presented a constant-round protocol for privately computing any probabilistic polynomial-time function. Denote the parties as Allice (A) and Bob (B), and denote their respective inputs by *x and y*. Let *f* be the function that they wish to compute. The protocol is based on expressing *f* as a combinatorial circuit with gates defined over some fixed base B. For example, B can include all the functions g: {0,1} x {0,1} $\rightarrow$ {0,1}. The bits of the input are entered into input wires and are propagated through the gates.

Encoding the Circuit Loosely speaking, Yao's protocol works by having one of the parties. First generate an "encrypted" or "garbled" circuit computing *f* and send its representation to Bob. The encrypted circuit is generated in the following way: First, Alice "hardwires" her input into the circuit, generating a circuit computing *f(x,.)*. She then assigns to each wire *i* of the circuit two random ("garbled") values W_i^0, W_i^1 corresponding to values 0 and 1 of the wire.

Consider a gate g which computes the value of the wire k as a function of wires *i* and *j*. Alice prepares a table T_g that encrypts the garbled value of the output wire using the output of pseudorandom function F keyed the garbled values of the input wires *i, j*. The table therefore has four entries, one entry for every combination of input values. The table enables computation of the garbled output of g, from the garbled inputs to g.

The representation of the circuit includes the wiring of the original circuit. The tables T_g, and tables that translate the garbled values of the output wires of the circuit to actual 0/1 values. In this form the representation reveals nothing but the wiring of the circuit, and therefore Bob learns nothing from this stage.

Encoding Bob's Input: Given these tables and the garbled values input wires of the circuit, Bob is able to compute the garbled values of its output wires and then translate them to actual values. In order for Bob to obtain the garbled values of the input wires, translate them to actual values. In order for Bob to obtain the garbled values of the input wires, Alice and Bob engage, for each input wire, in a 1-out-of-2 oblivious transfer. In this protocol Alice is the sender, and her inputs are the two garbled values of this wire, and Bob is the receiver, and his input is his input bit. As a result of the oblivious transfer protocol Bob learns the garbled value of his input bit and nothing about the garbled value of the other bit, and Alice learns nothing.

Computing the Circuit: At the end of the oblivious transfer stage Bob has sufficient information to compute the output of the circuit by his own. After computing f(x,y), he can send this value to Alice if she requires it.

To show that the protocol is secure it should be proved that the parties learn nothing that cannot be computed based on the input and output only. The main observation regarding the security of each gate is that every masking value. (e.g. output of the pseudo-random function F) is used only once, and that the pseudo-randomness of F ensures that without knowledge of the correct keys, i.e. garbled values of input wires, its output values look random. Therefore knowledge of one garbled value of each of the input wires discloses only a single garbled output value of the gate; while Bob cannot distinguish the other garbled value from random.

As for the security of the complete circuit the oblivious transfer protocol ensures that Bob learns only a single garbled value for each input wire, and Alice does not learn which value it was inductively, Bob can compute only a single garbled output value of each gate, and in particular of the circuit. The method in which the tables were constructed hides the values of intermediate results (i.e. of gates inside the circuit).

The Multi-party Case

In the multi-party scenario, there are protocols that enable the parties to compute any joint function of their inputs without revealing any other information about the inputs. That is, compute the function while attaining the same privacy as in the ideal mode. This was shown to be possible function while attaining the same privacy as in the ideal mode. This was shown to be possible in principle by Goldreich, Micali and Wigderson[6], Ben-Or, Goldwasser and Wigderson[1], and by Chaum, Crepau and

Damgard[2], for different scenarios. These constructions, too, are based on representing the computed function as a circuit and evaluating it. The constructions do have, however, some additional drawbacks, compared to the two-party case:

- The computation and communication overhead of the protocol is linear in the size of the circuit, and the number of communication rounds depends on the depth of the circuit1, unlike the two-party case where the number of rounds is constant. Furthermore, the protocol that is run for every gate of the circuit is more complex than the computation of a gate in the two-party case, especially in the malicious party scenario, and requires public-key operations;
- The multi-party protocols require each pair of parties to exchange messages (in order to compute each gate of the circuit). The required communication graph is, therefore, a complete graph, whereas a sparse communication graph could have been sufficient if no security was required. In many applications, for example applications run between a web server and many clients, it is impossible to require all pairs of parties to communicate.

These drawbacks prevent most applications from using the generic solutions for secure distributed computation.

THE TWO-PARTY CASE: COMPUTING ID3

Yao's two-party protocol is pretty efficient, as long as the size of the inputs, and the size of the circuit computing the function, are reasonable. In fact, for many functions the efficiency of Yao's generic protocol is comparable to that of protocols that are targeted for computing the specific function. We describe here a distributed scenario of computing the ID3 algorithm, where Yao's protocol is obviously too costly. On the other hand, a specialized protocol can be designed for computing this algorithm, which uses Yao's protocol as a primitive.

Classification Decision Trees and ID3: Classification is a classic problem in data mining, which is commonly solved using decision trees. ID3 is a basic algorithm for constructing decision trees. The input to a classification problem is a structured database comprised of attribute – value pairs. Each row of the database is a transaction and each column is an attribute taking on different values (for example, each row could represent a patient, and each column a different symptom). One of the attributes in the database in designated as the class attribute (e.g., it could denote whether the patient has a certain disease). The goal is to use the database in order to predict the class of a new transaction by viewing only the non-class attributes.

A decision tree is a rooted tree containing nodes and edges. Each internal node is a test node and corresponds to an attribute. The edges leaving a node correspond to the possible values taken on by that attribute. The elves of the tree contain the expected class value for transaction matching the path from the root to that leaf. Given a decision tree, one can predict the class of a new transaction by traversing the nodes from the root down, following the edges that correspond to the attribute values of the transaction. The value of the leaf is the expected class value of the new transaction.

The ID3 algorithm is used to design a design a decision tree based on a given database. The tree is constructed top-down in a recursive fashion. At the root, each attribute is tested to determine how Well it alone classifies the transactions. The "best" attribute (to be defined below) is then chosen and the remaining transactions are partitioned by it. ID3 is then recursively called on each partition.

Privacy Preserving Distributed Computation of ID3: We are interested in a scenario involving two parties, each one of them holding a database of different transactions, where all the transactions have the same set of attributes (this scenario is also denoted as a "horizontally partitioned" database). The parties wish to compute a decision tree by applying the ID3 algorithm to the union of their databases. An efficient privacy preserving protocol for this problem was described in.[7]

Computing ID3: A key observation is that each node of the tree can be computed separately, with the output made public, before continuing to the next node. In general, private protocols have the property that intermediate values remain hidden.

However, in the case of ID3 some of these intermediate values (specifically, the assignments of attributes to nodes) are actually part of the output and may therefore be revealed. Once the attribute of a given node has been found, both parties can separately partition their remaining transactions accordingly for the coming recursive calls. This means that private distributed ID3 can be reduced to privately finding the attribute with the highest information gain. (This is a slightly simplified argument as the other steps of ID3 must also be carefully dealt with. However, the main issues arise within this step.)

Computing Information Gains: Let t be a set of transactions. The exact test for determining the best attribute is defined as follows. Let C_1, ...,cl be the class-attribute values and let $t(c_i)$ denote the set of transactions with class c_i. Then the information needed to identify the class of a transaction in t is the entropy, given by $H_c(T)$ =

$$\sum_{i=1}^{l} -\frac{|T(c_i)|}{|T|}\log\frac{|T(c_i)|}{|T|}.$$

Let C be the class attribute and A be some non-class attribute. We wish to quality the information needed to identify the class of transaction in T given that the value of A has been obtained. Let A obtain values a1....,am and let T(aj) be the transactions obtaining value aj for A. Then, the conditional information of T given A

equal Hc(T/A) = $\sum_{j=11}^{m} -\frac{|T(a_i)|}{|T|} H_c(T(a_j))$.

Now, for each attribute A the information – gain is defined as Gain (A) = Hc(T) – Hc(T\A). the attribute A which has the maximum gain (or equivalently minimum Hc(T\A) value) over all attributes is then chosen.

Notice that the algorithm needs only to fined the name of the attribute A which minimises Hc(T\A); the actual value is irrelevant. Therefore, the coefficient $1/|T|$ can be ignored, and natural logarithms can be used instead of logarithms to base 2. Let TA and TB be the transactions in Alice's and Bob's databases, respectively. The values and $\left|T_A(a_j)\right|$ and $\left|T_A(a_j,c_i)\right|$ which are a function of the first database alone, can be computed by Alice independently, and a similar argument holds for Bob. Therefore the value Hc (T\A) can be written as a sum of expressions of the form $\vartheta_A + \vartheta_B$. In $\vartheta_A + \vartheta_B$, where ϑ_A is known to Alice and ϑ_B = $\left(\left|T_B(a_j)\right|\right)$ VB is known to Bob (e.g., $\vartheta_A = \left|T_A(a_j)\right|$, $\vartheta_B = \left(\left|T_B(a_j)\right|\right)$.

The protocol computes the information gain of every attribute, such that at the end of the computation Alice and Bob hold two random shares, whose sum is equal to the information gain. None of the parties learns the information gains themselves, but they can later compare the sum of the different shares and find the attribute with the maximum gain. The main technical component of the protocol is a private computation of x In x using a protocol that receives private inputs xA and xB such that XAXB = X and outputs random shares of an approximation of X in X. The shares are elements of a field F where it holds that x In x < $|F|$.

The x ln x protocol The protocol first computers random shares of ln x. The first step is computing random shares of the values n and ε such that $x=2^n(1+\varepsilon)$ and $-1/2 \leq \varepsilon \leq$ ½. Note that ln x = nln2+ln(1+ε). This computation is done using Yao's protocol, and is efficient since the circuit required for computing this function is very small (it basically sums the shares and checks for the location of the most significant bit of x).

The shares of the value e that are output from the previous step are used to privately compute the Taylor series for ln(1+ε), using the equation $\ln(1+\varepsilon) = \sum_{i=1}^{\infty} \frac{(-1)^{i-1} \varepsilon^i}{i} = \varepsilon - \frac{\varepsilon^2}{2} + \frac{\varepsilon^3}{3} - \frac{\varepsilon^4}{4} + \ldots\ldots$ This computation is done up to the power k that makes the approximation error sufficiently small. The parties therefore need to compute a polynomial of degree k and can do this using the oblivious polynomial evaluation primitive. All computations are done in F. In order to avoid dealing with fractions, the parties compute the results multiplied by the least common multiple of

1,..., k and therefore all intermediate values are integers (this means that the parties actually compute lcm (1,...,k) x ln x, but this does not matter since they are only interested in comparing the entropies).

After obtaining shares of ln x, the parties compute shares of x ln x using the oblivious polynomial evaluation primitive. To see how this is done, denote the shares of ln x as l_A and l_B. Therefore, $x ln x=(x_A+x_B)(l_A+l_B)=x_Al_A+x_Al_B+x_Bl_B$. Alice can define two linear polynomials $P_1(y) = x_Ay+r_1$ and $P_2(y)=l_Ay+r_2$, where r_1, r_2 are random. Bob runs oblivious polynomial evaluation protocols to obtain $P_1(l_B)$ and $P_2(x_B)$, and sets his share to be $P_1(l_B)+P_2(x_B) + x_Bl_B$. Alice sets her share to be $x_Al_A - r_1-r_2$.

Finding the best attribute Given shares for the different x ln x values, the parties should find the attribute with the best information gain. Each party first sums his or her shares that correspond to the same entropy value, in order to obtain a share of this entropy value. The parties then use Yao's protocol to compute the different information gain values and compare them, and output the index of the best attribute. Note that this is a simple circuit that has to perform one addition per attribute and then compare the results. Once the best attribute is found, the parties partition their databases according to the values of this attribute and run the algorithm recursively.

THE MULTI-PARTY CASE

The Multi-Party case involves three or more parties that wish to compute some function of their inputs without leakage any unnecessary information. To illustrate this point we consider the case of running a secure computation for computing the result of an auction, where there is an obvious motivation for privacy and security, and also certain restrictions on the operation of the parties. The auction application, discussed in[10], is not related to data mining, but it does exemplify some of he difficulties of the multi-party case.

The auction scenario is that of a "sealed bid" auction, and consists of an auctioneer and many bidders. Each bidder submits a single secret bid (i.e. the bid is sealed in an envelope). There is a known decision rule, whose inputs are the submitted bids, and whose output is the identity of the winning bidder and the amount that this bidder has to pay. For example, in an "English auction" the winning bidder is the bidder who offered the highest bid, and he has to pay the amount of his bid. In the second-price, or Vickrey, type of auction, the winner is the highest bidder and he has to pay the amount of the second highest bid. Bidding is allowed until some point in time, and at that stage the decision rule is applied to the submitted bids.

In the physical world bids are submitted in sealed envelopes that are kept secure until the end of the bidding period, and are then opened by the auctioneer. In the virtual world we would like to keep the bids secret during the bidding period, but we could also attempt to hide all information afterwards, except for the identity of the winning party and the amount he has to pay. For example, in the case of a Vickrey auction the auctioneer's output could be limited to the identity of the identity bidder and the value of the second highest bid. This is more privacy than can be achieved in the physical world.

The difficulty of applying the generic construction: A natural approach for achieving privacy is to run a secure multi-party construction involving the auctioneer and all bidders, where the inputs are the respective bids of the parties, and the output is the result of the auction. This approach seems promising in the auction scenario since the circuit that computes the result of the auction is typically small, as it involves only comparisons.

Applying the two-party solution in the multiparty scenario: Privacy preserving multiparty computation can be reduced to the two party case. Namely, it is possible to use the generic to party protocol to compute a function in the multiparty scenario. The protocol is run with the two special parties taking the roles of the two parties in the two-party case. The issuer prepares a circuit for computing the function. This circuit might have many inputs of different parties – for example, the inputs might be the bids of the different bidders. The issuer encodes the circuit as in the two-party case, by choosing garbled values for the wires and preparing tables for every gate. The other special party (the auctioneer) is responsible for computing the result of the circuit. In order to do that it should receive the tables that were prepared by the issuer, and one garbled value for every input wire, namely the value that corresponds to the input bit associated with that wire. Once it receives the garbled values of all input wires it can compute the output of the circuit.

In order to do that the parties run a protocol called "proxy oblivious transfer", which was introduced in.[10] This protocol is similar to oblivious transfer, but involves three parties; the chooser (which is the party who knows the value of the input wire), the sender (which is the issuer), and the receiver (the auctioneer). The input of the chooser is a bit σ, and the input of the sender consists of two items x_0,x_1. At the end of the protocol the receiver should learn x_0, and no information about $x_1 = \sigma$ or σ, and the other parties should learn nothing.

Given the proxy oblivious transfer protocol, the rest of the implementation is simple. Each bidder engages in a proxy oblivious transfer for each of its input bits. The input of the bidder to this protocol is the value of the input bit. The sender is the issuer, and its two inputs are the two garbled values that are associated with the corresponding input wire. The receiver is the auctioneer, and it learns the garbled value that corresponds to the input bit. This protocol consists of a single message that is sent from the bidder to the auctioneer, and then a round of communication between the auctioneer and the issuer. The auctioneer can actually wait until it receives messages from all the bidders effort it runs the round of communication with the issuer in parallel for all input bits. The main computational overhead of the protocol is incurred by the proxy oblivious transfers, and is the same as in the two – party case – a proxy oblivious transfer must be executed for every input wire. Estimates in[10] show that this method can be used to securely implement Vickrey auctions that involve hundreds of bidders.

CONCLUSION

In the paper we demonstrate basic ideas form a large body of cryptographic research on secure distributed computation, and their applications to data mining. We described in brief the definitions of security, and the generic constructions for the two-party and multi-party scenarios. We showed that it is easier to design an implementation based on the constructions for the two-party case than it is to design one based on the multi-party constructions.

REFERENCES

1. M. Ben-Or, s.Goldwasser and A.Wigderson, Completeness Theorems for Non-cryptographic Fault Tolerant Distributed Computation, *Proceedings of the 20th Annual Symposium on the Theory of Computing (STOC)*, ACM, 1988, pp. 1-9.

2. D.Chaum, C.Crepeau and I.Damgard, Multiparty Unconditionally Secure Protocols, *Proceedings of the 20th Annual Symposium on the Theorm of Computing (STOC)*, ACM, 1988, pp. 11-19.

3. S.Even, O.Goldreich and A.Lempel, A. *Randomised Protocol for Signing Contracts, Communications of the ACM*, Vol. 28, 1985, pp. 637-647.

4. R. Fagin, M. Naor and P.Winkler, *Comparing Information Without Leaking It, Communications of the ACM*, 39(5), pp. 77-85, 1996.

5. O.Goldreich, *Secure Multi-Party Computation*, Manuscript, 2002.

6. O.Goldreich S. Micali and A. Wigderson, How to Play any Mental Game — A Completeness Theorem for Protocols with Honest Majority, *Proceedings of the 19th Annual Symposium on the Theory of Computing (STOC)*, ACM, 1987, pp. 218-229.

7. Y. Lindell and B. Pinkas, *Privacy Preserving Data Mining, Journal of Cryptology*, Vol. 15, No. 3, pp. 177-206, 2002.

8. M. Naor and B. Pinkas, Oblivious Transfer and Polymonial Evaluation, *Proceeding of the 31st Annual Symposium on the Theory of Computing (STOC)*, ACM, 1999, pp. 245-254.

9. M. Naor and B. Pinkas, Efficient Oblivious Transfer Protocols, *Proceedings of 12th SIAM Symposium on Discrete Algorithms (SODA)*. January 7-9 2001, Washington DC, pp. 448-457.

10. M. Naor, B. Pinkas and R. Summer, *Privacy Preserving Auctions and Mechanism Design*, Proc. Of the 1st ACM Conference on Electronic Commerce, November 1999.

11. A.C. Yao, How to Generate and Exchange Secrets, *Proceedings of 27th Symposium on Foundations of Computer Science (FOCS)*, IEEE, 1986, pp. 162-167.

18

Applications of Data Mining in Libraries

Dr. D. Rajeswari*

Data Mining automatically and exhaustively explores large datasets, consequently uncovering otherwise hidden relationships among data. Data Mining refers to the extraction or "Mining" knowledge from large amount of data or data warehouse. An area of research that has been a recent surge in commercial development is data mining or knowledge discovery in databases. A number of terms have been used in place of data mining, including information harvesting, data archaeology, knowledge mining, and knowledge extraction. The knowledge is stored in data warehouse, which is the central store house of data that has been extracted from operational data over a time in a separate database.

There are four stages of the virtuous cycle of data mining:

- Identify the problem;
- Use data mining technique to transform the data into actionable information;
- Act on the Information;
- Measures the result.

The first and third stages raise mainly business issues. For data mining to be successful, these business issues must, of course properly addressed. There are two basic style of data mining:

* Associate Professor, Dept. of Library & Information Science, Sri Padmavathi Mahila Visvavidyalam, Tirupati.

(i) Hypothesis Testing;

(ii) Knowledge Discovery.

Hypothesis testing is what scientists and statisticians spend their lines doing. Testing the validity of a hypothesis is done by analysing data that may simply be collected by observation or generated through an experiment, such as test mailing.

The hypothesis method has several steps:

- Generate good ideas (hypothesis)
- Determine what data would allow these hypotheses to be tested
- Locate the data
- Prepare the data for analysis
- Build computer model based on the data
- Evaluates computers models to confirm or reject hypothesis

Knowledge Discovery can be either directed or undirected. Directed knowledge discovery is goal oriented. The directed knowledge discovery method has several steps:

- Identify sources of pre-classified data
- Prepare data for analysis
- Build and train the computer model
- Evaluate the computer model
- Apply the computer model to the new data

In undirected knowledge discovery the data mining tool is simply let loose on the data in the hope that it will discover meaningful structure. The undirected knowledge discovery method has several steps:

- Identify source of data
- Prepare data for analysis
- Build and train a computer model
- Evaluate the computer model
- Apply the computer model to the new data

- Identify potential targets for directed knowledge discovery
- Generate new hypotheses to test

University Libraries also have the good collection of information and din e-library there are organised collection of information which serves a rich resource for its user communities. Information resources appears in the library collection, users locate required information using catalog search system and bibliographic databases. The vast data stored in the databases of traditional and digital libraries represent the behavioural patterns of two important constituencies. Library staff and library users.

In the case of library staff mining available acquisitions and bibliographic data could provide important clue to understanding and enhancing the effectiveness of the library's own internal functions. Mining user data for knowledge about what information library users are seeking, whether they find what they need, and whether their questions are answered these kinds of information can have strategic utility within the large organisation in which the library is situated.

APPLICATION OF DATA MINING TO LIBRARIES

Now we are going to explore how data mining can be useful in the field of Library and Information Science. As per the fifth law of Library Science "Library is a Growing Organisation", so the volume of the library data is also growing with an enormous rate. For efficiently and effectively doing the library administration and extending library services the need of library automation and e-library occur. But simply automating the library or developing an e-library is not the only solution unless and until we are not able to explore the hidden information from the large amount of database. This can be done by applying the data mining in the library data. By applying data mining we can develop a computer programme that will replace the manual classification with automatic classification of library contents.

In a library setting one or more of the following patterns to be followed:

- Classification mimics library cataloging procedures by grouping structured and unstructured data according to certain criteria such as source (govt. bodies), document type (eg.maps), language, subject or a number of other criteria. Clustering is similar to classification clustering and classification are often used as a starting point for exploring further relationships in data.

- Link Analysis assumes that higher quality or otherwise more desirable documents will generally be linked to more frequently than other documents, and that links in a document reveal some thing about the content of a document. Link analysis can place frequently linked to documents at the top of a list or identify documents that are associated with each other.
- Sequence Analysis uses statistical analysis to identify unlinked documents that users are likely to want to read together. It examine the paths that users follow when searching for information and can help identify which documents users are likely to want together.

Next acquisition personnel obtain the information resources specified from this needs assessment. Once the library obtains requested new resources, cataloguing personnel create a catalogue record for the new resource. The circulation department then makes the resources available to end-users after an information resources appears in the library collection, users locate the required sources using catalogue search and bibliographic databases. In order to locate works in the library, users rely on the OPAC. Libraries often examine users comments and surveys to assess user satisfaction with these tools. Therefore, librarians may wish to examine the artifacts of those searches for problem areas instead of replacing on users comments and surveys in order to improve the user experience. When upgrading or changing library system interfaces, librarians can explore these patterns of common mistakes in order to make informed decisions about system improvement.

Data mining has been used successfully for several years in the scientific and business communities for tracking behaviour of individuals and groups, processing medical information, and a number of other applications and its use in libraries is limited.

ADVANTAGES

Data Mining offers two major advantages to libraries:

1. Data Mining can provide faster and more thorough access to materials than that provided by mammal cataloging;
2. It can be used by employees or users with basic computer and analytical skills so people can more easily find what they need without the assistance of highly skilled staff.

PROBLEMS

Data Mining also has some drawbacks as data mining tools are not standardised and very greatly in effectiveness. Besides, the technology is largely untested in a library setting most of the successful projects involved statistical data or relatively short records not the lengthy text documents and multimedia objects from a variety of sources that library users frequently seek. The most serious problems is that there are no established standards for data mining storage and retrieval. Before committing to data mining technologies on a large scale libraries need to determine how data mining fits with existing resources and organisational goals.

DATA MINING TECHNIQUES ENHANCE LIBRARY SYSTEM

Suppose a library system has the following goals:

(a) Increase books borrowing rate

(b) Attract more users to borrow books

(c) Assist library professionals in making policy on the acquisition of duplicate copies and new publications.

Acquisition: As per third law of Library Science "Every Books its Reader" by applying data mining in the library data it can be easily find out the required contents that are necessary to acquired next. This will reduce the work of library staff related to the acquisition as well as the efficient use of budget allocated to the library.

Classification: It will replace the manual classification of content of library with the computer assisted classification, so that classification task can be accomplished by less skilled person in a fast and efficient way this will simplify the classification task of the library.

Reference Service: i.e., Searching of Information since the data of library continuously growing with an exponential rate and the main problem is how one can use the required information from the large amount of redundant information of the library. This can be possible by applying data mining techniques. So one can say that the data mining is the future of reference service.

THE RELATIONSHIP BETWEEN DATA MINING AND LIBRARY MANAGEMENT

Consider a library where books database includes more than 10,000 volumes of books and the borrowing history of 6000 users who have borrowed books from the library. From this database we have developed a report system to represent the relationship between books and students. Then we use data mining association rule to analyse the books of the same cluster borrowed by the students. A Statistics chart of books will be produced so that the library professionals will find decision additionally the library collection may be used more effectively.

CONCLUSION

There is the need of data mining techniques that will be redesign and simplify the working of library to management like Acquisition, Classification, Circulation and Reference Service the main use of data mining is in referencing but it can be used for some other work of library and well so it is urgently needed that systematic efforts have been take place to develop data mining techniques and algorithms for library database.

REFERENCE

1. Adriaans, P. and Zantinge, D. 2001. Data Mining. Pearson Education Asia, Delhi.
2. Anahory, S. and Murray, D. 2001. Data Warehousing in the Real World: A Practical Guide for Building Decision Support Systems. Pearson Education Asia, Delhi.
3. Berry, Michael J.A. Linoff, G. Data Mining Techniques for Marketing, Sales and Customer Support, Wiley Computer Publishing.
4. Rangnathan, S.R. 1983. Five Laws of Library Science, Sarada Rangnathan Endowment for Library Science, Bangalore.

5. www.google.com
6. www.altavita.com
7. www.yahoo.com
8. www.infoseek.com

19

A Proposal for Classifying the Sanskrit Documents

R.J. Rama Sree*
B.Chandra Sekharam**
G. Sreedhar***
Dr. M.Usha Rani****

ABSTRACT

With the availability of abundant Sanskrit corpora on various schools of traditional Shastras in Rashtriya Sanskrit Vidyapeetha, Tirupati, there is a need to classify them according to the subject, which is an essential step for mining these documents.

Knowledge Management and Information Retrieval are the main problems of the present day due to information explosion. Most of the explicit knowledge of a particular organisation or an entity is stored in different documents and only few people know where to locate this knowledge.

This paper discusses the advantages of document classification; discusses the existing classification methods; and proposes how a model to classify the documents in Indian Languages in general and Sanskrit in particular. This may be useful to mine the documents of Indian languages and can further be extended to Indian web based applications.

* Reader in Computer Science.

** Junior System Analyst.

*** Lecturer in Computer Science, Rashtriya Sanskrit Vidyapeetha.

**** Associate Professor, Dept. of Computer Science, SPMVV,Tirupati.

INTRODUCTION

With the availability of abundant Sanskrit corpora on various schools of traditional Shastras in Rashtriya Sanskrit Vidyapeetha, Tirupati, there is a need to classify them according to the subject, which is an essential step for mining these documents.

Knowledge Management and Information Retrieval are the main problems of the present day due to information explosion. Most of the explicit knowledge of a particular organisation or an entity is stored in different documents and only few people know where to locate this knowledge.

We find that document classification is the basic task which helps in retrieving the relevant information from the existing Sanskrit corpora. Document classification is a process of assigning a predefined category to the given document.

In this paper, we propose a method to classify the Sanskrit documents under predefined categories.

THE EXISTING METHODS

In the domain of document mining, the classification techniques use machine learning approaches, so that new unseen document categorisation is also handled in an appropriate way.

Mostly, the document categorization approaches use decision trees, k-nearest neighbours, Bayesian approaches and neural networks. In this section we briefly describe these methods separately.

Decision Trees

Decision trees are used to partition large samples of data into a hierarchical structure. Commonly associated as a tool for classification [ApWe97], this method tries to construct the well defined true-false queries in the form of a tree structure where the nodes represent questions and the leafs the corresponding category of documents Once the tree is created, a new document can be categorised b putting it in a root node of the tree and let it run through the query structure until it reaches a certain leaf.

The predictive performance of trees is sometimes not nearly as strong on unseen data as that obtained from training data. This phenomenon is often described as over-fitting, where the tree is too specialised to the training data. This may arise due to the existence of high variance in the data.

k-Nearest Neighbour

In k-nearest-neighbour classification [EuVi] , the training dataset is used to classify each member of a "target" dataset. The structure of the data is that there is a classification (categorical) variable of interest and a number of additional predictor variables. Generally speaking, the algorithm is as follows:

1. For each row (case) in the target dataset (the set to be classified), locate the k closest members (the k nearest neighbours) of the training dataset. A Euclidean Distance measure is used to calculate how close each member of the training set is to the target row that is being examined;
2. Examine the k nearest neighbours—which classification (category) do most of them belong to? Assign this category to the row being examined;
3. Repeat this procedure for the remaining rows (cases) in the target set;
4. Additional to this, the system can let the user select a maximum value for k, builds models parallel on all values of k up to the maximum specified value and scoring is done on the best of these models.

The computing time goes up as k goes up, but the advantage is that higher values of k provide smoothing that reduces vulnerability to noise in the training data. In practical applications, typically, k is in units or tens rather than in hundreds or thousands.

Bayesian Approach

There are two groups of Bayesian approaches in document categorization: Naïve and non-naïve Bayesian Approaches.

Naive Bayes classifiers are based on probability models that incorporate strong independence assumptions which often have no bearing in reality, hence are naive. A more descriptive term for the underlying probability model would be *independent feature model*. Furthermore the probability model can be derived using Bayes' theorem. Non-naïve Bayesian arpproaches do not use this independent feature assumption.

There are some attempts [ZhHa05] to classify the documents and some good run-time behaviour is observed.

Neural Networks

There are many types of neural network approaches to solve the problem of document classification. Some systems use simplest form of neural networks, known as perceptrons, which consist of only input and output layers [NGL97], others use more sophisticated neural networks with a hidden layer between input and output layers[RuSr98]. Out of these methods, single layered perceptron approach is working well.

AN OVERVIEW OF ARCHITECTURE OF THE PROPOSED SYSTEM

In this section, we propose a document classifier for our Sanskrit corpus. The basic modules of document classifier is given below:

Document Pre-formatter

The text in Sanskrit documents exhibit the various phenomenon like Sandhi, Samasa etc and is highly inflectional. Hence the input text is to be pre-edited so as to reduce the compound words into simple Sanskrit inflective words so that these words can be handled by Sanskrit Morphological analyser.

For pre-editing, we can do it manually or we can use sandhi identifier and samasa splitter.

Training Document Classifier

The training documents are parsed to construct a dictionary of all words contained in the document. A training set is a set of documents that have already been assigned a category. The roots of the words are obtained either with the use of a morphological analyser or by an appropriate stemmer algorithm. Also stop words (which are not useful in determining the document class ex. a, an, the etc.) are identified and removed from the dictionary.

At this stage, we are free to choose any classification algorithm to train our test data. We prefer to use decision tree algorithms to classify our training data. This form of classification uses a *decision tree* algorithm for creating rules. Generally speaking, a decision tree is a method of deciding between two (or more, but usually two) choices. In document classification, the choices are "the document matches the training set" or "the document does not match the training set."

A decision tree has a set of attributes that can be tested. In this case, these include:

- words from the document
- stems of words from the document (as an example, the stem of *running* is *run*)
- themes from the document (if themes are supported for the language in use)

The learning algorithm builds one or more decision trees for each category provided in the training set. The categorical rules are created and indexed. These decision trees are then coded into queries suitable for use by a Rule index.

The advantage of the Decision Tree method is that it can generate rules that are easily inspected and modified by a human. Using Decision Tree classification makes sense when we want to the computer to generate the bulk of the rules, but we want to fine tune them afterward by editing the rule sets.

Testing New Documents

Once the rules are generated, we can test them by first indexing them and then using MATCHES to classify new documents.

CONCLUSION

This paper discusses the advantages of document classification; discusses the existing classification methods; and proposes how a model to classify the documents in Indian Languages in general and Sanskrit in particular. This may be useful to mine the documents of Indian languages and can further be extended to Indian web based applications.

REFERENCES

[ApWe97] C. Apte and S.Weiss. *Data Mining with Decision Trees and Decision Rules*. 1997. Future Generation Computer Systems, 13: 197-210.

[EuVi] Eui-Hong (Sam) Han George Karypis, Vipin Kumar. *Text Categorisation Using Weight Adjusted k-Nearest Neighbour Classification*. Department of Computer Science and Engineering, Army HPC Research Center,University of Minnesota, 4-192 EECS Bldg., 200 Union St. SE, Minneapolis, MN 55455, USA

[ZhHa05] Zhixiong Chen, and Hao Tang, *Member, IEEE. Sparse Bayesian Approach to Classification* at http://www.mercy.edu/Faculty/zchen/papers/icnsc2005.pdf

[NGL97] Ng H.T., Goh W.B., Low K.L. 1997. Feature Selection, Perceptron Learning, and a Usability Case Study for Text Categorisation. *Proceedings of the 20th Annual International ACM-SIGIR Conference on Research and Development in Information Retrieval*, pp. 67-73.

[RuSr98] Ruiz, M.E., Srinivasan P. 1998. Automatic Text Categorisatiom Using Nueral Network. *In Proceedings of the 8th ASIS SIG/CR Workshop on Classification Research*, pp. 59-72.

20

Security Issues in ATMs and Data Mining Techniques

P. Renuka*
Dr. T. Sudha**

ABSTRACT

This paper presents the study of ATM Systems, their security issues and application of Data Mining Techniques to improve the security of ATM Systems. Data about ATM Systems is collected from Bank Officials and Users of ATM Systems.

Data Mining is the non-trivial process of identifying valid, novel, potentially useful and ultimately understandable patterns in data. Data Mining Techniques support automatic exploration of data. Data Mining attempts to source out patterns and trends in the data and infers rules from these patterns. With these rules, the user will be able to support, review and examine decisions in related areas. This opens up the possibility of a new way of interacting with databases.

ATMs are Automated Teller Machines located either on or off Bank premises, which are capable of dispensing cash and handling routine financial transactions. ATMs can provide 24-hour access to routine banking operations such as deposits, cash withdrawals, transfer between accounts and loan repayments. ATMs can be installed in an apartment, shopping complex, factories or airports etc.

* Research Scholar, Department of Computer Science, SPMVV, Tirupati.

** Associate Professor and Head, Department of Computer Science, SPMVV, Tirupati.

There are incidents where ATM users faced security problems. While using ATM cards, the PIN and Password provide security for its users. But, others may know these through observation. Fraudulent persons use these methods to steel money from other's accounts.

By applying the Data Mining Techniques, another level security is generated for ATM Systems, which works on the database of an account holder and throws some questions and takes feedback from the users. This additional level of security can prevent mischievous handling of user's accounts by fraudulent people.

INTRODUCTION

Data mining is the non-trivial process of identifying valid, novel, potentially useful and ultimately understandable patterns in data. It uses machine learning, statistical and visualisation techniques to discover and present knowledge in a form, which is easily comprehensible to humans. Data mining techniques support automatic exploration of data. Data mining attempts to source out patterns and trends in the data and infers rules from these patterns. With these rules the user will be able to support, review and examine decisions in related areas. This opens up the possibility of a new way of interacting with databases.

The evolution of data mining began when business data was first stored in computers, and technologies were generated to allow users to navigate through the data in real time. Knowledge Discovery in Database was formalised in 1989, with reference to the general concept of being broad and high level in the pursuit of seeking knowledge from data. The term data mining was then coined.

There are two fundamental goals of data mining—Prediction and description. Prediction makes use of existing variable in the database in order to predict unknown or future values of interest and description focuses on finding patterns discovering the data and the subsequent presentation for user interpretation. The relative emphasis of both prediction and description differ with respect to the underlying application and the technique. There are several data mining techniques fulfilling these objectives. Some of these are associations, classifications, sequential patterns and clustering. The basic premise of an association is to find all associations, such that the presence of one set of items in a transaction implies the other items. Classification develops profiles of different groups. Sequential patterns identify sequential patterns subject to a user-specified minimum constraint. Clustering segments a database into subjects and clusters.

Banking sector is one of the major users of database systems. Automation of banking transactions is allowing this sector to minimise its cost of operations and to introduce new systems to improve the quality of service to its customers. ATM is one of such services introduced by banks in the recent past.

ATMs are Automated Teller Machines located either on or off bank premises, which are capable of dispensing cash and handling routine financial transactions. ATMs can provide 24-hour access to routing banking operations such as deposits, cash withdrawals, transfer between accounts and loan repayments. ATMs can be installed in an apartment, shopping center, factory, airport etc.

THE EXISTING ALGORITHM FOR ATM OPERATIONS

1. Insert card.
2. Is card in Stole list.

    If yes then Retail card and end the process.

    If no go to step 3.

3. Enter PIN
4. Is Pin matching

    If no

        Are all attempts over?

        If no then go to step 3.

        If yes then Retain card and end the process.

    If yes then go to step 5.

5. Enter request
6. If the request is:

    Deposit then

Take envelope, deposit cash or cheque, insert envelope and go to step 7.

Withdraw then

Enter Amount

Is amount with in limit?

If yes then cash delivery and go to step 7.

If no then go to step Enter Amount

7. Any more transactions

If yes then go to step 5.

If no then Card returned and print is given.

8. End the process.

SECURITY IN ATMS

Most security policies state that to access a network and its services, a user must enter a login ID and password that are authenticated by a security server. A security card is a physical device. PIN is an initial level of security that simply gives the user permission to use the card. The card provides a password that is used to access the corporate network for a limited time. The password is synchronised with a central security card server that resides on the network.

DESCRIPTION OF THE PROBLEM

There are incidents, where ATM users lost their money due to security problems. The PIN and Password provide security for the users while using ATMs. But, others may know these PIN and Password through observation. The mischievous persons use these methods to steel the money from others' account.

APPLICATION OF DATA MINING TECHNIQUES AND GENERATION OF NEW ALGORITHM

The data mining techniques are applied to find the association of current transaction with recent transactions such as time taken between two consecutive withdrawals on average during recent past and time difference between current withdrawal and most recent withdrawal etc.

By applying the data mining techniques a new algorithm is generated which is an extension to the existing one. This allows one more level of security to be generated for ATM systems, which works on the database of an account holder and throws some questions and takes feedback from the users when the suspicion is detected. This additional level of security can prevent mischievous handling of users' accounts by fraudulent people.

COMPARATIVE STUDY OF EXISTING AND NEW ALGORITHMS TO HANDLE ATM OPERATIONS

Once the entered amount is within limits, the existing system gives away the money. It will not check whether the user is genuine or fraudulent. But, new algorithm checks this. By displaying the question randomly every time a suspicion is encountered, the new system can be a better solution for highly secured transactions through ATMs.

CONCLUSION

As the number of users of ATMs are increasing day by day, the number of methods applied by fraudulent people to mishandle the accounts' of others are also increasing. The model presented through this paper, is only one way that can handle the security issues regarding ATMs. This model can be implemented with cheaper costs, within the servers, so there is no need to go for any costly physical devices to implement this system.

REFERENCES

1. *Data Mining Techniques*—Arun K. Pujari—University Press.
2. *Data Warehousing, Data Mining and OLAP*—Alex Berin Stephon J. Smith —Tata Mech Graw Hill
3. *Data Mining: Concept and Techniques*—Jiawei Han and Micheline Kambler—Morgan Kaufmann Publishers.

21

Data Mining
Trends and Applications

S. Sagar Imambi*
B. Sunaina Sravanthi**

INTRODUCTION

Data mining is the process of extracting hidden information knowledge from large volumes of data using algorithms. Data Mining helps to extracts useful information from great masses of data, which can be used for making practical interpretations for business decision-making. Data Mining is gaining a lot of importance because of its vast applicability. It is being used increasingly in business for understanding and then predicting valuable information like customer buying behaviour and buying trends, profiles of customers, industry analysis etc...Some of the main applications of Data Mining are direct marketing, e-commerce, customer relationship management, health care, the oil and gas industries, scientific tests, genetics, telecommunications, financial services and utilities and retail industries.

Many companies collect, refine and deduce massive quantities of data. Data Mining techniques can be implemented rapidly on existing software and hardware platforms to enhance the value of existing information resources, and can be integrated with new products and systems, as they become part of the system.

* M.C.A., M.Tech., M.Phil, Asst. Professor, Department of Computer Science, TJPS College, Guntur.

** M.C.A., Lecturer, Department of Computer Science, TJPS., College (P.G. Courses), Guntur.

TRENDS IN DATA MINING

Phenomenal Data Mining

Data Mining involves computer programmes that infer relations in different kinds of data in large databases. Data amounts to observations of the world, and it is possible to infer relations among entities in the world from the data. Such relations are likely to be as useful to know about, as are relations among the entities directly represented in the data. Phenomenal Data Mining finds relations between the data and the phenomena that give to rise to data rather than just relations among the data. One example of phenomenal data mining is that, using receipts from cash super market purchases, it is possible to identify various aspects of the customers who are marketing these purchases. Some of these phenomena include age, income, ethnicity and purchasing habits.

Constraint Based and Multidimensional Data Mining

Integrating both constraint-based and multidimensional mining into one framework provides an interactive, exploratory environment for effective and efficient data analysis and mining. By constraint-based Data Mining we mean, Data Mining process in which the user provides constraints that guide the mining in the databases. Constraint based Data Mining techniques can provide a more adhoc query-driven process that exploits the semantics of data, more efficiently than current stand-alone Data Mining system.

Multi-Relational Data Mining

Multi Relational Data Mining is the multi disciplinary fields dealing with knowledge discovery from relational databases consisting of multiple tables. Mining data which consists of complex/structured object also falls with in the scope of the field, since the normalised representation of such objects in a relational database requires multiple tasks.

Spatial Data Mining

The explosive growth of spatial data and widespread of spatial database emphasise the need for the automated discovery of spatial knowledge. Spatial Data Mining is the process of discovering interesting and previously unknown but potentially useful patterns from spatial databases. Efficient tools for extracting information from geo-spatial data sets, including NASA, the National Imaging and Mapping Agencies (NIMA), the National Cancer Institute (NCI). These organisations spread across many application domains including ecology and environmental management, transportation, earth science, epidemiology and climatology.

Geographical Data Mining

The immense explosion in geographically referenced data occasioned by developments in IT, digital mapping, remote sensing and the global diffusion of GIS emphasising the importance of developing data driven inductive approaches to geographical analysis and modelling to facilitate the creation of new knowledge and aid the processes of scientific discovery. Geographical data mining tools are useful for summarising the essential features of large spatial data sets to create geo-demographics classifications. Analysing spatial and geographic data include such tasks as understanding and browsing spatial data, uncovering relationships between spatial data items (and also between non-spatial and spatial items), and also analysing using spatial databases and spatial knowledge bases. The application of these would be useful in such fields as remote sensing, medical imaging, navigation, and related issues.

Hyper Text and Multimedia Data Mining

Multimedia data mining is the mining and analysis of various types of data, including image, video, audio and animation. Some of the important data mining techniques used for hypertext and hyper media data mining include classification, clustering, semi-structured learning and social network analysis.

Ubiquitous Data Mining

The advent of laptops, palmtops, cell phones, is making ubiquitous access to large quantity of data possible. After accessing, advanced analysis of data for extracting useful knowledge is the next step. The key issues include theories of UDM, advanced algorithms for mobile and distributed applications, data management issues, mark up language and other data representation techniques.

APPLICATIONS OF DATA MINING

Risk Analysis: Insurance companies and banks use data mining for risk analysis. An insurance company searches in its own insurants and claims databases for relationships between personal characteristics and claim behaviour. The company is especially interested in the characteristics of insurants with a highly deviating claim behaviour. With data mining these so-called risk profiles can be discovered.

Direct Marketing: Data mining can also be used to discover the relationships between one's personal characteristics ex: age, gender ,home town and the probability that one will respond to a mailing .Such relationships can be used to select those customers from the mailing database that have the highest probability of responding to a mailing. This allows the company to mail its prospects selectively, thus maximising the response.

Production Quality Control: Data mining can also be used to determine those combinations of production factors that influence the quality of the end product.

This information allows the process engineers to explain, why certain products fail the final test and to increase the quality of the production process.

Healthcare: Healthcare generates mountains of administrative data about patients hospitals, bed costs claims etc. Clinical trials, electronic patients records and computer supported disease management will increasingly produce mountains of clinical data. This data is a strategic resource for healthcare institutions. Clinically-based data warehouse product designed for use through out a hospital, bring the potential for specialized information production to the clinicians and manages desktop through use of clinical workstations and executive information systems (EIS) data mining products are designed to take this one stage further. It brings the facility to discover patterns and correlation hidden within data repository and assists professionals to uncover these patterns and put them to work.

Customer Relations: In customer relationship management (CRM), web mining is the integration of information gathered by traditional data mining methodologies and techniques with information gathered over the world wide web.

Customer relationship management centers around customer acquisition, retention and cross selling. Data mining tools can be employed very effectively to achieve both customer acquisition, product launch campaign and cross selling. Data mining will be essential for understanding customer behaviour on the web and for helping the websites of the world to create their personalized responses.

Financial Data Mining: Financial data mining is used to classify and cluster the customers for targeted marketing. Financial data collected in banks and financial institutions are often relatively complete, reliable, and of high quality. Multidimensional segmentation by nearest neighbor, classification, decision trees, etc, are used to identify customer groups or associate a new customer to an appropriate customer group. It is also used to detect money laundering and other financial crimes. Data mining tools like data visualisation linkage analysis, classification, clustering tools, outlier analysis and sequential pattern analysis tools are used to find unusual access sequences.

Retail Industry: Retail data mining applications are used to identify customer buying behaviours, discover customer shopping patterns and trends, improve the quality of the customer service, achieve better customer retention and satisfaction and design more effective goods transportation and distribution Policies.

CONCLUSION

There are a number of data mining trends in terms of technologies and methodologies which are currently being developed and researched. These trends include methods for analysing more complex forms of data as well as specific techniques and methods.

The main applications of Data Mining are direct marketing, e-commerce, customer relationship management, health care, the oil and gas industries, scientific tests, genetics, telecommunications, financial services and utilities and retail industries.

22

Clustering Algorithms for Data Mining

V. Sireesha*

ABSTRACT

Clustering in data mining is a discovery process that groups a set of data such that the intra cluster similarity is maximised and the inter cluster similarity is minimized. That is, a cluster is a collection of data objects that are similar to one another within the same cluster and are dissimilar to objects in other clusters. A cluster of data objects can be treated collectively as one group in many applications. Especially by clustering, one can identify dense and sparse regions and, therefore, discover overall distribution patterns and interesting correlations among data attributes.

The overall performance of clustering is dependent on the discovery of quality clusters of items. Thus a majority of algorithms are concerned with efficiently determining the set of clusters in a given transaction or relational database. The problem is essentially to generate the set of clusters in the database. Thus, different algorithms were introduced which aim at generating quality clusters. These algorithms differ from one another in the method of generating the clusters.

Tl is paper presents mainly four clustering algorithms such as K-Means, PAM, Nearest neighbour algorithm and minimum spanning tree algorithm which aims at generating the set of clusters from a given vehicle database.

* **(M.Tech-CST), Andhra University College of Engineering, Visakhapatnam,** ***Email id*****: v_sireesha2000@yahoo.com**

K-Means is an iterative partitioning clustering algorithm in which items are moved among sets of clusters until the desired condition is reached. Here each cluster is represented by the mean value of the objects in the cluster. PAM (Partitioning Around Medoids) algorithm, also called the K-Medoids algorithm represents a cluster by a medoid. Using a medoid is an approach that handles outliers well. Initially a random set of k-items is taken to be the set of medoids. In the Nearest neighbour algorithm, the items are iteratively merged into the existing clusters that are closest based on a threshold value. The minimum spanning tree algorithm is based on the agglomerative approach of clustering. It starts with each object forming a separate group and then successively merges the objects or groups close to one another, until all the groups are merged into one, or until a termination condition holds.

Thus, quality clusters can be produced using clustering algorithms like K-Means, PAM, Nearest neighbour algorithm and minimum spanning tree algorithm which are successfully implemented in Java and their performance is tested on vehicle dataset.

INTRODUCTION

The main reason that data mining has attracted a great deal of attention in the information industry in recent years is due to the wide availability of huge amounts of data and the imminent need for turning such data into useful information and knowledge. The information and knowledge gained can be used for applications ranging from business management, production control and market analysis to engineering design and science exploration.

Among the areas of data mining, Cluster Analysis has received a great deal of attention. Clustering analyses data objects without consulting a known class label. In general, the class labels are not present in the training data simply because they are not known to begin with. Clustering can be used to generate such labels. The objects are clustered or grouped based on the principle of maximising the intraclass similarity and minimising the interclass similarity. That is, the clusters of objects are formed so that objects within a cluster have high similarity in comparison to one another, but are very dissimilar to objects in another clusters. Each cluster that is formed can be viewed as a class of objects, from which rules can be derived. Clustering can also facilitate taxonomy formation, that is, the organisation of observations into a hierarchy of classes that group similar events together. There are numerous applications of data mining, which fit into this framework.

This paper *"Clustering Algorithms for Data Mining"* deals with grouping a set of data such that the intra cluster similarity is maximised and the inter cluster similarity is minimised. That is, collection of data objects that are similar to one another within the same cluster and are dissimilar to objects in other clusters.

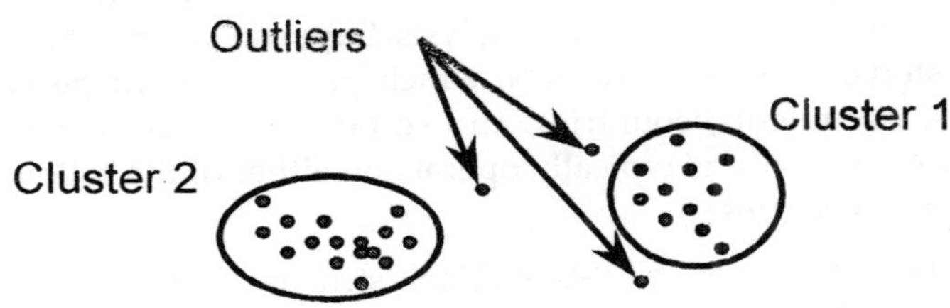

BASIC CONCEPTS OF CLUSTER ANALYSIS

Clustering in data mining is a discovery process that groups a set of data such that the intra cluster similarity is maximised and the inter cluster similarity is minimised. That is, a cluster is a collection of data objects that are similar to one another within the same cluster and are dissimilar to objects in other clusters. A cluster of data objects can be treated collectively as one group in many applications.

Applications

Clustering can be used as a stand alone tool to gain insight into the distribution of data, to observe the characteristic of each cluster, to focus on particular set of clusters for further analysis.

- Cluster analysis has been widely used in numerous application domains, including biology, medicine, anthropology, economics and market research.

- Clustering applications include plant and animal classification, disease classification, pattern recognition, data analysis, image processing etc.
- Recent uses include examining Web log data to detect usage patterns.

It may serve as a preprocessing step for other algorithms, such as characterisation and classification, which would then operate on the detected clusters.

Types of Data in Cluster Analysis

Different types of data occur in cluster analysis and they are to be preprocessed for such an analysis. Suppose that a data set to be clustered contains n objects, which may represent persons, houses, documents, countries, and so on. Main memory-based clustering algorithms typically operate on either of the following two data structures.

- *Data Matrix* (or object-by-variable structure): This represents n objects, such as persons, with p variables (also called attributes), such as age, height, weight, gender, race, and so on. The data matrix is often called *two-mode matrix*. The structure is in the form of a relational table, or n-by-p matrix:

$$\begin{bmatrix} x_{11} & \cdots & x_{1f} & \cdots & x_{1p} \\ \vdots & \vdots & \vdots & \vdots & \vdots \\ x_{i1} & \cdots & x_{if} & \cdots & x_{ip} \\ \vdots & \vdots & \vdots & \vdots & \vdots \\ x_{n1} & \cdots & x_{nf} & \cdots & x_{np} \end{bmatrix}$$

Dissimilarity Matrix (or object-by-object structure): This stores a collection of proximities that are available for all pairs of n objects. The dissimilarity matrix is often called *one-mode matrix* It is often represented by n-by-n table:

$$\begin{bmatrix} 0 & & & & \\ d(2,1) & 0 & & & \\ d(3,1) & d(3,2) & 0 & & \\ \vdots & \vdots & \vdots & & \\ d(n,1) & d(n,2) & \cdots & \cdots & 0 \end{bmatrix}$$

where d(i,j) is the measured difference or dissimilarity between objects i and j. In general, d(i,j) is a non-negative number that is close to 0 when objects i and j are highly similar or "near" to each other, and becomes larger the more they differ, Since d(i.j) = d(j,i), and d(i,i)=0.

Types of Data

Different types of data like Interval scaled variables, binary variables nominal variables, ordinal and ratio-scaled variables are to be preprocessed for cluster analysis. Interval scaled variables are continuous measurements of a roughly linear scale. The data for the variable must be standardised. In this paper I have considered Interval scaled variables.

Interval Scaled Variables: These variables are continuous measurements of a roughly linear scale. The data for the variable must be standardised. This can be performed by

1. Calculate the standard deviation, σ_A:

   $\sigma_A = ((\Sigma(A - \bar{A})^2)/n - 1)^{1/2}$

   where the mean of A is $\bar{A} = \bar{A} = (\Sigma A)/n$

2. Calculate the standardised measurement or Z-Score: In Z-score normalisation, the values for attribute A are normalised based on the mean and standard deviation of A. A value v of A is normalised to v′ by computing

   $v' = (v - \bar{A})/\sigma_A$

where $\bar{A}$ and σ_A are the mean and standard deviation, respectively, of attribute A. This method of normalisation is used when the actual minimum and maximum of attribute A are unknown, or when there are outliers that dominate the min-max normalisation.

After standardising the variables the *Dissimilarity Between Objects* has to be computed. Distances are normally used measures for computing similarity and dissimilarity between objects.

The following distance measures are used:

Minkowski Distance: It is a *generalisation* of both *Euclidean* distance and *Manhattan* distance . It is defined as:

$$d(i, j) = (|x_{i1} - x_{j1}|^q + |x_{i2} - x_{j2}|^q + \ldots + |x_{in} - x_{jn}|^q)^{1/q}$$

where $x_{i1}, x_{i2} \ldots\ldots x_{in}$ are n attributes of item i

$x_{j1}, xj_2 \ldots\ldots x_{jn}$ are n attributes of item j

If q = 2, d is Euclidean distance

If q = 1, d is Manhattan distance

$$= (|x_1 - y_1|^2 + |x_2 - y_2|^2 + |x_3 - y_3|^2 + |x_4 - y_4|^2 + |x_5 - y_5|^2)^{1/2}$$

Properties of Minkowski Distance:

- Distance is Non-negative when: $d(i,j) \geq 0$
- The distance of an object to itself is 0 $d(i,i) = 0$
- Distance is a Symmetric function: $d(i,j) = d(j,i)$
- Triangular inequality exists $d(i,j) \geq d(i,k) + d(k,j)$

If each variable is assigned a weight according to its perceived importance, the weighted Euclidean distance can be computed as

$$d(i,j) = (w_1 \mid x_{i1} - x_{j1} \mid^2 + w_2 \mid x_{i2} - x_{j2} \mid^2 + \ldots + w_p \mid x_{ip} - x_{jp} \mid^2)^{1/2}$$

Weighting can also be applied to the Manhattan and Minkowski distances.

Categorisation of Clustering Methods

The choice of clustering algorithm depends both on the type of data available and on the particular purpose and application. The clustering methods can be classified into categories like partitioning methods, hierarchical methods, density based methods, grid based and model based methods. Among these categories I have presented the algorithms relating to partitioning and hierarchical based methods:

- ***Partitioning Methods:*** Given a data base of n objects, a partioning method constructs k partitions of the data, where each partition represents a cluster and $k \leq n$. That is, it classifies the data into k groups, which together satisfy the following requirements: (1) each group must contain at least one object, and (2) each object must belong to exactly one group.

It then uses an iterative relocation technique that attempts to improve the partitioning by moving the objects from one group to another. K-Means, PAM nearest neighbour algorithms are some of the examples of this category.

- ***Hierarchical Methods:*** A hierarchical method creates a hierarchical decomposition of the given set of data objects. A hierarchical method can be classified as being either agglomerative or divisive, based on how the hierarchical decomposition is formed. The agglomerative approach, also called the bottom-up approach, starts with each object forming a separate group. It successively merges the objects or groups close to one another, until all the groups are merged into one, or until a termination condition holds. The divisive approach, also called the top-down approach, starts with all the objects in the same cluster. In each successive iteration, a cluster is split up into smaller clusters, until eventually each object is in one cluster, or until a termination condition holds. The Minimum spanning tree algorithm is based on the agglomerative approach of clustering.

It suffers from the fact that once a step is done, it can never be undone. This rigidity is useful in that it leads to smaller computation costs by not worrying about a combinatorial number of different choices. However, a major problem is that they cannot correct erroneous decisions. The quality of hierarchical algorithms can be improved by some of the algorithms like CURE, Chameleon, BIRCH.

BASIC CONCEPTS OF IMPLEMENTED ALGORITHMS

In this paper, I have discussed four clustering Algorithms namely K-Means, PAM, Nearest neighbour algorithm, minimum spanning tree algorithms.

K-Means Algorithm

It is an iterative clustering algorithm in which items are moved among sets of clusters until the desired set is reached. A high degree of similarity among elements in clusters is obtained, while a high degree of dissimilarity among elements in different clusters is achieved simultaneously.

The cluster mean of $K_i = \{ t_{i1}, t_{i2}, \ldots, t_{im} \}$ is defined as

$$m_i = (1/m)\sum_{j=1}^{m} t_{ij}$$

This algorithm assumes the desired number of clusters, k, is an input parameter. The initial values for the means are arbitrarily assigned. These could be assigned randomly or perhaps could use the values from the first k input items themselves. The items are assigned to a cluster which has the closest mean. Then the new means are calculated. This process is repeated until a convergence criteria is met. The convergence criteria may be condition where the clusters generated in the last two iterations are same.

K-means Algorithm

Input

$D = \{ t_1, t_2, \ldots, t_m \}$ // set of elements

K // Number of desired clusters

Output

K // set of clusters

Algorithm

Assign initial values for means $m_1, m_2, \ldots m_k$;

repeat

assign each item t_i to the cluster which has the closest mean;
calculate new mean for each cluster;

Until convergence criteria is met;

The time complexity of K-means is O(tkn) where t is the number of iterations. K-Means does not work on categorical data because the mean must be defined on the attribute type. Only convex-shaped clusters are found. It also does not handle outliers well.

Partitioning Around Medoids Algorithm

The PAM (Partitioning Around Medoids) algorithm, also called the K-Medoids algorithm represents a cluster by a medoid. Using a medoid is an approach that handles outliers well. Initially a random set of k-items is taken to be the set of medoids. Then at each step, all items from the input dataset that are not currently medoids are examined one by one to see if they should be medoids. By looking at all pairs of medoid, non-medoid objects, the algorithm chooses the pair that improves the overall quality of the clustering the best and exchanges them. Quality here is measured by the sum of all distances from a non-medoid object to the medoid for the cluster it is in. An item is assigned to the cluster it is represented by the medoid to which it is closest(minimum distance). We assume that K_i is the cluster represented by medoid t_i. Suppose t_i is a current medoid we wish to determine whether it should be exchanged with a non-medoid t_h. We wish to do this swap only if the overall impact to the cost (sum of the distances to the cluster medoids) represents an improvement. Let C_{jih} be the cost change for an item t_j associated with swapping medoid t_i with non-medoid t_h. The cost is the change to the sum of all distances from items to their cluster medoids. There are four cases that must be examined when calculating this cost:

1. $t_j \in K$, but $\ni$ another medoid t_m where $dist(t_j, t_m) \leq dist(t_j, t_h)$;
2. $t_j \in K_i$, but $dist(t_j, t_h) \leq dist(t_j, t_m)$ for all other medoids t_m;
3. $t_j \in Km$, does not belong to K_i and $dist(t_j, t_m) \leq dist(t_j, t_h)$; and
4. $t_j \in Km$, does not belong to K_i and $dist(t_j, t_h) \leq dist(t_j, t_m)$.

The total impact to quality by a medoid change TC_{ih} then is given by

$$TC_{ih} =_{j=1}^{n} \sum C_{jih}$$

PAM Algorithm

Input

D= { t_1, t_2,..., t_m} // set of elements

A // Adjacency matrix showing distance between elements

K // Number of desired clusters

Output

K // set of clusters

Algorithm

Arbitrarily select k medoids from D;

repeat

for each t_h not a medoid do

for each medoid t_i do

calculate TC_{ih};

find i,h where TC_{ih} is the smallest;

if $TC_{ih} < 0$, then

replace medoid t_i with t_h;

Until $TC_{ih} \geq 0$;

For each $t_i \in D$ do

Assign t_i to K_j, where dist(t_i, t_j) is the smallest overall medoids;

PAM does not scale well to large datasets because of its computational complexity. For each iteration, we have k(n-k) pairs of objects i,h for which a cost, TC_{ih} , should be determined . Calculating the cost during each iteration requires the cost be calculated for all other non-medoids t_j. There are n-k of these. Thus the total complexity per each iteration is $k(n-k)^2$. The total number of iterations can be quite large, so PAM is not an alternative for large databases.

Nearest Neighbour Algorithm

In this algorithm the items are iteratively merged into the existing clusters that are closest. A threshold value is used to determine if items will be added to existing cluster or if a new cluster is created.

Nearest Neighbour Algorithm

Input

D={ }

A // adjacency matrix showing distance between elements

Output

K // set of clusters

Algorithm

k1={t_1};

k={ k_1};

k=1;

For i= 2 to n do

find the t_m in some cluster k_m in k such that dist (t_i , t_m) is the smallest;

if dist(t_i , t_m) ≤ t then

$k_m = k_m \cup t_i$

else

k = k+1;

k_k = { t_i };

The complexity of the nearest neighbour algorithm actually depends on the number of items. Each item must be compared to each item already in a cluster. Obviously, this is n in worst case. Thus, the time complexity is $O(n^2)$ and space complexity is $O(n^2)$.

Minimum Spanning Tree Algorithm

The Minimum spanning tree algorithm is based on the agglomerative approach of clustering where a series of successive fusions of data are performed until the final number of clusters is obtained. This hierarchial method starts by considering each component of the data set to be a cluster. Next, the two clusters with the minimum distance between them are fused to form a single cluster. This process is repeated until a termination condition holds, that is all components are grouped into the final required number of clusters.

Minimum Spanning Tree Algorithm

Input

D = { t_1 , t_2,..., t_m} // set of elements

A // Adjacency matrix showing distance between elements

K // Number of desired clusters

Output: K // set of clusters

Algorithm

Read the number of clusters;

Calculate the distance between each pair of items.

repeat

Merge the items with minimum distance;

Update the attributes of merged items by taking means;

Until convergence criteria is met;

The time complexity of this algorithm is $O(n^2)$.

IMPLEMENTATION DETAILS

The algorithms which I have implemented aims at generating the set of clusters from the given vehicle database. The whole process of generating clustering can be divided into two modules, which are construction of a normalised file using the norm algorithm and generation of clusters using one of the algorithms (K-Means/PAM/Nearest neighbour algorithm/Minimum spanning tree).

The first module, construction of a normalised file, is done starting with reading the vehicle data base file. Means, variances and Z-Scores are then computed. Each and every attribute of an item is replaced with the corresponding Z-score. Then finally the resultant data is written to an output file which will be used as input by the clustering algorithms.

The second module, generation of clusters, is done using the following methods. If user chooses K-means algorithm to generate frequent clusters, following steps are used. First step is to read the number of clusters. The next step is to read the normalised file of the vehicle data base . Next after initialising the means the clusters are computed based on the means. Next the means of the items are updated based on the clusters computed. Next, new clusters are formed based on the new means. This activity continues until the previous cluster is equal to the present cluster. Then finally the resultant set of clusters are displayed as output.

Input for K-Means Algorithm: vehicle dataset with 9 records and number of clusters 4.

95	48	83	178	72	10	162	42	20	159	176	379	184	70	6	16	187	197
119	54	106	220	65	12	213	31	24	167	223	675	232	66	20	1	192	202
98	55	101	228	70	9	210	31	24	168	236	661	245	72	1	6	188	197
84	47	75	153	64	6	154	43	19	145	175	354	184	75	0	3	185	192
85	44	70	205	103	52	149	45	19	144	241	325	188	127	9	11	180	183
107	57	106	172	50	6	255	26	28	169	280	957	264	85	5	9	181	183
97	43	73	173	65	6	153	42	19	143	176	361	172	66	13	1	200	204
90	43	66	157	65	9	137	48	18	146	162	281	164	67	3	3	193	202
86	34	62	140	61	7	122	54	17	127	141	223	112	64	2	14	200	208

Output for K-Means Algorithm

k0= 0, 4

k1= 1

k2= 2, 5

k3= 3, 6, 7, 8

If the user chooses PAM algorithm to generate clusters, following steps are used. First step is to read the number of clusters. The next step is to read the normalised file of the vehicle data base. Next, after initialising the medoids clusters are computed based on the medoids. Next step is to compute the swapping cost as a result of swapping a medoid with a non-medoid. Then, medoids of the items are updated and new clusters are formed based on the new medoids. The above activity is repeated until swapping cost is greater than zero. Then finally the resultant set of clusters are displayed as output.

Input for Partitioning Around Medoids Algorithm: vehicle dataset with 9 records as above and number of clusters 5.

Output for Partitioning Around Medoids Algorithm

k0= 5

k1= 1

k2= 2

k3= 7, 0, 3, 6, 8

k4= 4

If the user chooses nearest neighbour algorithm to generate clusters, following steps are used. First step is to read the threshold value. The next step is to compute the distances between the items in the normalised data base. Then finally the set of clusters which are within the threshold value are displayed.

Input for Nearest Neighbour Algorithm: vehicle dataset with 9 records as above and Threshold value 5

Output for Nearest Neighbour Algorithm

k: 0

k: 1 2 3 5 6 7 8

k: 4

If the user chooses minimum spanning tree algorithm to generate clusters, following steps are used. First step is to read the number of clusters. The next step is to read the normalised file of the vehicle data base. The next step is to merge the items with minimum distance and then update the means of the items which are merged. The activity of merging the clusters and updating means is repeated until the number of clusters present before merging is greater than or equal to the number of clusters. Then finally the resultant set of clusters are displayed as output.

Input for Minimum Spanning Tree Clustering Algorithm: vehicle dataset with 9 records as above and number of clusters 2.

Output for Minimum Spanning Tree Clustering Algorithm

k: 0, 3, 4, 6, 7, 8

k: 1, 2

CONCLUSIONS AND FUTURE ENHANCEMENTS

Conclusion

Clustering data is a canonical task, fundamental for many data mining and other applications including biology, medicine, anthropology, economics, market research, plant and animal classification, disease classification, pattern recognition, data analysis, image processing etc. Especially by clustering, one can identify dense and sparse regions and, therefore, discover overall distribution patterns and interesting correlations among data attributes. K-Means, PAM, Nearest neighbour and Minimum Spanning Tree Algorithm implemented in Java in this project are useful in displaying the set of clusters identified in the data base files.

The proposed algorithm K-Means is an iterative partitioning clustering algorithm in which items are moved among sets of clusters until the desired set is reached. Here each cluster is represented by the mean value of the objects in the cluster. PAM (Partitioning Around Medoids) algorithm, also called the K-Medoids algorithm represents a cluster by a medoid. In the Nearest neighbour algorithm, the items are iteratively merged into the existing clusters that are closest based on a threshold value. The Minimum Spanning Tree Algorithm is based on the agglomerative approach of clustering. It starts with each object forming a separate group and then successively merges the objects or groups close to one another, until all the groups are merged into one, or until a termination condition holds. K-Means algorithm does not handle outliers well. PAM algorithm does not scale well to large datasets because of its computational complexity.

Future Enhancements

In this project the items in the dataset with all the eighteen attributes are considered for clustering. We can further reduce the high dimensionality by considering only a subset of the attributes for the items based on a purpose so that the quality of clusters may be improved. Other partitioning clustering algorithms like CLARA and CLARANS which improves the time complexity of PAM can be added to the set of clustering algorithms. Hierarchical clustering algorithms like Chameleon and BIRCH can also be added to improve the quality of clusters. To find clusters of arbitrary shape density based clustering algorithm like DBSCAN can also be added.

REFERENCES

1. Jiawei Han, Micheline Kamber, *Data Mining and Concepts*.
2. Margaret H. Dunham, *Data Mining and Introductory to Advanced Topics*.
3. Vehicle Data Set. http://www.ncc.up.pt/liacc/ML/statlog/datasets/veh.dat
4. Data mining: http://www.statsoft.com/textbook/stdatmin.html
5. Cluster Analysis: http://www.statsoft.com/textbook/stcluan.html
6. K-meansAlgorithm: http://cne.gmu.edu/modules/dau/stat/cluatalgs/clust5_frm.html
7. *Minimum spanning tree method*: http://cne.gmu.edu/modules/dau/stat/clustgalgs/clust4_frm.html

23

CRM and Data Mining

N. Sri Rajani*
Dr. C.S.G. Krisnamacharyulu*

ABSTRACT

Customer Relationship Management (CRM) has become the buzzword for most of the managers. Growing competition and increasing marketing costs have given the realisation that retention is important as much as attracting new customers. The IT technology advances -data warehousing and data mining tools—have opened new avenues of consumer knowledge processing—have been facilitating the companies to be market driven and consumer centric. In this paper the role of data mining in CRM is examined.

INTRODUCTION

Customer relationship marketing—also called as relationship marketing is the use of wide array of communication and sales technology to identify and manage relationship with the targeted customers.

Gronroos who advocated the concept defines:

"Customer relationship management is to establish, maintain, and enhance relationship with customers and other partners at a profit so that the objective of the parties involved are met. This is achieved by a mutual

* Research Scholar, Department of M.B.A., SPMVV, Tirupati.

** Professor in Management, S.V.University, Tirupati.

exchange and fulfillment of promises. Such relationships are usually but not necessarily always long term".

Table 23.1 Shows differences between the traditional and relationship marketing approaches.

Table 23.1: Differences Between Conventional and CRM

Conventional Marketing	*CRM*
Mass Marketing is given more emphasis	Personal marketing is given more emphasis
Customer is passive and rational	Customer is active and emotional
Limited use of technology	Widespread use of technology
Serve customers well	Serve customers Differently
Success measured by current profits/ market shares	Success measured by lifetime profits/market shares
Customer acquisition is given more emphasis'	Customer retention is given more emphasis

WHY CRM?

The following arguments justify investment in marketing for CRM.

(i) Recent Trends

Business process re-engineering, automation and downsizing reduced the manpower costs.

Financial restructuring and efficient fund management reduced the financial costs.

Production and operation costs have been reduced through Total Quality Management (TQM), Just in Time (JIT) inventory, Flexible Manufacturing Systems (FMS), and efficient Supply Chain Management (SCM).

Studies have shown that while manufacturing costs declined from 55% to 30% and management costs declined from 25% to 15%, the marketing costs have increased from 20% to 55% (Sheth, 1998).

The practice of relationship marketing has the potential to improve marketing productivity through improved marketing efficiencies and effectiveness.(Sheth and Parvatiyar, 1995).

(ii) Retention Best Policy

CRM can be cost effective, as it emphasises to retain the customers rather than only acquiring new customers. As per a research survey, companies lose roughly 15 per cent of their customers every year. This implies that in three years the company will be left with half the customers it started with. In addition, it is often said in America that selling to an exiting customer is successful at least for the first time when tried for two times. This is much more different in the context of a new customer because here the success rate is 1 in 16 times. On average, businesses spend six times more to acquire customers than they do to keep them (Gruen, 1997).

(iii) Attraction Intermediary Step

Attracting customers is considered to be an intermediary step in the relationship building process with the ultimate objective of increasing loyalty of profitable customers. This is because of the applicability of the 80-20 rule. According to Market Line Associates, the top 20 per cent of typical bank customers produce as much as 150 per cent of overall profit, while the bottom 20 per cent of customers drain about 50 per cent from the bank's bottom line and the revenues from the rest just meeting their expenses.

(iv) Lifetime Relationship

In CRM, every customer is viewed on the terms of his lifetime value. This implies that if a customer keeps buying the same product over his entire lifetime, it adds up to a decent amount. As per a survey conducted by Hindustan Thompson Associates (HTA), an advertising agency, the lifetime value of one cigarette smoker is Rs. 1.10 lakhs over a 10-year period.

CUSTOMER CENTRIC MARKETING

In customer-centric marketing, marketers assess each customer individually to determine whether to serve that customer directly or via a third party. Therefore it is very important to have an understanding of all the linkages between the customers and the business processes, which help fulfill the customer needs.

The Life-cycle model for customer relationship management has four steps as shown in Chart-23.1.

1. Customer acquisition through referrals;
2. Customer development through personalisation and customisation;
3. Leveraging customer equity through cross-selling and up-selling;
4. Customer retention and referrals.

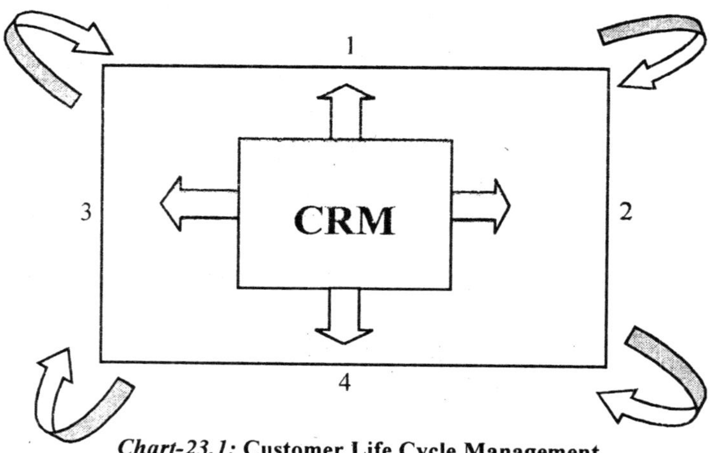

Chart-23.1: **Customer Life Cycle Management**

CRM STRATEGY

It also is important to realise that developing an effective CRM operational capability is not about technology alone. Success requires a tight integration of People, Process and Technology.

Raymond is one example:

The premium suiting and shirtings are supported by air-conditioned, decent retail outlets and classy ads with the punch line: 'The Perfect Man'.

Successful implementation of CRM requires a strategic approach which encompasses customer information and knowledge generation capabilities to differentiate them.

Marketing Initiatives

The marketing measures taken by different companies in India are:

- *Club Formation*—Maggie club, Barbie club, Saffola healthy heart club etc.
- *Frequent Marketing Programmes*—Free flights to frequent fliers by British airways.
- *Special Facilities*—Opel astra card to car owners to provide special facilities like 24 hours service breakdown etc.
- Customer Training—Hawkins with a dealer network of more than 500 dealers provides training to customers on how to cook effectively and variedly in Hawkins pressure cooker.
- *Relationship Cells*—Apollo tyres have developed a separate relationship marketing cell specially functioning to develop and maintain relationship with the customers.
- *Mystery Shopping Programme*—Bank of America is using mystery shopping to identify, appraise and reward on interpersonal skills and relationship building abilities of marketing personnel.
- *Awards*—Welcome Group gives away awards to the most loyal customers.

Technology Initiatives

Developments in information technology, data warehousing and data mining have made it possible for firms to maintain a one to one relationship with their customers. Firms can now manage every single contact with the customer from account management personnel, call centers, interactive voice response systems, on-line dial-up applications, and websites to build lasting relationships. These interactions can be used to glean information and insights about customer needs and their buying behaviour to design and develop services, which help create value for the customers as well as the firms.

REFERENCES

G. Sridhar, *Customer Relationship Management*, JIMS 8 M, Vol. 7, No. 1, January-March 2002, pp. 37-43.

Deepali Singh, *Information Technology Enabled Customer Relationship Management*, JIMS 8 M, Vol. 6, No. 1, January-March 2001, pp. 31-37.

24

Web Usage Mining
Preprocessing and Pattern Discovery

N. Sudhakar Reddy*
A.V. Sreeharsha**

ABSTRACT

Web usage mining is the application of data mining techniques to discover usage patterns from Web data, in order to understand and better serve the needs of Web-based applications. Web usage mining consists of three phases, namely preprocessing, pattern discovery, and pattern analysis. Preprocessing is a process of cleaning and correcting the data, pattern discovery and analysis involves various methods of statistics and machine learning. This paper has presented the details of preprocessing tasks that are necessary for performing Web Usage Mining, the application of data mining and knowledge discovery techniques to WWW server access logs. In this paper some exploratory methods are explained with internal details of the phases that benefit the Web-community. Experimental results on synthetic data for the purpose of comparing transaction identification approaches and on real-world industrial data to illustrate some of its applications were also discussed.

Keywords: Data Mining, World Wide Web, Web Usage Mining.

1. **Assistant Professor, nsreddysvec@yahoo.com, Department of Computer Science and Engineering, Sree Vidyanikethan Engineering College, A.Rangampet.**

2. **Assistant Professor, avsreeharsha@gmail.com, Department of Computer Science and Engineering, Sree Vidyanikethan Engineering College, A.Rangampet.**

INTRODUCTION

The ease and speed with which business transactions can be carried out over the Web has been a key driving force in the rapid growth of electronic commerce. Specifically, e-commerce activity that involves the end user is undergoing a significant revolution. The ability to track users' browsing behaviour down to individual mouse clicks has brought the vendor and end customer closer than ever before. It is now possible for a vendor to personalise his product message for individual customers at a massive scale, a phenomenon that is being referred to as mass customisation.

The scenario described above is one of many possible applications of Web Usage mining, which is the process of applying data mining techniques to the discovery of usage patterns from Web data, targeted towards various applications. Data mining efforts associated with the Web, called Web mining, can be broadly divided into three classes, i.e. content mining, usage mining, and structure mining. Web Structure mining projects such as structural information and link topologies; Web Content mining projects such as filtering the content, seeking content; are the basic scope of the survey carried in Web mining arena. An early taxonomy of Web mining is directed in providing the pattern discovery of web usage, which also describes the architecture of a typical *WebMiner* system, one of the first systems for Web Usage mining.

This paper provides an up-to-date survey of Web Usage mining, including both academic and industrial research efforts, as well as commercial offerings. Section 2 describes the various kinds of Web data that can be useful for Web Usage mining. Section 3 discusses the challenges involved in discovering usage patterns from Web data. The three phases are preprocessing, pattern discovery, and patterns analysis. Section 4 provides an overview of the systems that track web usage and Section 5 concludes the paper.

WEB DATA

One of the key steps in Knowledge Discovery in Databases is to create a suitable target data set for the data mining tasks. In Web Mining, data can be collected at the server-side, client-side, proxy servers, or obtained from an organisation's database (which contains business data or consolidated Web data). Each type of data collection differs not only in terms of the location of the data source, but also the kinds of data available, the segment of population from which the data was collected, and its method of implementation.

There are many kinds of data that can be used in Web Mining. This paper classifies such data into the following types:

- *Content:* The real data in the Web pages, i.e. the data the Web page was designed to convey to the users. This usually consists of, but is not limited to, text and graphics.
- *Structure:* Data that describes the organisation of the content. Intra-page structure information includes the arrangement of various HTML or XML tags within a given page. This can be represented as a tree structure, where the HTML tag becomes the root of the tree. The principal kind of inter-page structure information is hyper-links connecting one page to another.
- *Usage:* Data that describes the pattern of usage of Web pages, such as IP addresses, page references, and the date and time of accesses.
- *User Profile:* Data that provides demographic information about users of the Web site. This includes registration data and customer profile information.

Data Sources

The usage data collected at the different sources will represent the navigation patterns of different segments of the overall Web traffic, ranging from single-user, single-site browsing behaviour to multi-user, multi-site access patterns.

Server Level Collection

A Web server log is an important source for performing Web Usage Mining because it explicitly records the browsing behaviour of site visitors. The data recorded in server logs rejects the (possibly concurrent) access of a Web site by multiple users. These log files can be stored in various formats such as Common log or Extended log formats. An example of Extended log format is given in Fig. 24.2 (Section 3). However, the site usage data recorded by server logs may not be entirely reliable due to the presence of various levels of caching within the Web environment. Cached page views are not recorded in a server log. In addition, any important information passed through the POST method will not be available in a server log. Packet sniffing technology is an alternative method to collecting usage data through server logs. Packet sniffers monitor network traffic coming to a Web server and extract usage data directly from TCP/IP packets. The Web server can also store other kinds of usage information such as cookies and query data in separate logs. Cookies are tokens generated by the Web server for individual client browsers in order to automatically track the site visitors. Tracking of individual users is not an easy task due to the stateless connection model of the HTTP protocol. Cookies rely on implicit user cooperation and thus have raised growing concerns regarding user privacy, which is a sensitive topic, where different policies are maintained for the different demographies of users. Online visitors while searching for pages relevant also typically generate query data to their information needs. Besides usage data, the server side also provides content data, structure information and Web page meta-information (such as the size of a file and its last modified time).

The Web server also relies on other utilities such as CGI scripts to handle data sent back from client browsers. Web servers implementing the CGI standard parse the URI of the requested file to determine if it is an application programme. The URI for CGI programmes may contain additional parameter values to be passed to the CGI application. Once the CGI programme has completed its execution, the Web server sends the output of the CGI application back to the browser.

Client Level Collection

Client-side data collection can be implemented by using a remote agent (such as Java scripts or Java applets) or by modifying the source code of an existing browser (such as *Mosaic* or *Mozilla*) to enhance its data collection capabilities.

The implementation of client-side data collection methods requires user cooperation, either in enabling the functionality of the Java scripts and Java applets, or to voluntarily use the modified browser. Client-side collection has an advantage over server-side collection because it ameliorates both the caching and session identification problems. However, Java applets perform no better than server logs in terms of determining the actual view time of a page. In fact, it may incur some additional overhead especially when the Java applet is loaded for the first time. Java scripts, on the other hand, consume little interpretation time but cannot capture all user clicks (such as reload or back buttons). These methods will collect only single-user, single-site browsing behaviour. A modified browser is much more versatile and will allow data collection about a single user over multiple Web sites. The most difficult part of using this method is convincing the users to use the browser for their daily browsing activities. Offering incentives to users who are willing to use the browser can do this, similar to the incentive programmes offered by companies that offer lucrative rewards for clicking on the banner advertisements or using the link for any sort of message communication.

Proxy Level Collection

A Web proxy acts as an intermediate level of caching between client browsers and Web servers. Proxy caching can be used to reduce the loading time of a Web page experienced by users as well as the network traffic load at the server and client sides using proxy servers. The performance of proxy caches depends on their ability to predict future page requests correctly. Proxy traces may reveal the actual HTTP requests from multiple clients to multiple Web servers. This may serve as a data source for characterising the browsing behaviour of a group of anonymous users sharing a common proxy server.

Data Abstractions

The information provided by the data sources described above can all be used to construct/identify several data abstractions, notably users, server sessions, episodes, click streams, and page views. In order to provide some consistency in the way these terms are defined, the W3C Web Characterisation Activity

(WCA) has published a draft of Web term definitions relevant to analysing Web usage. A user is defined as a single individual that is accessing file from one or more Web servers through a browser. While this definition seems trivial, in practice it is very difficult to uniquely and repeatedly identify users. A user may access the Web through different machines, or use more than one agent on a single machine. A *page view* consists of every file that contributes to the display on a user's browser at one time. Page views are usually associated with a single user action (such as a mouse-click) and can consist of several files such as frames, graphics, and scripts. When discussing and analysing user behaviours, it is really the aggregate page view that is of importance. The user does not explicitly ask for"*n*" frames and "m" graphics to be loaded into is or her browser, the user requests a "Web page". All of the information to determine which files constitute a page view is accessible from the Web server. A *click-stream* is a sequential series of page view requests. Again, the data available from the server side does not always provide enough information to reconstruct the full click-stream for a site. Any page view accessed through a client or proxy-level cache will not be "visible" from the server side. A user session is the click-stream of page views for a singe user across the entire Web. Typically, only the portion of each user session that is accessing a specific site can be used for analysis, since access information is not publicly available from the vast majority of Web servers. The set of page-views in a user session for a particular Web site is referred to as a server session (also commonly referred to as a visit). A set of server sessions is the necessary input for any Web Usage analysis or data mining tool. The end of a server session is defined as the point when the user's browsing session at that site has ended. Again, this is a simple concept that is very difficult to track reliably. The W3C WCA refers to any semantically meaningful subset of a user or server session as an episode.

WEB USAGE MINING

As shown in Fig. 24.1, there are three main tasks for performing Web Usage Mining or Web Usage Analysis. This section presents an overview of the tasks for each step and discusses the challenges involved.

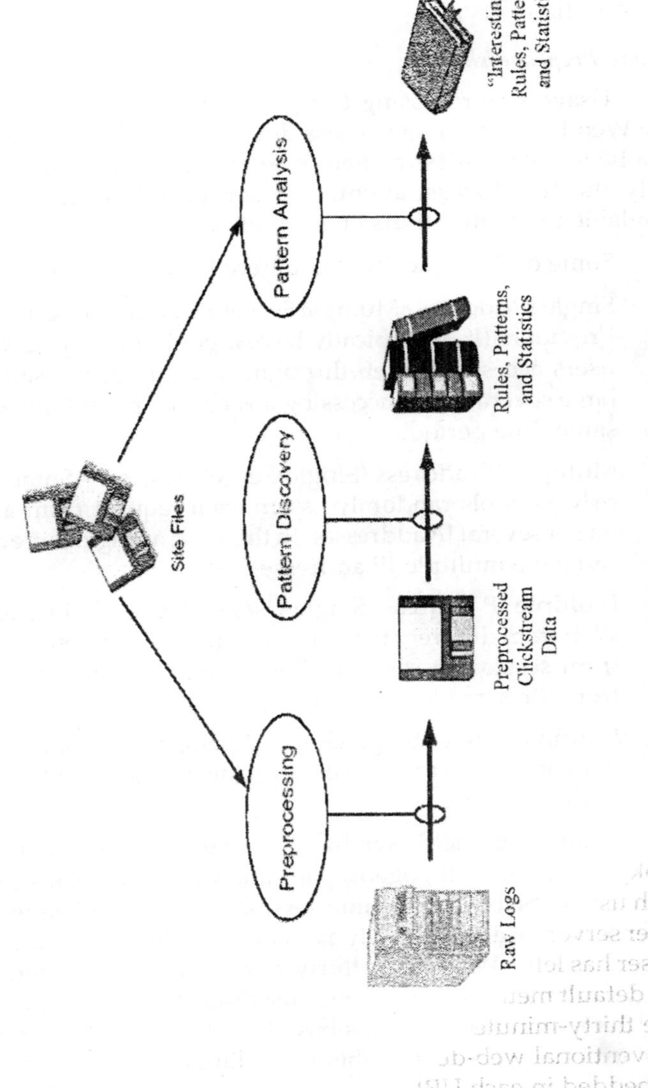

Fig. 24.1: **High level *Web Usage Mining* Process**

Preprocessing: Preprocessing consists of converting the usage, content, and structure information contained in the various available data sources into the data abstractions necessary for pattern discovery.

Usage Preprocessing

Usage preprocessing is arguably the most difficult task in the Web Usage Mining process due to the incompleteness of the available data. Unless a client side tracking mechanism is used, only the IP address, agent, and server side click-stream are available to identify users and server sessions.

Some of the typically encountered problems are:

- Single IP address/Multiple Server Sessions—Internet Service Providers (ISPs) typically have a pool of proxy servers that users access the Web through. A single proxy server may have several users accessing a Web site, potentially over the same time period.
- Multiple IP address/Single Server Session—Some ISPs or privacy tools randomly assign each request from a user to one of several IP addresses. In this case, a single server session can have multiple IP addresses.
- Multiple IP address/Single User— A user that accesses the Web from different machines will have a different IP address from session to session. This makes tracking repeat visits from the same user difficult.
- Multiple Agent/Singe Users - Again, a user that uses more than one browser, even on the same machine, will appear as multiple users.

Assuming each user has now been identified (through cookies, logins, or IP/agent/path analysis), the click-stream for each user must be divided into sessions. Since page requests from other servers are not typically available, it is difficult to know when a user has left a Web site. A thirty-minute timeout is often used as the default method of breaking a user's click-stream into sessions. The thirty-minute timeout is based on the results obtained from conventional web-development standards. When a session ID is embedded in each URI, the content server sets the definition of a session.

#	IP Address	User ID	Session ID	Time	Method	Status	Size	Referrer	Agent
1	123. 456. 78.9	-	805A13D44	[25/Apr/2006:09:00-0550]	"GET"	200	1820	A.html	Mozilla/3.01(Win95,I)
2	123. 456. 78.9	-	805A13D44	[25/Apr/2006:09:05-0781]	"GET"	200	3290	-	Mozilla/3.01(Win95,I)
3	123. 456. 78.9	-	805A13D45	[25/Apr/2006:09:15-0781]	"GET"	200	620	B.html	Mozilla/3.01 (Win95,I)
...	...	...	...	...	...	...	...	...	...
...	...	...	...	...	...	...	...	...	...
100	123. 456. 78.2	-	815613E50	[25/Apr/2006:09:15-0781]	"GET"	200	125	C.html	Mozilla/3.01(Win95,I)

***Fig. 24.2:* A Sample Web Server Log**

While the exact content served as a result of each user action is often available from the request field in the server logs, it is sometimes necessary to have access to the content server information as well. Since content servers can maintain state variables for each active session, the information necessary to determine exactly what content are served by a user request is not always available in the URI. The final problem encountered when preprocessing usage data is that of inferring cached page references. As discussed in Section 2.2, the only verifiable method of tracking cached page views is to monitor usage from the client side. The referrer field for each request can be used to detect some of the instances when cached pages have been viewed.

Fig. 24.2 (*See on page 235)* shows a sample log that illustrates several of the problems discussed above (The first column would not be present in an actual server log, and is for illustrative purposes only). IP address 123.456.78.9 is responsible for three server sessions, and IP addresses 209.456.78.2 and 209.45.78.3 are responsible for a fourth session. Using a combination of referrer and agent information, lines 1 through 11 can be divided into three sessions of A-B-F-O-G, L-R, and A-B-C-J. Path completion would add two page references to the first session A-B-F-O-F-B-G, and one reference to the third session A-B-A-C-J. Without using cookies, an embedded session ID, or a client-side data collection method, there is no method for determining that lines 12 and 13 are actually a single server session.

Content Preprocessing

Content preprocessing consists of converting the text, image, scripts, and other files such as multimedia into forms that are useful for the Web Usage Mining process. Often, this consists of performing content mining such as classification or clustering. While applying data mining to the content of Web sites is an interesting area of research in its own right, in the context of Web Usage Mining the content of a site can be used to filter the input to, or output from the pattern discovery algorithms. For example, results of a classification algorithm could be used to limit the discovered patterns to those containing page views about a certain subject or class of products. In addition to classifying or clustering page views based on topics, page views can also be classified according to their intended use. Page views can be intended to convey information (through text, graphics, or other multimedia), gather information from the user, allow navigation (through a list of hypertext links), or some combination uses. The intended use of a page view can also filter the sessions before or after pattern discovery.

In order to run content mining algorithms on page views, the information must first be converted into a quantifiable format. Some version of the vector space model is typically used to accomplish this. Text files can be broken up into vectors of words. Keywords or text descriptions can be substituted for graphics or multimedia. Parsing the HTML and reformatting the information or running additional algorithms as desired can easily preprocess the content of static page views. Dynamic page views present more of a challenge. Content servers that employ personalisation techniques and/or draw upon databases to construct the page views may be capable of forming more page views than can be practically preprocessed. A given set of server sessions may only access a fraction of the page views possible for a large dynamic site. Also the content may be revised on a regular basis. The content of each page view to be preprocessed must be "assembled", either by an HTTP request from a crawler, or a combination of template, script, and database accesses. If only the portions of page views that are accessed are preprocessed, the output of any classification or clustering algorithms may be skewed.

Structure Preprocessing

The structure of a site is created by the hypertext links between page views. The structure can be obtained and pre-processed in the same manner as the content of a site. Again, dynamic content (and therefore links) pose more problems than static page views. A different site structure may have to be constructed for each server session.

Pattern Discovery

Pattern discovery draws upon methods and algorithms developed from several fields such as statistics, data mining, machine learning and pattern recognition. However, it is not the intent of this paper to describe all the available algorithms and techniques derived from these fields. This section describes the kinds of mining activities that have been applied to the Web domain. Methods developed from other fields must take into consideration the different kinds of data abstractions and prior knowledge available for Web Mining. For example, in association rule discovery, the notion of a transaction for market-basket analysis does not take into consideration the order in which items are selected. However, in Web Usage Mining, a server session is an ordered sequence of pages requested by a user. Furthermore, due to the difficulty in identifying unique sessions, additional prior knowledge is required (such as imposing a default timeout period, as was pointed out in the previous section).

Statistical Analysis

Statistical techniques are the most common method to extract knowledge about visitors to a Web site. By analysing the session file, one can perform different kinds of descriptive statistical analyses (frequency, mean, median, etc.) on variables such as page views, viewing time and length of a navigational path. Many Web traffic analysis tools produce a periodic report containing statistical information such as the most frequently accessed pages, average view time of a page or average length of a path through a site. This report may include limited low-level error analysis such as detecting unauthorised entry points or finding the most common invalid URI. Despite lacking in the depth of its analysis, this type of knowledge can be potentially useful for improving the system performance, enhancing the security of the system, facilitating the site modification task, and providing support for marketing decisions.

Association Rules

Association rule generation can be used to relate pages that are most often referenced together in a single server session. In the context of Web Usage Mining, association rules refer to sets of pages that are accessed together with a support value exceeding some specified threshold. These pages may not be directly connected to one another via hyperlinks. For example, association rule discovery using the *Apriori* algorithm (or one of its variants) may reveal a correlation between users who visited a page containing electronic products to those who access a page about sporting equipment. Beside from being applicable for business and marketing applications, the presence or absence of such rules can help Web designers to restructure their Web site. The association rules may also serve as a heuristic for prefetching documents in order to reduce user-perceived latency when loading a page from a remote site.

Clustering

Clustering is a technique to group together a set of items having similar characteristics. In the Web Usage domain, there are two kinds of interesting clusters to be discovered: usage clusters and page clusters. Clustering of users tends to establish groups of users exhibiting similar browsing patterns. Such knowledge is especially useful for inferring user demographics in order to perform market segmentation in *e*-commerce applications or provide personalised Web content to the users. On the other hand, clustering of pages will discover groups of pages having related content. This information is useful for Internet search engines and Web assistance providers. In both applications, permanent or dynamic HTML pages can be created that suggest related hyperlinks to the user according to the user's query or past history of information needs.

Classification

Classification is the task of mapping a data item into one of several predefined classes. In the Web domain, one is interested in developing a profile of users belonging to a particular class or category. This requires extraction and selection of features that best describe the properties of a given class or category. Classification can be done by using supervised inductive learning algorithms such as decision tree classifiers, naïve Bayesian classifiers, *k*-nearest neighbor classifiers, Support Vector Machines etc. For example, classification on server logs may lead to the discovery of interesting rules such as: 30 per cent of users who placed an online order in /Product/Music are in the 18-25 age group and live on the West Coast.

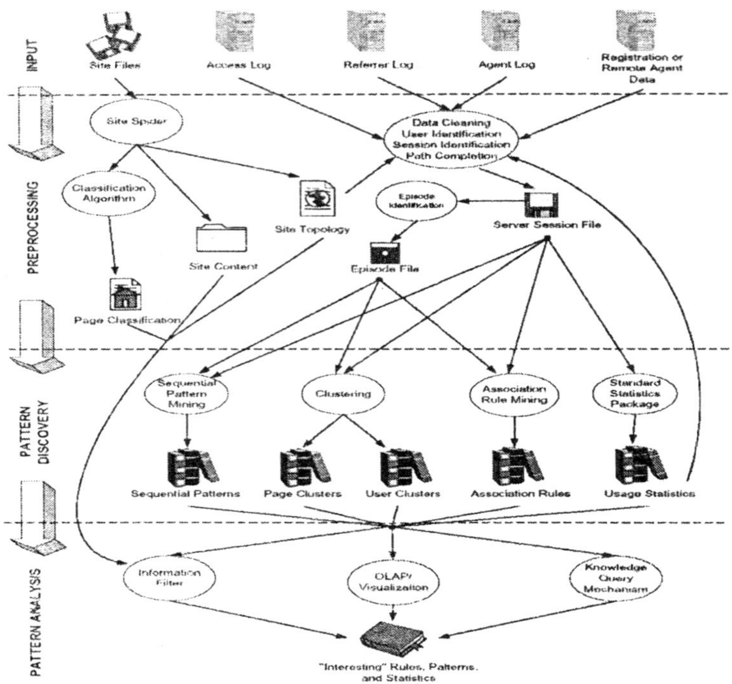

Fig.24.3: **Illustrating the Typical Web Usage**

Sequential Patterns

The technique of sequential pattern discovery attempts to find inter-session patterns such that the presence of a set of items is followed by another item in a time-ordered set of sessions or episodes. By using this approach, Web marketers can predict future visit patterns that will be helpful in placing advertisements aimed at certain user groups. Other types of temporal analysis that can be performed on sequential patterns include trend analysis, change point detection, or similarity analysis.

Dependency Modelling

Dependency modelling is another useful pattern discovery task in Web Mining. The goal here is to develop a model capable of representing significant dependencies among the various variables in the Web domain. As an example, one may be interested to build a model representing the different stages a visitor undergoes while shopping in an online store based on the actions chosen (i.e. from a casual visitor to a serious potential buyer). There are several probabilistic learning techniques that can be employed to model the browsing behaviour of users. Such techniques include Hidden Markov Models and Bayesian Belief Networks. Modelling of Web usage patterns will not only provide a theoretical framework for analysing the behaviour of users but is potentially useful for predicting future Web resource consumption. Such information may help develop strategies to increase the sales of products offered by the Web site or improve the navigational convenience of users.

Pattern Analysis

Pattern analysis is the last step in the overall Web Usage mining process as described in Fig. 24.1. *(See on page 233)* The motivation behind pattern analysis is to filter out uninteresting rules or patterns from the set found in the pattern discovery phase. The exact analysis methodology is usually governed by the application for which Web mining is done. The most common form of pattern analysis consists of a knowledge query mechanism such as SQL. Another method is to load usage data into a data cube in order to perform OLAP operations. Visualisation techniques, such as graphing patterns or assigning colors to different values, can often highlight overall patterns or trends in the data. Content and structure information can be used to filter out patterns containing pages of a certain usage type, content type, or pages that match a certain hyperlink structure.

CONCLUSION

This paper has attempted to provide an up-to-date survey of the rapidly growing area of Web Usage mining. With the growth of Web-based applications, specifically electronic commerce, there is significant interest in analysing Web usage data to better understand Web usage, and apply the knowledge to better serve users. This has led to a number of commercial offerings for doing such analysis. However, Web Usage mining raises some hard scientific questions that must be answered before robust tools can be developed. This article has aimed at describing such challenges, and the hope is that the research community will take up the challenge of addressing them.

REFERENCES

1. Accrue. http://www.accrue.com.
2. Alladvantage. http://www.alladvantage.com.
3. Andromedia aria. http://www.andromedia.com.
4. Broadvision. http://www.broadvision.com.
5. Hit list commerce. http://www.marketwave.com.
6. Likeminds. http://www.andromedia.com.
7. Netgenesis. http://www.netgenesis.com.
8. Netperceptions. http://www.netperceptions.com.
9. Netzero. http://www.netzero.com.
10. Platform for privacy project. http://www.w3.org/P3P/.
11. Surfaid analytics. http://surfaid.dfw.ibm.com.
12. Truste: Building a web you can believe in. http://www.truste.org/.
13. Webtrends log analyser. http://www.webtrends.com.
14. World wide web committee web usage characterisation activity. http://www.w3.org/WCA.

25

Knowledge Discovery in Spatial Databases

P. Sumalatha*
R. Chandrakala**

INTRODUCTION

Knowledge discovery in databases has been defined as the process of discovering valid, novel, and potentially useful patterns from large data. *Spatial Databases Systems* (*SDBS*) are used for the management of spatial data. Spatial data mining algorithms are very important to find implicit regularities, rules or patterns hidden in large spatial databases, e.g. for traffic control or environmental studies. Most existing data mining algorithms integrating with a *Data Base Management System* (DBMS) has the fallowing advantages.

- Redundant storage
- Potential inconsistencies can.be avoided
- Index structures can be used to speed-up the execution of data mining algorithms

In this paper, we introduce

- A set of database primitives for mining in spatial database primitives for mining in spatial databases. (Section 2)

* M.C.A. (V Semester), M.C.A. (II Semester), S.P.M.V.V., Tirupati, *e-mail:* sumamca_2004@yahoo.co.in

** M.C.A (II Semester), S.P.M.V.V., Tirupati, *e-mail:* Chandu_madhu80@yahoo.com

- Algorithms for spatial data mining (Section 3)
- Techniques for efficiently supporting databases primitives by a DBMS (Section 4)
- Summarises the contribution and discusses several issues for future research.

DATABASE PRIMITIVES FOR SPATIAL DATA MINING

The major difference between mining in relational database and mining in spatial databases is that attributes of neighbours of some object of interest may have an influence on the object itself. So, database primitives are based on the concept of spatial neighbourhood relations.

Neighbourhood Relations

The mutual influence between two objects depends on factors such as the topology, the distance or the direction between the objects. For instance, a new industrial plant may pollute its neighbourhood depending on the distance and on the major direction of wind.

Figure 25.1 depicts a map used in the assessment of possible locations for a new industrial plant. The map shows three regions with different degrees of pollution (indicated by the different colours) caused by the planned industrial plant.

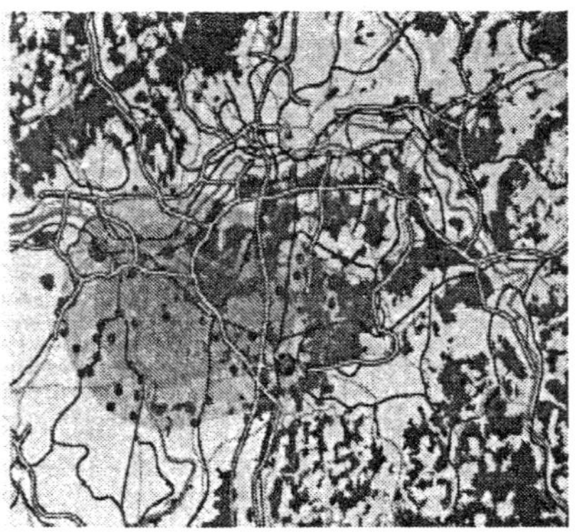

Fig. 25.1

We introduce three basic types of binary spatial relations: topological, distance and direction relations.

Topological Relations

The topological relations between two objects A and B are derived from the nine intersections of the interiors and the boundaries. The relations are A disjoint B, A overlaps B, A equals B, A covers B, A covered-by B, A contains B, A inside B.

Distance Relations

Distance relations are those relations comparing the distance of two objects with a given constant using one of the arithmetic operators.

Definition

Let *dist* be a distance variable, let $ be one of the arithmetic predicates <, >, =, Let 'C' be a real number and let A & B are spatial objects. Then a distance relation "A distance $c B holds iff dist (A, B)$c".

Direction Relations

Here let rep(A) be the representative of a source object and all the points of destinations is object B. Generally representative point of a source object is used as the origin of the virtual coordinate system and its quadrants are directions.

Definition

- B northeast A holds, iff for all *b E B: bx >= rep (a)x ^ by >= rep(a)y*

  Similarly, southeast, southwest and northwest are defined.

- B north A holds iff for all *b E b: by >=rep(a)y* Similarly, south, east, west are defined.

Complex Neighbourhood Relations

Topological, distance and direction relations may be combined by the logical operators to express C.N.R.

Definition: If r1 and r2 are Neighbourhood Relations then r1^r2 and r1 v r2 are complex neighbourhood relations.

Neighbourhood Graphs and Their Operations

Based on the neighbourhood relations, now we introduce neighbourhood graphs and neighbourhood paths and same basic operations.

Neighbourhood graphs and paths: Let *neighbour* be a neighborhood relation and DB be a database of spatial objects.

(a) *Neighbourhood Graph* G= (N, E) is a graph where the set of nodes N corresponding to the set of objects O E DB. The set of edges E contains the pair of nodes (n_1,n_2) iff neighbour (n_1,n_2)holds.

(b) *Neighbourhood path:* It is a sequence of nodes $(n_1,n_2,\ldots.n_k)$ where neighbour(ni,ni+1) holds forall n_i E N. The number K denotes the length of the path.

The number of neighbourhood paths may become very large. Therefore, the operations on neighbourhood paths will provide parameters to further reduce the no.of paths actually created.

In this paper, we introduce only the two most important of these operations.

Neighbours: Ngraphs* objects* predicates

Extensions: Ngraphs* $2^{Npaths*}$ Integer*predicates

The operation neighbours (Graph , object, pred) returns the set of all objects connected to object via some edge of Graph satisfying the conditions expressed by the predicate pred.

The operation extensions (graph, paths, max, pred) returns the set of all *paths* extending one of the elements of paths by at most *max* nodes of graph .All the extended paths must satisfy the predicate *pred*. Therefore, the predicate pred in both the operations acts as a *filter* to restrict the no.of paths created using domain knowledge about the relevant paths.

ALGORITHMS FOR SPATIAL DATA MINING

Here, we introduce three different types of algorithms:

- Spatial clustering
- Spatial characterisation
- Spatial Trend Detection

Spatial Clustering

Clustering is the task of graphing the objects of a database into meaningful subclasses, so that numbers of the cluster are similar and members of all the different clusters differs.

Different types of spatial clustering algorithms have been proposed

Single Scan Algorithm: The basic idea is to group neighbouring objects of the database into clusters based on a local cluster condition performing only one scan through the database. Single scan clustering algorithms are efficient. Algorithmic schema of Single Scan Clustering is as follows:

```
Singlescanclustering (database db, Nrelation rel)
Set graph to create-graph (db, rel);
Initialize a set currentobjects as empty;
For each node O in graph do
    If O is not yet member of some cluster then
        Create a new cluster C;
        Insert O into currentonjects;
        While currentobjects not empty do
            Remove the first element of currentobjects as O;
            Set neighbours to neighbors (graph,O,TRUE);
            If neighbours satisfy the cluster condition do
                Add O to cluster C;
                Add neighbours to current objects;
End Singlescanclustering.
```

Spatial Characterisation

The task of *characterisation* is to find a compact description for a selected subset of the database. A *spatial characterisation* is a description of the spatial and non-spatial properties.

- The *characterisation algorithm* usually starts with a small set of target objects, selected *for instance* by a condition on some non-spatial attribute such as "rate of retire people=HIGH".

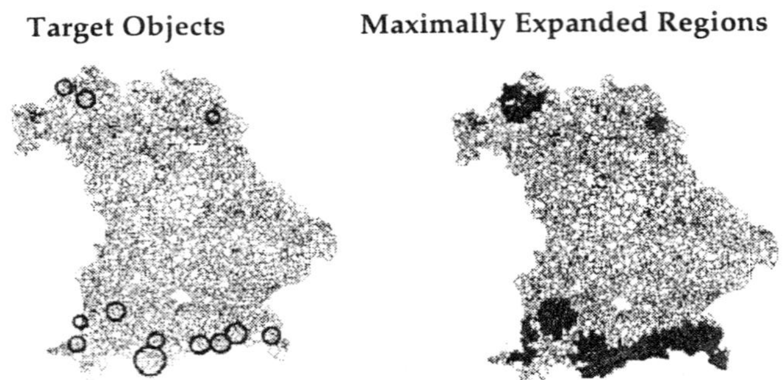

Fig 25.2: **Characterising wrt. high rate of retired people**[8]

- Then, the algorithm expands regions around the target objects, simultaneously selecting those attributes of the regions for which the distribution of values differs significantly from the distribution in the whole database.
- In the last step of the algorithm, *characterisation rule* is generated describing the target regions.

Spatial Trend Detection

A *spatial Trend Detection* is as a regular change of one or more non-spatial attributes when moving away from a given start object 'O'.

There are two different types of algorithms:

1. Global-trend
2. Local-trend

Fig. 25.3: **Trends of the "average rent" starting from the city of Regensburg**

Algorithm *global-trends* detects global trends around a start object 'o'. The existence of a global trend for a start object 'O' indicates that if considering all objects on all paths starting from 'O' the values for the specified attribute in general tend to increase with increasing distance.

Algorithm ***local-trends*** detects single paths starting from an object 'O' and having a certain trend. The paths starting from 'O' may show different pattern of change.

The following figure depicts the result of algorithms *global-trend* and *local-trends* for the trend attribute "average rent" and start object representing the city of Regensburg.

EFFICIENT DBMS SUPPORT BASED ON NEIGHBOURHOOD INDICES

Spatial index structures are used in an SDBMS to speed up the processing of queries. Many SDBMS are rather static since there are not.many update on objects such as geographic maps or proteins. Therefore materialising the relevant neighbourhood graphs may be worthwhile.*

Neighbourhood Indices

Our concepts of neighbourhood indices is related to the concepts of spatial join indices, and extends spatial join indices by associating each pair of objects with their distance.

Neighbourhood indices means extends distance associated join indices with the following new contributions:

- A specified maximum distance restricts the pairs of objects presented in a neighbourhood index.
- For each of the different types of neighbourhood relations, the concrete relation of the pair of objects is stored.

Neighbourhood Index: Let *DB* be a set of spatial objects and let *max* and *dist* be real numbers. Let *D* be a direction relation and *T* be a topological relation. The neighbourhood index for *DB* with maximum distance *max* denoted by *I* is defined as follows:

$I=\{O1, O2, dist, D, T \mid O1,O2\ E\ DB \wedge O1 distance_{=dist}\ O2 \wedge dist>=max \wedge$

$O2\ D\ O1 \wedge O1TO2\}$

A simple Neighborhood Index is as follows:

Object-Id	*Neighbour*	*Distance*	*Direction*	*Topology*
O1	O2	2.7	Southwest	Disjoint
O1	O3	0	Northwest	Overlap
...	...	...	...	...

A neighbourhood index supports not only one but a set of neighborhood graphs.

Applicable Neighbourhood Index

A neighbourhood index is said to be applicable for a given neighbourhood graph if the index contains an entry for each of the edges of the graph.

Critical Distance of a Neighbourhood Relation

To fin applicable neighbourhood index for some neighbourhood graph, we use of the critical distance of a neighbourhood relation.The *critical distance* of a neighbourhood relation 'r' is the maximum possible distance for a pair of objects O1 and O2 satisfying O1 r O2.

Smallest Applicable Neighbourhood Index

If two neighbourhood indices I_{c1} & I_{c2} with c1<c2 are applicable, using I_{c1} is more efficient because it has less entries than I_{c2}.

The smallest applicable neighbourhood index for some neighbourhood index for some neighbourhood graph is the applicable index with the smallest critical distance.

The *algorithm* for processing the *neighbours* operation, which makes use of the smallest applicable neighbourhood index.

Neighbours (graph G,object O,predicate pred)

Select as I the smallest applicable neighbourhood index for G //*index selection*

If such I exists then //*filter step*

Use the neighbourhood index I to retrieve as *candidates* the set of objects C having an entry (O,C,dist,D,T) in I;

Table 25.1: **Parameters of the cost model**

Name	*Meaning*	*Typical Values*
n	number or nodes in the neighbourhood graph	$[10^3..10^5]$
f	average number of edges per node in the graph (fan out)	$[1..10^2]$
v	average number of vertices of a spatial object	$[1..10^3]$
ff	ratio of fanout of the index and fanout (*f*) of the graph	[1..10]
c_{index}	capacity of a page in terms of index entries	128
c_v	capacity of a page in terms of vertices	64
P_{index}	probability that a given index page must be read from disk	[0..1]
P_{data}	probability that a given data must be read from disk	[0..1]
t_{page}	average execution time for a page access	$1*10^{-2}$ sec
t_{float}	execution time for a floating point comparison	3*10-6 sec
s	system overhead	depends on DBMS

T_{page} — The execution time of a page access.

T_{float} — The execution time of a floating point comparison.

The system *overhead* S includes client-server communication.

The p_{index} & p_{data} denote the probability that a requested index page and data, page, respectively, have to be read from disk.

Table 25.2: Cost model for the neighbours operation

Step	*Cost without neighbourhood index*	*Cost with neighbourhood index*
Selection	s	s
Filter	$f\left\lceil \log_{c_{index}} n \right\rceil . P_{index} . t_{page}$	$f\left\lceil \log_{c_{index}} (f.n) \right\rceil . P_{index} . t_{page}$
Refinement	$(1+f).\lceil v/c_v \rceil . p_{data} . t_{page} + f.v^2.t_{\text{float}}$	$ff.f.p_{data}.t_{page}$

Else

Use the R-tree to retrieve as *candidates* the set of objects C satisfying O or C;

Initialise an empty set of neighbours; //*refinement step*

For each C in *candidates* do

If O or C and *pred(C)* then add C to neighbours Return *neighbours;*

The first step of the algorithm *neighbours,* the *index selection,* selects a neighbourhood index. The second step, *Filter step,* returns a set of candidate objects, which may satisfy the specified neighbourhood relation. The last step, *the refinement step,* for all these candidates the neighbourhood relation as well as the additional predicates *pred* are evaluated and all objects passing this test are returned as the resulting neighbours.

The *extensions* operation can obviously be implemented by iteratively performing *neighbours* operation. Therefore, it is obvious that the performance of the *neighbours* operation is very important.

Cost Model

To predict the cost of performing a *neighbours* operation, we develop a *cost model.* In order to develop a cost model we use different parameters. (*See Tables 25.1 and 25.2*).

CONCLUSION

In this paper, we defined neighbourhood graphs and paths and a small set of database primitives for spatial data mining. We showed that spatial data mining algorithms as spatial clustering, spatial characterisation and spatial trend detection are well supported by the proposed operations. Finally, we introduced neighbourhood indices to speed-up the processing of our database primitives. The efficiency of the neighbourhood indices was evaluated by using an analytical cost model.

So far, the neighbourhood relations between two objects depend only on the properties of the two involved objects. In future, we will extend our approach to neighbourhood relations such as "being among the k-nearest neighbours" which depend on more than two related objects. Finally, a tighter integration of the database primitives with the DBMS should be investigated.

REFERENCES

1. Ester M., Gundlach S., Kriegle H-P., Sander J.:" *Database Primitives for Spatial Data Mining"*.
2. Ester M., Kriegel H-P., Sander J.:"*Spatial Data Mining: A Database Approach"*.
3. Gueting R.H.:"*An Introduction to Spatial Database Systems"*.
4. Koperski K., Adhikary J.:"*Knowledge Discovery in Spatial Databases:Progress and Challenges"*.

http://www.bs.informatik.unimuenchen.dc/Forschung/KDD/SpatialKDD